Controversies in Crime and Justice
series editor Victor E. Kappeler Eastern Kentucky University

Controversies in

Critical Criminology

edited by Martin D. Schwartz
Suzanne E. Hatty
Ohio University

 anderson publishing co.
2035 Reading Road
Cincinnati, OH 45202
800-582-7295

Controversies in Critical Criminology

Copyright © 2003
     Anderson Publishing Co.
     2035 Reading Rd.
     Cincinnati, OH 45202

   Phone 800.582.7295 or 513.421.4142
Web Site www.andersonpublishing.com

Library of Congress Cataloging-in-Publication Data

Controversies in critical criminology / edited by Martin D. Schwartz and Suzanne E. Hatty.
        p. cm. -- (Controversies in crime and justice)
     Includes bibliographical references and index.
     ISBN 1-58360-521-5 (pbk.)

Cover design by Tin Box Studio, Inc.

Editor Gail Eccleston
Acquisitions Editor Michael C. Braswell

Dedication

To Robert Blum and Carl Preston, the two right-wing old men who keep my arguments sharper by disagreeing vociferously and debating with me on everything.

MDS

To James Hatty and Winifred Caldwell Hatty, who taught me that left of center is a good place to be.

SEH

Acknowledgments

This book is, of course, a complete product of the Division on Critical Criminology of the American Society of Criminology, one of the most active divisions ever seen in the field. With up to 20 critical panels at the national meetings, an e-mail list server (Jim Thomas and Ken Mentor getting kudos), *The Critical Criminologist*, the best newsletter in criminology (thanks to Barbara Sims and Rick Matthews), and an excellent refereed journal, *Critical Criminology*, now on an even keel thanks to Jeff Walker and Paul Leighton, this large division is keeping critical criminology alive and well.

Many of the authors here have won one of the research awards of the Division. They are invariably the best known representatives of their subfield or least one of the top representatives. Of course, these authors did the bulk of the work on this book and deserve all of the praise.

Table of Contents

Introduction

Martin D. Schwartz & Suzanne E. Hatty

This book, which is composed of original essays, has been designed to introduce students to the complex and influential field of critical criminology. This fairly new field has become quite important to the field at large, and involves a substantial number of criminological theorists. Just as an indicator, the main criminology organization in North America—the American Society of Criminology—has a large and active Division on Critical Criminology. This division maintains a large membership base and a very active membership. It has a journal with 30 editorial board members from about 10 countries (*Critical Criminology: An International Journal*), a large and active intellectual newsletter (*The Critical Criminologist*), about 20 panels (more than 100 papers) delivered each year at the annual meetings of the American Society of Criminology, and an active web site (*www.critcrim.org*). The counterpart organization in criminal justice, the Academy of Criminal Justice Sciences, also has a similar Section on Critical Criminology. Thus, critical criminology is an important and integral part of criminology itself.

But how do we define critical criminology? The problem is that there are as many types of critical criminology as there are writers and teachers in the area. One thing we can be sure about is that modern critical criminology has its roots in the long tradition of Marxist criminology that exploded into an enormously complex and rich field of radical criminology in the 1960s and the 1970s. In this volume, Rick Matthews discusses this history of criminologists trying to follow a Marxist tradition when Karl Marx himself said so little on the subject.

By the end of the 1970s, however, a number of criminologists began to agree with the self-description of David Friedrichs, another contributor to this volume. He said at the time that he was a "soft-core Marxist," in that he really liked the questions that the Marxists were asking, but he disagreed with their analyses. What drew together those criminologists somewhat like Friedrichs was their critical regard for the way in which modern capitalist society is constructed. Slowly through the 1980s, the term "critical" criminology became applied to a broad range of criminologists who, like Friedrichs, agreed to challenge the mainstream assumptions, policies and practices of academic criminology, but who might not be Marxists. Critical criminology became an "umbrella" term—describing an intellectual space in which a broad variety of people could come together to think through issues related to power, crime and punishment. Marxists were just one of the many groups under this umbrella.

Although few critical criminologists would self-identify as Marxists, all critical theorists share in common is a concern with class, or at least the economic structure of society, and the manner in which the inequalities of modern capitalist society influence crime. Race has been important to many theorists, and increasingly scholars in this area take gender into account when developing their theories. The most cutting-edge work today not only includes race, class, and gender, but also specifically attempts to locate the intersections between these identities and experiences (see, e.g., Schwartz & Milovanovic, 1996). For example, in some circumstances being an African-American might be the primary influence on a person's behavior, but in others it might be the fact of being a woman, or being an African-American woman, or being a poor African-American woman or even just being a poor woman. She is the same woman, but in different circumstances she may call upon different resources. The same applies, of course, to rich white men, or any other combination.

Readers of this volume will discover two things that will make understanding critical criminology both easier and harder. First, there are many critical criminologies, and quite a few will be represented here. Second, they are not completely distinct from each other. Because they all have at least some roots back in radical criminology, and they all are critical of mainstream criminology, there are a large number of shared beliefs, methodologies, goals, and interpretations. This is how hundreds of professionals can share an organization, publications, and social events together. Yet, the "mix and match" nature of the field can be highly confusing, not only for students but for the criminologists themselves. Many criminologists create for themselves identities that cross over several of these subfields simultaneously. Thus, some are feminist criminologists, some are Marxist criminologists and some are peacemaking criminologists. But, there are people who consider themselves feminist Marxist peacemaking criminologists.

Some people are just able to balance more than one belief at the same time, much like professional soldiers who have strong religious beliefs that require them to turn the other cheek but military beliefs that require them to practice to be trained killers. Others find that the problems or "holes" in their favorite theory are in fact filled by the analysis provided by other theories, and that an amalgam of two or more theories satisfies them best intellectually.

Of course, for the purposes of a book like this, we chose to avoid the hundreds of variations and instead somewhat artificially asked the contributors to contribute to the "pure" form of their field. It is rather important, though, for the reader to understand that although many people exist within the "pure" form of any theory, perhaps more agree with parts of any theory.

One of the strengths of this book is that each author has been asked to discuss some of the most important attacks on her or his favorite theory. They were allowed, of course, to answer these attacks, but as a reader you are certainly welcome to assess for yourself what you think of any particular strain of critical criminology. You should think in terms of which theories lend themselves, in your own mind, to combination with others.

Another strength of this book is that theory books have a tendency to be a tiny bit abstract. If readers see the theories as disconnected from an everyday experience of crime, they sometimes have trouble seeing just how these theories would be applied. Although in each chapter the authors have tried to give some flavor of the value of these theories, in Part II of this book we have asked several authors to discuss some very specific critical criminology topics so that readers can see ways in which a critical criminologist would approach the field.

Part I—Some Types of Critical Criminology

Marxist Criminology. We have included as the first substantive theory chapter Rick Matthews' discussion of Marxist criminology. As noted above, Marxist criminology is definitely a minority position in criminology, but Matthews does an outstanding job of developing the roots of the discipline, and, as he puts it, "the twists and turns of its evolution." He notes that, in general, Marxist theories are broad-based theories that pay primary attention to the economy, capitalist structure, and the relations of people within that structure. Simple Marxism would suggest that as economic conditions deteriorate, crime would increase. Further, the very nature of competitive capitalism virtually requires the rich to continually scramble for more, usually at the expense of the working people. As far back as 1916, predating modern mass advertising campaigns, the Dutch Marxist Willem Bonger argued that, by its nature, capitalism created a strong desire for material accumulation, and that this was the cause of much crime. More complex Marxist formulations take a broad variety of other social and political factors into account, such as Richard Quinney's 1970s account of ruling-class crimes of repression, and working-class crimes of resistance. Structuralists such as Stephen Spitzer argued that some parts of the population need to be socially controlled so that the capitalist class can maintain its power. This requires both the labeling of some groups as deviant, and also processes of regulating those who are not dangerous to capitalists and suppressing those who are.

Feminist Criminology. Jody Miller, perhaps the best young feminist criminologist in North America, explains feminist criminology in the second substantive chapter. This is another area that was completely marginalized years ago, but now at least at the level of lip service is completely mainstream. What this means is that it has begun to influence criminologists at every level of the system, although that influence is not very deep in many areas. Still, while the influence of feminist scholarship and teaching is widespread, what is more important is the extent to which feminist scholarship has begun to slowly permeate the rest of the criminology enterprise.

The material above noted that many schools of thought rarely exist in isolation; authors commonly combine two or more critical criminologies to develop their own writings. Nowhere is this truer than with feminist criminology. Nevertheless, there are some basic assumptions upon which all feminists can agree. Although rooted in some biological facts, Miller explains to us that gender is a constructed and relative reality, based on historical, cultural and social influences. Feminists reject any notion that men or women act in a certain way, except as influenced in particular times by particular cultural or subcultural or personal influences. Gender relations in modern society tend to be based on systems of male dominance, and these relations fundamentally affect social life. In fact, our very systems of common sense and ways of knowing are gendered (Hatty, 2000).

As Miller points out, a key tenet of feminist theory has always been that women should be at the center of intellectual inquiry, not peripheral or invisible. As a first move in that direction 20 to 30 years ago, there was some tendency for feminists to mainly study female criminals and female victims. The most important insight then was the discovery that theories thought to be theories of criminals were in fact theories about men. More recently, feminists have broadened their scope of inquiry. Both male and female criminologists have discovered that male behavior is as gendered as female behavior. With generations of criminological study, we still have not found a factor more statistically associated with criminality than simply being male.

Feminist criminologists claim that their unique perspective makes them particularly capable of looking at the intersection of race, class, and gender in criminology. Whether this is true or not, it is certainly true that most of the intersections work has arisen out of this perspective.

Left Realism. One of the most important critical criminologies in the English-speaking world has not, interestingly, been deeply powerful in the United States. Left realism has been extremely important in the United Kingdom, Canada, Australia, and New Zealand, but less powerful in the United States. One of the reasons for this, no doubt, is that one of the world's best-selling left realists, Elliott Currie, is an American who does not use that term to describe himself. In this book, Walter DeKeseredy, who is widely considered the leading North American proponent of left realism, tries to situate this school of thought in the specific context of inner-city violence, by showing the advantages and disadvantages of using left realist theory in this fashion.

Actually, left realism was originally a response to British Marxists who excused inner-city violence and ignored victims of such crimes. Such theorists as Jock Young in England argued that inner city poor were the ones

most victimized by their neighbors, in addition to victimizations from capitalists. Left realists attacked those who worried more about providing support for the criminal justice system than about providing support for the victims of lower-class and working-class crime. For example, opponents of left
realism have called it racist to point out that African-Americans commit a disproportionate amount of American homicide, but left realists point out that
African-Americans also have a particularly high rate of victimization in a wide
range of crimes in the United States, including homicide.

Early on, left realism adopted the position that relative poverty, rather
than absolute poverty, was a powerful determinant of crime. After all, many
poor people do not commit crimes. Relative deprivation, plus the rampant
competitive individualism of capitalism combine to provide discontent and
a search for solutions that often include actions labeled as criminal. Although
left realism has often been seen as less relevant to women because it did not
theorize women's experiences, DeKeseredy suggests that more recent work
has suggested that violence against women is facilitated when individualistic men suffering from relative deprivation simultaneously come under the
influence of masculinist subcultural dynamics.

Finally, DeKeseredy points out, while some on the left have been content
to wait for massive social change to take place at once to make broad
sweeping changes, left realists have generally been highly concerned with
short-term policy suggestions to "chip away" at patriarchal capitalism.

Postmodern Criminology. Postmodernists are unlikely to develop a
theory of why people commit crimes. Rather, as Bruce Arrigo shows here,
their analysis centers on why we consider some things crimes, and why we
consider some people criminals. Arrigo is exceptionally well published in
this area and is widely considered a top spokesman for this school of
thought, which is actually somewhat fragmented into many postmod-
ernisms. Still, all of them are concerned with language, and the role it plays
in creating our understanding of the world around us (as opposed to language being a neutral reflection of our understandings). The dominant
structures in society have more influence than others on the language we
use, which means that truth is not absolute, but partial and reflective of
power structures. What we think is fixed, or common sense, is instead relative. Perhaps already, without even getting into the chapters here, the
reader can already see how a feminist and a postmodernist analysis can be
combined. Of course, there is no automatic reason why a postmodernist has
to agree that the power structures involved are male dominated.

Arrigo shows us here some of the attractions and advantages of a postmodern viewpoint, and covers both some of the techniques (such as deconstruction) and some of the cutting edge theoretical approaches (such as
chaos theory). He admits that there is some "truth" to the objection that
postmodernist writing is at times cumbersome and confusing, but explains
why from his perspective there is a logic to this prose.

Constitutive Criminology. Closely related to postmodern criminology is another broad-ranging critical theory that has its roots in Marxism and postmodernism. Dragan Milovanovic is widely considered North America's most prominent postmodern criminologist, but with the very widely published Stuart Henry, he has developed an entirely new field—constitutive criminology—that also includes a broad variety of other influences ranging from chaos theory from physics, to French psychoanalytic thought, to textual analysis. They place a great deal of emphasis on the ways in which humans shape their social world, in addition to being shaped by it. Rather than a simple question of whether criminals are to blame for committing crimes (the standard mainstream definition), or whether society victimizes certain people and labels them as criminals (a standard 1970s radical criminology approach), these theorists look at the broad interrelationships between the individual and society. Crime has its roots in unequal power relations, which can cause some people to suffer a loss, or others to suffer crimes of repression. Constitutive criminology is very concerned with the processes by which crime is "constructed" rather than caused.

Cultural Criminology. Critical criminologists have been highly concerned with the influence of culture and mass media since at least the 1920s. Today, a group of critical criminologists has been looking directly at crime control through the lens of media analysis. The major theoretical writer in this field, Jeff Ferrell, in this book explains the field he essentially invented, cultural criminology.

Within cultural criminology, the traditional topics of criminology are supplemented by a careful examination of the ways in which the mass media and popular culture create public understandings of human behavior. These understandings end up shaping public policy toward such things as drug use. Cultural criminology is closely aligned with the general field of cultural studies, and is influenced by the postmodern insights that the image generated by the media is in fact seen by many people as reality. Cultural criminologists are influenced by a broad array of other types of critical criminologists in developing their research methods and modes of analysis.

Peacemaking Criminology. Another of the powerful and widely discussed, if not particularly influential, perspectives is peacemaking criminology. This is a perspective that does not ponder why people commit crimes, but rather asks questions about how we might rethink our responses to crime and offending. The term "peacemaking" derives from the full generation we now have had of "wars" against crime, none of which have been successful. These theorists suggest that we make "peace" on crime.

John Randolph Fuller, who has written the only textbook on the subject, suggests here that peacemaking criminology shares with several other perspectives the concern with mainstream criminology's split of people into criminals and noncriminals. He attempts to bridge the theories that emphasize individual responsibility with those that emphasize crime being caused by societal influence. Peacemakers are concerned, like other critical theorists, with the effects of unequal power relations on the effects of the criminal justice system. However, it also calls upon offenders to take responsibility for their actions, and their need to stop harming others.

This perspective owes its rather young roots to Richard Quinney and Harold Pepinsky, although the strongest statement of the perspective comes from Fuller's own Peacemaking Pyramid. He suggests that solutions to problems of the criminal justice system must include examinations of nonviolence, social justice, issues of inclusion, a search for better means to settle cases, a deep concern to make sure that participants fully understand the process, and the development of a consistent and predictable viewpoint.

Restorative Justice. Closely related to peacemaking criminology, and perhaps even a part of it, is restorative justice. The theme of this movement is to design programs that bring people together through informal community mechanisms in an attempt to restore and repair the relationships between people. Rick Sarre, an Australian law professor who has written extensively on this theme, argues that although criminal justice professionals would still be important, the goal is to oppose the popular retributive punishment (casting out) model in use today with one that emphasizes reconciliation and the restoration of relationships. An important goal is to rely less on formal punishment and imprisonment as reactions to crimes.

Perhaps the best-known application of this model has been numerous experiments in Australia and New Zealand with family group conferences with juveniles that brings together relatively minor offenders and their extended families with their victims and their supporters. An independent facilitator requires the offender to deal with their own wrongdoing, and to negotiate a settlement, with the goal being reconciliation rather than penalty.

Part II—Some Examples of Critical Criminology

Crimes of the State. Overall, the first and foremost contribution of critical criminologists has been to note that mainstream criminology has been primarily concerned with the crimes of the poorest and politically weakest people in any society, while simultaneously ignoring the crimes of the politically powerful. Although there are now a number of books and articles available on white-collar crime (by people in positions of trust) and corporate crime (by corporations themselves in furtherance of corporate goals), there has been significantly less work done on crimes of the state (the government generally) itself. In their chapter, David Kauzlarich and David Friedrichs examine this phenomenon.

Criminologists have begun to recognize that when a corporation commits a crime to further one of its goals (e.g., profits) that this can be a problem. What if the entity committing that crime to further one of its goals is a governmental unit itself? Of course, the easy examples have always been Nazi Germany, Idi Amin's Uganda, the current government in Iraq, and many more. Kauzlarich and Friedrichs point out that no matter how dangerous street criminals may be, the most physically dangerous, murderous, and threatening crimes are those committed by criminal governments. One can rant about the Mafia, or youth gangs, or any criminal groups, but none can match the horror of having an atomic bomb dropped on your home city. No group can match the Nazis for genocide, although evidently not for lack of trying.

Numerous other examples of state crime are reviewed here, along with a discussion of the controversial nature of even the notion of state crime, and potential methods of controlling it even when we agree upon it. Kauzlarich and Friedrichs show how various strands of critical criminology come together in this area, which, in perhaps their one understatement of the chapter, they call "immensely consequential."

Crime and the Body. A very different form of critical criminology investigation is undertaken by Victoria Pitts, who has been studying a variety of criminal actions against the body. Mainly influenced by feminism, but also postmodernism and a variety of other influences, Pitts shows how we have begun to look at the body as the place of social control. We have become very concerned with what people do to their own bodies, and in particular have defined as deviant a variety of behaviors such as homosexuality, sadomasochistic actions, abortion, prostitution, female promiscuity, cross-dressing, and much more. Pitts' particular interest has been in deviant body art, such as tattooing, piercing, and scarification. Such practices have become associated with a variety of other social problems, such as drug taking. When women, homosexuals, or lesbians engage in body modification, it is particularly likely to be defined as sick and in need of serious medical or psychological treatment—or even legal intervention.

Masculinities Theory. Although criminological theory is filled with theoretical notions of what factors might best predict criminal activity, what seems to have been ignored until fairly recently has been that the single best predictor of being a criminal is being male. As feminist theorists pointed out, most criminals are male. Not all, certainly, but most. Kenneth Polk, an American who teaches in Australia, has studied at length the male behavior involved in homicide, and here takes up some of the more recent materials on masculinities and homicide.

In most textbooks and approaches to masculinity there has been a presumption in both sociology and psychology that there is a single concept or sex role of masculinity that a particular society teaches an individual male person, who grows up to more or less exhibit these traits. Masculinities theories, however, have more recently been adopted by many criminologists to look at the fact that there are many masculinities, and that many men have to accomplish masculinity in different ways at different times (e.g., during school hours, but later on the street corners), or at different times of life (e.g., as a teenager, as a father, as a grandfather).

Polk takes on the differences between male and female violence, and gets engaged in the debate in the field between sociologists and socio-biologists (often called the evolutionary perspective). He discusses the different uses of violence for men and women, and discusses the utility for understanding of violence of concepts of masculinity and masculinities.

Hate Crimes. Barbara Perry argues, in the final example, that critical criminology provides a variety of theoretical advantages over the use of other more mainstream theoretical explanations to describe why hate crime occurs. Hate crime, she argues, is an assertion of the relative power relationships of the parties involved. It is a crime of the relatively privileged asserting both their power and contributing to the further marginalization of already marginalized groups.

Perry argues that structured action theory best describes hate crime today. The power to impose the hate criminal's definition of what is happening, the desire to maintain unequal relations, and the use of violence to continue the privilege of race and class, are all important variables to consider. Of course, sexuality is always an important American arena of power politics, whether it consists of male violence against women, or male violence against gays.

Thus, the central goal of this book is to introduce the reader to an important, but too often neglected, segment of criminology theory. Critical criminology is not only a popular and essential component of criminology in North America, but it may be even more important in the criminologies of Canada, Europe, and Australia. The scholarship that is produced by critical criminologists has become much more sophisticated and can now be found published in the very best mainstream academic journals such as *Criminology, Justice Quarterly* and *Theoretical Criminology*. As noted above, specialized journals such as *Critical Criminology: An International Journal* are now being published, and most large, mainstream presses are now publishing critical criminology books.

As this book will make clear, the various components of critical criminology draw heavily on each other and share many sensibilities. There is no question that the most important newer development is in the intersections literature, as researchers attempt to simultaneously include race, class, and gender into their analyses. Further, critical scholars share a viewpoint that retributive justice, in the form of an overuse of imprisonment, is unproductive and in fact likely to exacerbate our current problems. Although some theorists point to the need for changes in those who are generally defined as criminals in our society, all feel that changes in society are needed to change the conditions that produce and foster crime.

CHAPTER 1

Marxist Criminology

Rick A. Matthews

Introduction

The problem anyone faced with the task of summarizing Marxist criminology is that Marx himself wrote very little on crime. The general lack of attention Marx paid to crime has led to a somewhat uneven development within Marxist criminology, and has also led to many disagreements among Marxists.[1] For example, because the bulk of Marx's writings are concerned with linking economic development to political, social, and historical change, some have argued that the term Marxist criminology is somewhat of a misnomer, and that "crime and deviance vanish into the general theoretical concerns [of Marxism] and the specific scientific object of Marxism" (Hirst, 1975:204). Further complicating matters are the beliefs that people have about Marxism—that it is inherently nondemocratic, that the former Soviet Union was the "pinnacle" of Marxist development, and that quite simply the project of Marxism has "lost" to capitalism. In short, most people do not understand that there are many forms of Marxism, and that many Marxists disagree with one another.

In this chapter I will first briefly describe general Marxist theory. This discussion will be used as the foundation for answering the most important question in this chapter: What does Marxism have to do with crime? Next, I will turn to the development of Marxist criminology, tracing the twists and turns of its evolution. In the last two sections of the chapter, I will discuss some of the problems surrounding Marxist criminology, and the future of Marxism within the field of criminology.

General Marxist Theory

> ... Marx had the good fortune, combined of course, with the necessary genius, to create a method of inquiry that imposed his stamp indelibly on the world. We turn to Marx, therefore, not because he is infallible, but because he is inescapable (Heilbroner, 1980:15).

Marx's analysis of capitalism is very complex, and a complete analysis is well beyond the scope of this chapter.[2] Nevertheless, a brief explanation of some of the central concepts within Marx's writings is in order so that we may build upon them later. If the large body of Marx's writings can be boiled down to a few components, one must include his theory of exploitation and his theory of capitalist development and crisis (Gottlieb, 1992).

In Marx's view, there exist two primary classes in any capitalist society; the proletariat (i.e., working class), and the bourgeois (i.e., capitalist ruling class). The bourgeoisie, or capitalist ruling class, own the means of production (e.g., factories). The proletariat, on the other hand, own very little and must sell their labor to the bourgeois to make ends meet. The bourgeoisie, according to Marx, exploit the proletariat because they pay them far less than the value of what they produce. As such, Marx claimed that the interests of bourgeoisie and proletariat are fundamentally different—the bourgeoisie want to keep labor prices down to maximize profit, and the proletariat seek higher wages to sustain themselves.

The second key concept found in Marx's writings is that of crisis. Because the bourgeoisie are continually trying to maximize profits at the expense of the proletariat, capitalism develops very unevenly with periods of "boom" and "bust." For example, if the working class is not paid enough to afford the products they are producing, underconsumption occurs. Underconsumption slows the overall economy down, increases unemployment, and leads to a recession or depression. In turn, rates of profit fall for the capitalist ruling class. When this happens, less money is invested, and unemployment rates increase. With increased unemployment, fewer goods are consumed, and there is less need for production. Eventually, many businesses fail and the unemployment rate becomes so high that the cost of labor is driven down. With less competition among the capitalist owners, and the willingness of the working class to accept lower wages to have any job, production and consumption patterns begin to increase. Over time, these cycles of boom and bust lead to the concentration of wealth in the hands of the capitalist owners, corporate monopolization, intermittent periods of high unemployment, the attrition of small businesses, and increased use and dependency on technology (Gottlieb, 1992).[3]

A few points are now in order. First, as Marx noted, the boom and bust nature of capitalism is inherent within the system itself and is unavoidable. As history clearly demonstrates, capitalist economic systems and gravity are governed by the same law: that which goes up eventually comes down. Second, whether or not the working class realizes their class interests are different from the capitalist ruling class, they are. According to Marx, many in the working class may not recognize that their interests are the opposite of those of the capitalist ruling class because of ideological barriers which prevent them from understanding they are being exploited. Others, however, understand their class position and the exploitive nature of social relations. This creates instability and potential class conflict. In turn, class conflict may potentially lead to a socialist revolution by the working class, but only if large-scale class consciousness is born. Third, and perhaps most importantly, the antagonisms between the working class and the ruling class, and the antagonism between boom and bust periods in the overall economy are due to existing social relations which are incompatible with one another. These "contradictions" work to destabilize the overall system, and cannot be avoided: they are inherent within existing social relations.

What Does Marxism Have to Do with Crime?

Intuitively it makes sense that economic conditions are related to crime rates, particularly property crimes: if people do not have access to the things they need and/or want, then they may be more likely to steal them. Thus, as economic conditions deteriorate, crime rates should increase. While this may appear to make sense (and has been supported fairly well from an empirical standpoint), the relationship between economic conditions and crime is more complex than this. For example, not all people who are poor or unemployed commit serious or chronic crimes, and many people who commit crimes (particularly white-collar and corporate criminals) are economically privileged. Obviously, then, there are other factors that must be considered.

From a Marxian perspective, crime can only be understood as occurring within a specific set of social and economic conditions. As such, the nature, form and extent of crime is dependent on the way in which society organizes itself, and the aim of Marxist criminologists must be to understand the ways in which capitalism itself creates the conditions in which crime is likely to occur. As Greenberg (1981) has pointed out, this is precisely what separates Marxian theories of crime from traditional theories of crime. He notes,

> as crime does not exist in isolation, it must be analyzed in the context of its relationship to the character of the society as a whole. With only a handful of exceptions, non-Marxian work on criminology does not attempt to do this. Most of it tends, instead, to focus on the attributes of individuals (such as the psychological traits) or on their immediate social settings . . . The possibility that its organization—its way of producing and distributing material

goods, and of organizing its political and legal institutions, for example—might have major implications for the amount and kinds of crime present in a society as well as for the character of its crime control apparatus, is not even considered (Greenberg, 1981:17).

With this in mind, we now turn to an examination of the ways in which criminologists have attempted to develop a Marxian criminology.

The Evolution of Marxist Criminology

Willem Bonger's 1916 work, titled *Criminality and Economic Conditions*, offered one of the first Marxian accounts of the causes of criminal behavior. Bonger argued that egoism, created by the capitalist economic system, was the source of crime. Crime, in Bonger's view, was the natural result of an economic system and subsequent culture which produced a "need" for material accumulation and excess. This need for material accumulation and consumption was not only seen as the cause of "street" crimes (i.e., interpersonal crimes of violence and property), but also the cause of crime for those in positions of relative wealth and prosperity (i.e., business owners). From this perspective, nearly all members of society are prone to crime because of the egoism created by capitalism, which arises from the emphasis that is placed on individual success and competition.

In the context of poverty and deprivation, Bonger argued that the poor in society were likely to commit crimes for two primary reasons, both of which center around class divisions created by capitalism. First, the poor may have to commit crimes in order to survive in an economic system which unequally distributes its wealth and resources. Because wealth and resources are always unequally distributed in capitalist economies, demarcations along class lines result. Those members of society who are impoverished are thus more likely to commit crimes (particularly property crimes) in order to survive economically (Bonger, 1916).

The second reason crime may be committed by the poor has to do with the demoralizing effect of being impoverished. In large part, the demoralizing effect of impoverishment is created through capitalism's emphasis on material consumption. Showing that Bonger's work is still relevant today, Currie's (1985) writes:

> Seventy years ago, the noted Dutch criminologist Willem Bonger warned that a single-minded emphasis on market values breeds crime because it "weakens the social instincts of man." The United States has always been distinctive, even among other societies based on market capitalism, for the intensity of that emphasis and the absence of countervailing traditions and institutions to mediate and humanize it. That difference, moreover, has intensi-

fied in the political climate of the past decade (1980s). This affects the whole tenor of social life in America; its impact on crime and violence is hard to measure, but the connection is difficult to ignore. In a society that values its people for what they can acquire rather than what they can contribute and that encourages predatory and manipulative behavior in the service of immediate gain as the guiding principle of economic life, we should not be altogether surprised if more explosive forms of the same ethos are expressed among the most deprived. (1985:277)

Although Bonger's (1916) work has been profoundly criticized,[4] it offered critical criminologists of the 1960s and 1970s a beginning point for Marxian and conflict explanations of crime, and many criminologists took up the task of developing a Marxian theory of crime.

Taylor, Walton, and Young (1973) argued that crime can only be understood within the context of the society's political economy. In reaction to labeling theory (particularly the work of Lemert), they argued that it was premature to cast away macro-level explanations of crime. Accordingly, any understanding of crime must include an analysis of the macro-level origins of crime within a given economic system, such as capitalism, as well as a social psychological component which addresses the precipitating causes of crime (Taylor et al., 1973). Like other critical theorists of their time, they argued that the poverty caused by the normal operation of the system produces and exacerbates the crime problem.

The work by Taylor et al. (1973) was important in the newly developing area of Marxian criminological theory. First and foremost, their work pointed criminologists in the direction of the political economy as a criminogenic force. Prior to this, a great deal of criminological theory had ignored the impact of the political economy on crime. What Taylor et al. (1973) offered was a detailed critique of mainstream perspectives (i.e., anomie, social learning, and strain), and other left-liberal perspectives (i.e., labeling and social constructionism). As the title *The New Criminology* suggests, they sought to move criminological theory beyond what had been done so far and develop a political economy of crime perspective.

The Tale of Two Marxisms in Criminology

As was noted earlier, the development of Marxian criminology has not been without disagreement. Within Marxist criminological circles, there were early debates between two groups of Marxist proponents. The first group of theorists includes those who are instrumental Marxists who assume that the state is an instrument of the ruling class. From this perspective state policies (which include the definition of certain behaviors as criminal and punishments for such behavior) are manipulated either directly or indirectly by those in power (see Gold, Lo & Wright, 1975). Therefore, instrumentalists see little state autonomy, as the policies of the state are manipulated in favor of the interests of powerful segments of society. Structuralist Marxists, on the other hand, have argued that the role of the state is to resolve the inherent contradictions in the capitalist system. Those such as Gold et al. (1975) claim that there are struggles and conflicts of interest both within and between classes and the state.

Many early Marxist criminological theories were rooted in the instrumentalist tradition, in that they focused on ruling class interests in defining certain behaviors as criminal. For example, Chambliss' (1975) argued in his work *Toward a Political Economy of Crime* that the class divisions within capitalist systems create unequal economic conditions based on class. Crime, then, is functional for the ruling class because it diverts attention from the exploitative nature of the capitalist system and causes people to focus their attention on crime. While the difference between classes in committing crimes may be insignificant if one considers all the behaviors of the ruling class which are harmful but not defined as criminal, there is a tendency for people to focus on the lower classes when it comes to crime (Chambliss, 1975). Thus, while attention is focused on street crimes associated with the lower classes, the exploitive nature of capitalism and the privileged position of the ruling class goes unnoticed.

Most of the instrumental elements in Chambliss' theory center around how behavior is classified as criminal. Because the ruling-class has control over the legal process, it is able to define a wide variety of activities as being criminal, which serves to promote their own self interests. Chambliss (1975) suggested that criminal behavior is a direct consequence of one's relation to the means of production, and that the unequal distribution of wealth in capitalist societies creates social conditions favorable to crime.

At the same time Chambliss' work came out, so too did works by structuralist Marxists such as Spitzer (1975). He attempted to construct a general Marxian theory of deviance which viewed "deviance production (as) involving all aspects of the process through which populations are structurally generated, as well as shaped, channeled into, and manipulated within social categories defined as deviant" (1975:640). Arguing that such a theory must include an analysis of the economic conditions of society, he suggested that:

> . . . the starting point of our analysis must be an understanding of the economic organization of capitalist societies and the impact of that organization on all aspects of social life. . .it [the capitalist mode of production] contains contradictions which reflect the internal tendencies of capitalism. These contradictions are important because they explain the changing character of the capitalist system and the nature of its impact on social, political and intellectual activity. The formulation of a Marxist perspective on deviance requires the interpretation of the process through which the contradictions of capitalism are expressed. In particular, the

theory must illustrate the relationship between specific contradictions, the problems of capitalist development and the production of a deviant class. (Spitzer, 1975:641)

From this perspective, crime is a function of deviant definitions, problem populations, and social control systems. As Spitzer (1975) notes, deviant
definitions are applied to those who "disturb, hinder or call into question"
the reproduction of the economic system (1975:642). The problem populations he identifies as needing to be controlled in order for the capitalist
class to maintain its position of power are social junk and social dynamite.
Social junk refers to those populations which represent a control cost, but
are relatively harmless to the capitalist class. Social junk is controlled by the
welfare state through programs which are "designed to regulate and contain
rather than eliminate and suppress the problem" (Spitzer, 1975:645). Thus,
while problematic at times, social junk is not specifically deviant. Social
dynamite, on the other hand, represents populations that have the potential
to "call into question established relationships, especially relations of production and domination" (Spitzer, 1975:645). For this reason, laws and
social control institutions such as the police and prisons are used to quell
those deviant groups which call into question such things as the mode of
appropriating the product of human labor (Spitzer, 1975:642).

Another structuralist was Richard Quinney, who attempted to outline a
Marxian theoretical perspective on crime that went beyond Chambliss' earlier work by presenting a more detailed argument of the development of
crime in capitalist systems. Quinney's starting point was to differentiate
between crimes of repression and crimes of resistance. Crimes of domination and repression are those committed by either the state or ruling class
in order to maintain their position of power (Quinney, 1977). Crimes of resistance, on the other hand, are crimes committed by lower- and working-class
persons which stem directly from their class position. For example, Quinney
argued that both predatory and personal crimes were committed by lower-
class persons against other lower-class persons because of their economic
and class position. Thus, as inequality between classes increased, one could
expect to find increases in both predatory and personal crimes.

While instrumental Marxian explanations have often examined the
preservation of ruling class interests through law, and paid less attention to
street crimes, some structuralists specifically focused their attention on the
role which inequality plays within the capitalist system in generating street
crimes (see Michalowski, 1985). A key issue for Michalowski was whether
poverty itself caused crime, or the condition of relative inequality within a
given system causes crime, because economic distress can take many forms.
For instance, at the individual level, economic distress may occur from
being unemployed, subemployed, or underemployed. At the community
level, economic distress may arise from downturns in the larger economy of
the state or nation, as well as when industries leave communities through

deindustrialization. Any combination of the previously listed factors may lead to poverty, inequality, or both. However, as Michalowski pointed out, there is a difference between inequality and poverty and their possible effects on crime. He argued that many societies and communities have been "poor," but had low rates of crime. However, in the context of affluence, relative poverty is related to crime in several ways. The ways in which they are related include the increase of material "wants" by the relatively impoverished, loss of a social bond, as well as feelings of low self-esteem, alienation, frustration, and hostility (Michalowski, 1985:407-409).

Marxist Feminism and Left Realism

Critical criminologists inspired by Marxist criminology but unsatisfied with the tendency of theorists working within the perspective to privilege economic conditions over other important issues like gender and culture have expanded the scope of traditional Marxist criminology. For example, while the instrumental and structural Marxists were debating among themselves in the 1970s, some feminist scholars of crime were turning their attention toward developing Marxist feminism.[5]

Marxist feminists generally begin their analysis of crime from the position that gendered divisions of labor result from larger class divisions of labor. Because men have controlled the means of production in capitalist societies, Marxist feminists argue that they have also controlled most social institutions. As such, women are dominated and controlled first and foremost by the social relations created by the mode of production in capitalism, and secondarily by men.

According to Marxist feminists, those activities which are defined by society as criminal tend to be those which threaten the existing capitalist/patriarchal order. To illustrate this point, they have argued that much female criminality that is sexual in nature is defined as such because it threatens men's control over women's bodies and sexuality. Additionally, some have argued that the oppressive nature of the capitalist/patriarchal system for women leads them to commit crime because they feel trapped in subordinate social roles (Radosh, 1990). Finally, in terms of male crime committed against women, Julia and Herman Schwendinger (1983) argued that rape is a crime that is characteristic of those societies that are generally more violent. The Schwendingers also argued that in more egalitarian societies rape, in particular—and violence in general—are less common. Thus, in order to reduce rape and other forms of violence in society, they have argued that structural changes must be made in the mode of production.

During this same period, yet another Marxian inspired perspective began to emerge. This perspective, known as left realism, has taken up the task of explaining street crime within the context of the larger political economy. Left realists were generally dissatisfied with the relative lack of attention traditional Marxists paid to street crime, and charged instrumental Marxian theorists in particular, with failing to pay adequate attention to its harmful effects. Furthermore, they have criticized the tendency of some structuralist Marxists to "romanticize" criminals as being a revolutionary class. While not ignoring crimes of the powerful, left realists have taken the position that the effects of street crime are both serious and real, that the criminal class is not revolutionary, and that critical (i.e., Marxian, conflict, feminist, and postmodern) criminologists must pay attention to it. What ties left realism to Marxian criminology, however, is its emphasis on understanding crime within the larger political economy.

Young (1997), for example, has argued that the social and economic conditions favorable to street crime include such things as high unemployment rates and an individualistic ethos for righting such perceived social injustices. He notes that:

> there is no evidence that absolute deprivation (e.g., unemployment, lack of schooling, poor housing, and so forth) leads *automatically* to crime. Realist criminology points to relative deprivation in certain *conditions* as being the major causes of crime; i.e., when people experience a level of unfairness in their allocation of resources and utilize individualistic means to attempt to right this condition. . . . To say that poverty in the present period breeds crime is not to say that all poor people are criminals. Far from it: most poor people are perfectly honest and many wealthy people commit crimes. Rather, it is to say that *the rate of crime is higher in certain parts of society under certain conditions.* (1997:30-31; emphasis added)

Young (1997) has also argued that oftentimes the victims of street crime are persons within the same social class as the offender. Therefore, to place emphasis on understanding the etiology of street crime is to not necessarily uncritically accept the role of the ruling class in creating laws, but to pay adequate attention to the harmful nature of street crime.

In addition to a critical examination of the economic forces which create the conditions likely to produce crime, many left realists have emphasized equally the problematic nature with the cultural ethos of capitalism. Young (1999) reminds us that relative deprivation alone does not increase crime, but rather it is "the lethal combination is relative deprivation *and individualism*" (2000:48, emphasis added).

Elliott Currie's (1997) work has also pointed forcefully in the direction of the political economy to explain high crime rates, arguing that the development of what he terms "market societies" has led to high levels of crime. Market societies, according to Currie (1997) are characterized by "the pursuit of private gain increasingly becoming the organizing principle for all areas of social life—not simply a mechanism that we use to accomplish certain circumscribed economic ends" (1997:37). Market societies quickly become imbalanced, with the need for personal autonomy overriding common goals, values, and solidarity. Within this context we see increases in inequality, the destruction of the autonomy of local communities, the fragmentation of the family, and the rise of a culture of Darwinian competition that urges levels of consumption which cannot be supported (Currie, 1997).

Opponents of Marxist Criminology

Just as a complete description of Marxism is beyond the scope of this chapter, so too is a complete analysis of the myriad of criticisms which have been leveled at it. Opponents of Marxist criminology generally fall into one of three categories: (1) traditional (i.e., mainstream criminologists), (2) critical criminologists, and (3) Marxists themselves.

One of the major problems which mainstream theorists have with Marxist criminology is that Marxist criminologists make a number of assumptions about human nature which run contrary to utilitarian-based notions of why people commit crime. For example, there is a long tradition within mainstream criminology that suggests (at least implicitly) that humans are prone to crime by their very nature. Thus, without any type of social control in place, humans will engage in behavior which is harmful to themselves and others, particularly if the perceived "rewards" of engaging in the behavior outweigh the potential "costs." This line of reasoning, typified by the classical school of criminology and its continued influence on many contemporary criminologists, locates the causes of criminal behavior within the individual and the choices he or she makes. Marxist criminologists, on the other hand, begin with the assumption that humans are not by their very nature prone to crime, but rather are more likely to commit crime under certain social and economic conditions. As such, many mainstream criminologists have claimed that Marxist criminology is overly deterministic, and that it fails to fully take into account "free will" (i.e., the ability for humans to choose between "right" and "wrong").

Other problems which mainstream criminologists have with Marxist criminology include its "unscientific," "utopian," and "moralistic" nature (Greenberg, 1981). Marxists, however, have been quick to point out that their explanation is no more or less "utopian" or "moralistic" than those of traditional criminologists. Additionally, as critical criminologists of all stripes have pointed out, value statements, whether explicitly addressed or not, are implicit in the assumptions theorists make about the causes and nature of crime. In the final analysis though, there is little question that the reason why most mainstream criminologists find Marxism unpalatable is likely due in large part to the social and economic implications of adopting a Marxist approach. In short, a Marxist understanding of crime calls into question many of our most basic assumptions about human nature and the way in which society is organized.

While Marxist criminology has been criticized by mainstream criminologists, it has also come under fire from others under the umbrella of critical criminology. Some feminists have argued that Marxism privileges the oppression of class over gender. A similar criticism has also been made that Marxism privileges class over race. While there is little doubt that Marxist criminologists use class as their starting point, this does not preclude them from making insightful analysis about the ways in which class effects both gender and race.

Other areas of concern for critical criminologists have been (1) the tendency of some Marxist criminologists to "romanticize" criminals as a "revolutionary class" (2) the overly deterministic nature of some Marxists (3) the tendency of some Marxists to give undue weight to the state as an "instrument" of ruling class oppression, and finally (4) the tendency of some Marxists to claim that people's fears of crime are only symptoms of "false consciousness" manufactured by the state to keep people's attentions diverted from the root of all problems: the capitalist system itself. While any one or more of these criticisms may apply to a particular "Marxian" work, it does not mean that all Marxists are prone to them. In fact, many Marxist criminologists would agree with these criticisms.

Within the critical tradition postmodernists have also leveled several criticisms toward Marxist criminology, two of which will be discussed here. The first, and most central is that postmodern criminologists view Marxist criminology as a "meta-narrative." Postmodernists have rejected the "totalizing" nature of meta-narratives, and their adherence to truth in favor of more "localized" and "subjective" truths. Secondly, postmodernists have tended to engage in cultural, structural, and linguistic critiques, many of which trace today's problems back to the Enlightenment (specifically, the values of modernity). As such, they have serious concerns with the inherently modernist nature of Marxism itself.

Marxist criminologists have been quick to respond to the postmodernists, and have raised the question of whether or not postmodern criminology should even fall under the umbrella of critical criminology because of its apolitical, and conservative undertones. As Russell (1997) has recently argued,

> if one is truly passionate about eradicating injustices and promoting a transformative politics, postmodernism provides no guidance . . . bereft of any transcendental praxis, and due to its many other fatal flaws, postmodernism becomes another variant of intellectual and political conservatism. Ultimately, it is conservative because of its tacit acceptance of the status quo, and the belief that it is not possible for humanity to construct a better future (1997:78-79).

The most damning criticisms of Marxist criminology, however, probably come from Marxists themselves. Many Marxists who do not study crime believe that "true" Marxists should pay little attention to crime at all. Crime, for many Marxists who aren't criminologists is merely an unfortunate consequence of capitalism, and little if anything can be gained by Marxists spending time analyzing a "problem" like crime which is peripheral at best to the primary issue of class struggle.

Finally, as Greenberg (1981) noted nearly 20 years ago, the development of Marxist criminology in the United States was hampered by the fact that some scholars did not have a solid grounding in general Marxist theory. Many of Marx's works were either unavailable or not well-known prior to the 1960s. As such, in their haste to develop a Marxist criminology, some scholars merely applied Marx to crime in crude and mechanical ways.

Wither Marxist Criminology?[6]

Marxism in general, and Marxist criminology in particular, have survived many internal and external attacks. While some have argued that Marxist criminology has seen its better days, many continue to make excellent inroads in developing a more complete Marxist criminology, both theoretically (e.g., Chambliss & Zatz, 1993) and empirically (e.g., Carlson & Michalowski, 1997). While some have been quick to hail the defeat of Marxist criminology, and Marxism in general, the deepening crisis of late twentieth-century capitalism, marked by increased inequality and poverty (both in the United States and globally), has made Marxism even more relevant today than ever. In the end, as long as capitalism persists as a dominant economic force that exerts influence over human relations, Marxist criminology will offer a fruitful method of inquiry to help us understand crime.

Notes

[1]   Most of Marx's writings on crime can be found in Greenberg (1981), and Taylor, Walton, and Young (1973). Other original writings of Marx concerning crime and law can be found in Cain and Hunt (1979).

[2]   Volumes have been dedicated to the understanding and development of Marx's work. Two very accessible texts which outline Marx's core concepts and ideas include Gottlieb (1992) and Heilbroner (1980).

[3]   In short, technology which replaces human labor increases profit rates for capitalists because machines are more efficient, more durable, and less volatile than humans—particularly when it comes to the repetitive and mundane tasks found in many factory settings.

4   See Taylor, W., Walton, I., & Young, J. (1973) pp. 222-236 and B. Mike (1976).

5   It must be emphasized here again that there are many varieties of feminist criminology; see Chapter 2.

6   This subtitle has been used by other Marxist criminologists, most notably Greenberg (1981).

Discussion Questions

1. How might one explain white-collar crime from a Marxist perspective?

2. From a Marxist perspective, how might changes in the larger economy such as increased unemployment cause crime rates to go up?

3. How would a structuralist Marxist explain Enron?

4. In your view, which form of Marxism offers a more compelling explanation of the relationship of the state to the ruling class: instrumental or structural? Provide reasons to support your answer.

5. Some Marxists have argued that some harmful actions of the ruling class are not labeled "criminal" because the ruling class has close ties to the legal apparatus. Can you identify some behaviors that might fall under this category?

6. From a Marxist perspective, how might a large gap between the rich and the poor create fertile grounds for street crime?

7. Explain domestic abuse from a Marxist-feminist perspective.

8. What are the primary differences between instrumental Marxist and structural Marxist explanations of crime?

9. On what grounds might the public find left-realist explanations of crime palatable? (e.g., in what ways is it "practical," "useful," etc.).

10. Some have argued that Marxist criminology has "served its purpose," but is currently no longer a promising area of theoretical inquiry. How would a dedicated Marxist respond to this assertion?

CHAPTER 2

Feminist Criminology

Jody Miller

Feminist criminology refers to a body of research and theory that situates the study of crime and criminal justice within a complex understanding that the social world is systematically shaped by relations of sex and gender. Though feminist scholarship emerges from diverse theoretical traditions— for example, liberal, Marxist, radical, socialist, postmodern and poststructural feminist traditions (see Tong, 1998)—there are a number of central beliefs that guide feminist inquiry. Daly and Chesney-Lind (1988:504) list five aspects of feminist thought that distinguish it from traditional criminological inquiry. These include the recognition that:

- Gender is not a natural fact but a complex social, historical, and cultural product; it is related to, but not simply derived from, biological sex difference and reproductive capacities.

- Gender and gender relations order social life and social institutions in fundamental ways.

- Gender relations and constructs of masculinity and femininity are not symmetrical but are based on an organizing principle of men's superiority and social and political-economic dominance over women.

- Systems of knowledge reflect men's views of the natural and social world; the production of knowledge is gendered.

- Women should be at the center of intellectual inquiry, not peripheral, invisible, or appendages to men.

In addition, contemporary feminist scholars strive to be attentive to the interlocking nature of race, class, and gender oppression, recognizing that women's experiences of gender vary according to their position in racial and class hierarchies (see Daly & Maher, 1998; Maher, 1997; Schwartz & Milovanovic, 1996; Simpson, 1991).

Feminist criminology has made a number of important contributions to the discipline. It is clear that feminist criminologists do not simply study female offenders. Instead, feminist scholarship addresses a broad range of issues. For example, it examines and interrogates traditional theories of crime and the androcentric (male-centered) biases shaping those theories; it examines both female *and* male offending—recognizing that gender is as relevant for understanding men's and boys' lives as women's and girls'. Feminist scholars are also concerned with how gender shapes females' and males' treatment within the juvenile and criminal justice systems as both offenders and workers, and feminist criminology addresses violence against women—including, for example, rape, intimate partner violence, and sexual harassment. With this caveat in mind, my primary focus in this chapter concerns feminist research and theory on gender and offending.

Theories of Crime

Beginning with work in the 1970s, one of feminist scholars' most important contributions has been to analyze and critique the ways traditional criminological theory constitutes "the female offender." Every theoretical perspective has both explicit and implicit assumptions about human nature and the individuals or groups in question. In criminology, assumptions about gender—and about the "nature" of females and males—have shaped the evolution of theories about women and crime. Often these assumptions are grounded in longstanding cultural stereotypes about women and men. Feminist critiques of traditional criminological approaches are grounded in the recognition that this work is limited in its ability to adequately address women's involvement in crime (see Chesney-Lind, 1997; Daly & Chesney-Lind, 1988; Simpson, 1989). Several limitations in particular have been highlighted.

First, much criminological theory has either ignored women—focusing exclusively or implicitly on explaining male participation in crime and defining females as unimportant or peripheral—or has ignored gender. The tendency to ignore *women* results, in part, because the most serious criminal offenders are male. As a consequence, the field of criminology is primarily concerned with understanding and explaining men's offending. Ignoring *gender* results both when theories of male crime don't seek to account for how gender helps to structure and shape male involvement in crime, and when theories assume to be generalizable—that is, theories derived from the study of men are assumed to be able to account for female crime or female offenders. As theories derived from studies of women are not seen as generalizable to men, implicit in the assumption that male theories are generalizable to women is the notion that women are a subcategory of men.

A second critique is aimed at theories that do the opposite: theories that are based on beliefs about fundamental differences between women and men—for instance, men are more rational, women more emotional; men are more aggressive, women more passive; men are stronger, women weaker. As taken-for-granted suppositions, these stereotypes about what distinguishes women from men often are reflected in criminological theory. It is precisely women's greater emotionality, passivity and weakness, according to these theories, which account for both their involvement (or lack thereof) in crime and the nature of their criminal activities. Early theories about female crime, for example, focused on individual pathologies such as personality disorders and sexual or emotional maladjustment. This approach contrasts with theories of male crime, which have historically been much more likely to define males in relation to the broader social world around them.

Because many of the gender-based assumptions that have guided criminological theories are hidden or taken-for-granted, it has taken a feminist lens to bring many of these biases to light. In the context of feminist critiques of traditional theory, several key issues emerged and have guided many feminist inquiries and debates about gender and offending. First is the issue of generalizability. As I have just described, for nearly a century, theories developed to explain why people commit crime have actually been theories of why *men* commit crime. Feminist scholars have been interested in the question of whether (or to what extent) these theories can explain *women's* participation in crime. If not, what alternative explanations can account for women's offending?

Second is the "gender-ratio" problem: what are the reasons behind men's much greater participation in crime as compared to women? Despite debates that routinely emerge about whether women's rates of crime are increasing at a faster pace than men's, or whether the gender gap in offending is narrowing, it is nonetheless the case that gender—specifically being male—is one of the strongest correlates of criminal offending. This is especially the case, the more serious and more violent the crime in question. Traditional approaches, as I have detailed, explained these differences drawing on stereotypical images of women's supposed inferiority, and viewed gender as an individual trait. In contrast, feminist scholars offer theoretical accounts that recognize gender as a key element of social organization. Each of these issues—the question of generalizability and the gender-ratio problem— merit further consideration.

The Issue of Generalizability

Theories that seek to explain why people commit crime are quite diverse. One thing they have routinely shared, however, is a primary orientation toward explaining men's or boys' crime. In many cases, this orientation is not outwardly stated; instead, the theory is assumed to be gender-neutral, and it is often taken for granted that the theoretical approach can be applied to males or females. Given the recognition of gender as a structuring feature of society, feminists, however, have posed the questions: "Do theories of men's crime apply to women? Can the logic of such theories be modified to include women?" (Daly & Chesney-Lind, 1988:514). Scholars who have attempted to test whether these theories can be generalized to women have focused on such constructs as the family, social learning, delinquent peer relationships, and to a lesser extent strain and deterrence. For the most part, these studies have found mixed results (for an overview, see Smith & Paternoster, 1987). As Kruttschnitt (1996:141) summarizes, "it appears that the factors that influence delinquent development differ for males and females in some contexts but not others."

Feminist scholars have posed several critiques of the generalizability approach. First, while theorists in this tradition look to find out whether the same processes are at work in explaining women's and men's crime, they can't account for the gender-ratio of offending—that is, men's disproportionate involvement in most crime. The dramatic gender differences in rates of offending suggest that a general etiological process is not occurring. Moreover, as I noted above, feminist scholars recognize gender as an important feature of the social organization of society, and consequently of women's and men's experiences. Theories that attempt to be gender-neutral are unable to address this pivotal issue (see Daly & Chesney-Lind, 1988). For instance, in much of the generalizability research, it is often taken for granted that variables or constructs (for instance, "family attachment" or "supervision") have the same meaning for males and females, but in fact this is an empirical question that cannot be taken for granted or simply assumed. Because of the gendered nature of women's and men's lives, some factors take on different meanings and have different consequences for the lives and experiences of females and males. Thus, feminists insist that while some of the theoretical concepts found in presumably gender-neutral theories of crime may be relevant or useful for understanding women's offending, gendered theories—i.e., those that take into account gender and gender stratification—are preferable to gender-neutral approaches (Daly, 2000; Simpson, 2000).

Second, the intersections of gender with racial and economic inequalities are sometimes overlooked in this work. Given that women (and men) live in diverse structural conditions—conditions that are shaped especially by race and class inequality—approaches that seek to find general causal patterns in women's and men's offending beg the question of how these causal factors differentially shape offending across race, class *and* gender (see Simpson, 1991). For instance, there is evidence of a link between "underclass" conditions and urban African-American women's offending that does not hold explanatory value for women's offending in other contexts. Hill and Crawford (1990) report that structural indicators appear to be most significant in predicting the criminal involvement of African-American women, while social-psychological indicators are more predictive for white women.

They conclude: "the unique position of black women in the structure of power relations in society has profound effects not shared by their white counterparts" (Hill & Crawford, 1990:621). In fact, the most common means of testing generalizability across race and gender is to hold race constant for gender, and gender constant for race. This approach fails to recognize the distinctive ways in which race and gender intersect to shape the experiences of specific racial-gender groups—for instance, African-American males, white males, African-American females, white females. Thus, theories that attempt to generalize across gender often miss the importance of racial and class inequalities, and their intersections with gender, in the causes of crime. These are issues of increasing interest to feminist scholars, as I will illustrate later in this chapter.

The Gender-Ratio Problem

One problem with attempts to generalize theories across gender, as I noted, is that all of this work begs the question of why it is that women and men have vastly divergent rates of criminal offending. This is the gender-ratio problem. Scholars who address this issue raise the following questions: "Why are women less likely than men to be involved in crime? Conversely, why are men more crime-prone than women? What explains [these] gender differences?" (Daly & Chesney-Lind, 1988:515). These questions have led scholars to pay attention to gender differences, and to develop theories that can account for variations in women's and men's offending (see Hagan, Gillis & Simpson, 1985; Heimer & De Coster, 1999).

With men as the starting point, the question of interest is what factors limit or block women's involvement in crime? But to only ask this question again reflects an androcentric perspective that makes men the norm upon which women deviate through their limited offending. Inverting this question, and attempting to account for why men have considerably higher rates of offending than women, raises an important set of additional queries. For feminists, one key question, then, is what is it about being male—and about masculinity specifically—that accounts for men's disproportionate levels of offending?

One theoretical perspective brought to bear on the issue is the analysis of gender as situated accomplishment. From this approach, gender is "much more than a role or individual characteristic: it is a mechanism whereby situated social action contributes to the reproduction of social structure" (West & Fenstermaker, 1995:21). Specifically, these theorists argue that women and men "do gender"—or behave in gendered ways—in response to normative beliefs about femininity and masculinity. The performance of gender is a response to gendered social hierarchies and expectations, but it also reproduces and reinforces them. This approach has been incorporated into feminist accounts of crime in order to explain differences in women's and men's offending (Messerschmidt, 1993; Simpson & Elis, 1995). Specifically, crime is described as "a 'resource' for accomplishing gender—for demonstrating masculinity within a given context or situation" (Simpson & Elis, 1995:50).

For example, Messerschmidt (1993) describes robbery as a quintessentially masculine crime, and he argues that men commit robberies as a means of constructing a masculine identity:

> The robbery setting provides the ideal opportunity to construct an 'essential' toughness and 'maleness'; it provides a means with which to construct that certain type of masculinity—hardman. Within the social context that ghetto and barrio boys find themselves, then, robbery is a rational practice for 'doing gender' and for getting money (Messerschmidt, 1993:107).

Examining crime as masculine accomplishment can help account for men's greater involvement in particular types of crime, and can help account for women's limited involvement in crime. Facets of this approach also offer useful insights regarding how gendered opportunities shape women's involvement in particular types of crime. For example, cultural definitions of femininity and women's sexuality, coupled with gender stratification on the streets, contribute to the narrowing of women's offending options and help explain women's higher levels of involvement in sex work than other forms of street offending. Nonetheless, the way this theory has been applied to explain male crime is of limited utility in explaining women's offending: it would be difficult to argue, for example, that women engage in street-level sex work as a means of constructing a feminine identity, particularly given the dangers and stigma attached to such activities. Rather, gender helps to narrow those options available to women on the streets, making sex work one of the few money-generating activities open to women (see Maher, 1997). Nonetheless, the concept of "gender accomplishment" remains a useful theoretical explanation for male crime. Even though it is a gendered theory, this does not mean it must be generalizable in its application across gender.

Because the gender-ratio problem highlights differences between women and men, it has also led to feminist scholarship focusing on those factors distinctive in explaining women's offending. One predominant school of feminist thought in this regard is the examination of the "blurred boundaries" between the victimization of women and girls and their participation in crime. This approach has been used in several ways to explain female offending (see Daly & Maher, 1998). Perhaps the clearest illustration of the overlap of victimization and crime is women who have killed their abusive partners. In this instance, what are often long-term patterns of serious abuse culminate in a "criminal" event that is a direct result of women's victimization (see Richie, 1996). An additional area in which the "blurred boundaries" approach has been used is to explain the criminalization of adolescent girls. There is evidence that a number of young female offenders have histories of childhood abuse within their families. When young women run away from home to escape violence, their running away, as well as the strategies they use on the streets to survive, are then classified as crimes. In effect, young women's efforts to escape and resist abuse are criminalized, resulting in a process that punishes girls for their victimization (see Chesney-Lind, 1997).

Some feminist criminologists argue that all or much of women's use of violence is a consequence of and response to gendered victimization. They suggest that women's use of violence is qualitatively different than men's. While men's violence, as noted above, is described as a means of enacting a masculine identity, these scholars argue that women use violence as a protective measure, in response to their vulnerability or actual victimization. For example, Campbell (1993:131-133) differentiates between male and female gang members' use of violence. She argues that for young men, "[v]iolence is power, and it is directed at other gangs and local youth because gang members want recognition and respect on their own turf. Violence is a measure of being someone in a world where all hope of success in conventional terms is lost." In contrast, she describes young women's aggression in a very different manner:

> Fear and loneliness—in their families, their communities, and their schools—are the forces that drive young women toward an instrumental view of their aggression. They know what it is to be victims, and they know that, to survive, force must be met with more than unspoken anger or frustrated tears. Less physically strong and more sexually vulnerable than boys, they find that the best line of defense is not attack but the threat of attack.

As Campbell's example illustrates, the emphasis on gender differences—and its justification through the gender-ratio problem—often leads to feminist accounts of female offending that are in marked contrast with traditional "gender neutral" approaches.

Critiques of Feminist Criminology

The work of feminist criminologists has not gone unchallenged. Among traditional criminologists, the key critique of feminist scholarship is that it is perceived to result in a dogmatic emphasis on gender and gender inequality, to the exclusion of other significant theoretical constructs. In particular, it is viewed by its critics as a perspective that derives from a political agenda rather than from the perspective of "objective" scientific investigation. However, as other chapters in this volume illustrate, the post-Enlightenment move within social science has called into serious doubt whether any social research can ever be objective or value-free, as the detractors of feminist scholarship suggest (see Harding, 1987). Instead, the belief in objectivity and value-free research is itself a particular political stance. Given this, the outright rejection of feminist criminology as "too political" holds little ground as a legitimate critique.

This is not to suggest, however, that some of the critiques waged at particular theoretical frameworks or emphases within feminist criminology are baseless. In fact, some of the most important critiques of feminist criminology have come from debates *among* feminists, rather than from traditional criminologists. These critiques—sometimes but not always mirrored in traditional criminological critiques—have led to new work in response to such challenges, and have helped to further strengthen and refine feminist scholarship within criminology. Here I will highlight three overlapping critiques of feminist criminology: universalizing tendencies within feminist research; problems resulting from an overemphasis on gender differences; and the limitations of a narrow victimization model for understanding women's offending. I will conclude this chapter by presenting several examples of recent feminist scholarship in criminology to illustrate feminist efforts to overcome these problems and develop theoretically and empirically rich understandings of gender and offending.

I noted that one of the critiques feminists have raised about the generalizability approach and its application is that it fails to take into account the unique positions that individuals and groups in society are placed in by relations of gender, but also race and class inequalities. Feminists have consistently made a convincing case that theories need to be *gendered*—there is no "universal" human being; rather, our experiences, opportunities and lives are ordered by relations of sex and gender. If traditional criminology can be critiqued for overlooking gender, one limitation of some feminist scholarship within criminology is a tendency to emphasize *only* gender, without recognizing the interlocking nature of race, class and gender. Consequently, theories have been generated to explain how gender shapes women's and men's experiences and actions, with either little attention to the impact of race and class or with the belief that race and class can be "added on" as additional burdens facing, for instance, African-American women or poor women.

One consequence of this approach is that it implies that there is a "universal" woman—i.e., that all women have a shared set of gendered experiences, regardless of their position in various social hierarchies within society. Moreover, gendered theories that do not integrate race and class imply that white, middle class women are the norm upon which other women deviate. Universalizing tendencies within feminist scholarship are often one outcome of an approach that overemphasizes gender differences. A strengthened feminist approach is one that instead can grapple with and understand variations in women's experiences, including variations based on race and class inequalities. This involves looking at race and class, not as additional burdens facing women of color and/or poor women, but as structuring unique positions within the system, and consequently unique experiences of gender. It also involves looking at the unique positions and privileges that accrue from being white and/or middle class or wealthy. Such an approach can help feminist scholars overcome the "additive" model of race, class, and gender (see Harding, 1987).

The overemphasis on gender differences leads to additional problems as well. Traditional criminologists in particular have accused feminist scholars of "throwing out the baby with the bathwater"—that is, failing to be attentive to those aspects of traditional scholarship that may actually illuminate our understandings of women's offending. Recently feminist scholars likewise have argued that in addition to examining gender differences (and within-gender variations), it is also important to examine similarities across gender (Miller, 2001; Thorne, 1993). In fact, examining both differences *and* similarities across gender is an important means of uncovering the precise impact of gender in various social contexts. As Simpson (2000) explains, "many seminal ideas that have emerged in criminological thought can be integrated and/or elaborated in ways that can inform gendered criminological theory." Consequently, a number of feminists now recognize the utility of re-examining this issue.

Finally, as my earlier discussion of the "blurred boundaries" approach suggests, a strength *and* limitation of feminist criminology is its emphasis on the overlapping nature of victimization and offending among women and girls. Recognition of women's victimization within male-dominated society is a necessary feature of any theory that attempts to take gender seriously and place relations of sex and gender at the foreground of inquiry. Nonetheless, focusing narrowly on women's victimization is problematic because it "tend[s] to create the false impression that women have *only* been victims, that they have never successfully fought back, that women cannot be effective social agents on behalf of themselves or others" (Harding, 1987:5). Moreover, even when feminist inquiries focus on *resistance* to victimization, women's lives—or their criminal activities—are still framed as governed exclusively by gendered victimization, or fear and response to such victimization. While women's victimization is important, feminist research on women's offending is strengthened when it also addresses other facets of women's offending and women's lives. Let me now turn to a discussion of recent developments in feminist criminology, to illustrate the ways in which feminist scholars have incorporated these challenges into their studies of gender and crime.

Current Directions in Feminist Criminology

Critiques of traditional criminological theory, along with debates about generalizability and the gender-ratio of offending, have been longstanding in feminist responses to the discipline. There is consensus among feminists that criminological theory must be gendered. In addition, middle-range theories, or those that attempt to explicate the operation of gender within particular facets of the social world, are preferred to "grand theories" of social life (Daly, 2000). In several recent papers, Daly (1998:94-99; 2000) outlines four areas of inquiry within contemporary feminist scholarship:

- *Gender Ratio of Crime:* What is the nature of, and what explains gender differences in lawbreaking and arrests for crime?

- *Gendered Pathways:* What is the nature of, and what explains the character of girls'/women's and boys'/men's pathways to lawbreaking?

- *Gendered Crime:* What are the contexts and qualities of boys'/men's and girls'/women's illegal acts? What is the social organization of particular offenses?

- *Gendered Lives:* How does gender organize the ways in which men and women survive, take care of themselves and others, and find shelter and food? How does gender structure thinkable courses of action and identities?

Within each area of inquiry outlined by Daly, many scholars have incorporated insights from the critiques raised above in order to build upon previous feminist scholarship and strengthen the feminist contribution to criminology. To illustrate, I conclude this chapter by discussing two examples of excellence in feminist scholarship. The first is a quantitative study examining "the gendering of violent delinquency" (Heimer & De Coster, 1999). The second is an ethnographic study of the gendered social organization of a drug market (Maher, 1997). Combined, these studies represent distinct areas of investigation among feminist scholars, and they show the diversity of methodological approaches utilized by feminist criminologists in the study of gender and crime.

The Gendering of Violent Delinquency

In their article "The Gendering of Violent Delinquency," Heimer and De Coster (1999) address two key issues of importance to feminist criminologists: *within-gender* variations in the use of violence and variations in violence *across gender* (i.e., the gender-ratio of offending). As I noted above, one critique raised against feminist scholarship is that it sometimes overemphasizes gender differences. Heimer and De Coster provide a theoretical model of the causes of violent delinquency that can address differences across and within gender, as well as between-gender similarities. They accomplish this by blending insights from a traditional criminological theory—differential association theory—with feminist theory about the definitions, meanings, and impact of gender.

Heimer and De Coster outline a complex causal model of violent delinquency based on the differentiated experiences of young women and young men that result from gender inequality. They focus specifically on the interplay between social structure and culture, and argue that different social structural position—based on gender, race, social class—results in variations in two significant cultural processes: family controls and peer associations. With regard to family controls, Heimer and De Coster differentiate between two types of family controls, which they suggest operate differently for males and females. First, *direct parental controls* include such things as supervision and coercive discipline. On the other hand, *emotional bonding* is a more indirect form of control that results from emotional attachment to families. Particularly as young women are taught to value interpersonal relationships to a greater extent than young men, Heimer and De Coster argue that indirect controls resulting from emotional bonds to the family are the primary controls over girls' behavior, whereas direct controls have a stronger impact for boys.

With regard to peer associations, they suggest that boys are more likely to have exposure to friends who engage in aggressive activities than are girls. This means boys are also more likely to be exposed to norms favorable to violence than are girls. These two cultural processes—family control and peer associations—along with prior histories of violent behavior, influence two cultural outcomes: the extent that youths learn violent definitions (e.g., definitions of violence as an appropriate behavior) and gender definitions (traditional beliefs about the proper behavior of males and females, or of masculinity and femininity). The greater youths' cultural definitions of violence, the more likely they are to engage in delinquency. However, cultural definitions of violence also run counter to traditional definitions of femininity, which stress "nurturance, passivity, nonaggressiveness, and physical and emotional weakness" (Heimer & De Coster, 1999:283). Thus the attitudes and beliefs young women learn about appropriate femininity will have a direct impact on their likelihood of engaging in violence.

Through a sophisticated quantitative analysis of the National Youth Survey—a longitudinal probability sample of youths in the United States—Heimer and De Coster tested their theoretical model and found strong support for its ability to explain variations in girls' and boys' use of violence, as well as variations in the use of violence within gender, based on the causal pathway of social structural factors (positions tied to race, class, gender) shaping cultural processes (family controls, peer associations), shaping cultural outcomes (violent definitions, gender definitions), shaping the likelihood youths participate in violence. They (1999:305) explain:

> In short, the conclusion of our research is that violent delinquency is "gendered" in significant ways. Adolescent violence can be seen as a product of gendered experiences, gender socialization, and the patriarchal system in which they emerge. Thus, consistent with feminist arguments, gender differences in violence are ultimately rooted in power differences.

Sexed Work

Heimer and De Coster's study examines *gendered pathways* into offending, utilizing quantitative research methods. In contrast, Lisa Maher's *Sexed Work: Gender, Race and Resistance in a Brooklyn Drug Economy* examines *gendered crime,* based on several years of ethnography and in-depth interviews with women in a street-level drug economy. Her study provides a complex, layered account of women's participation in drug markets. It is particularly exemplary due to Maher's consistent examination of the intersections of race, class, and gender in shaping women's experiences and lives, and is illustrative of the strength of feminist scholarship that moves beyond a universalizing emphasis on gender. In addition, like Heimer and De Coster, Maher blends feminist theory with a traditional theoretical approach—cultural reproduction theory.

Revealing the interdependence of formal and informal economies, including the illicit drug economy, the study focuses on the impact of stratification within formal and informal market economies, and the consequent truncation of women's economic opportunities. Though some (primarily non-feminist) scholars have suggested the drug trade has opened new opportunities for women, Maher's study provides compelling evidence to the contrary. Gender inequality, as she demonstrates, is institutionalized on the streets: gender segregation and stereotypes of women as unreliable and weak limit women's participation in informal economic street networks. Specifically, the study documents a rigid gender division of labor in the drug economy, shaped as well along racial lines, in which women are "clearly disadvantaged compared to their male counterparts" (1997:54).

Describing the three spheres of income generation on the streets—drug business hustles, non-drug hustles, and sex work—Maher details the ways in which women are excluded from more lucrative opportunities, and find sex work one of their few viable options for making money. Moreover, the introduction of crack cocaine into urban drug markets has further disadvantaged women by increasing competition, as well as the degradation and mistreatment women often experience on the streets. In addition, she shows how racial stratification further differentiates the opportunities and experiences of white, African-American and Latina women within street-level sex work.

Sexed Work challenges several dimensions of previous work on women's participation in drug markets—including both previous feminist studies and traditional criminological approaches. First, it contradicts "the highly sexualized images of women crack users that dominate the social science literature" (1997:195). This sexualized imagery—of desperate women willing to do "anything" for their next hit—is part and parcel of the dominant view of drug users (and especially women) as pathological, dependent, and lacking any control over their lives. In contrast, Maher shows that women are involved in a wide array of income-generating activities within the drug economy, with occupational norms governing their activities, despite the rigid division of labor on the streets.

The counterpoint to scholarship that provides overly sexualized imagery of women crack users is scholarship that suggests the advent of crack is linked to increases in women's use of violence. Here the concern among traditional criminologists is with a convergence in male and female offending rates. However, Maher counters the stereotype of the "new" violent female offender through her documentation of the contexts of women's use of violence. She suggests that much of women's violence was in response to the increased denigration they faced as a result of the changes brought about by the introduction of crack. For example, Maher adopts the term "viccing" to describe women's robberies of clients in the sex trade—a practice adopted to resist women's increased vulnerability to victimization and the cheapening of sex markets within the drug economy. While Maher emphasizes the overlapping nature of victimization and offending among women, she takes particular care to emphasize women's strategies of resistance and agency.

Conclusion

Feminist criminology provides a series of important contributions to the field of criminology and the study of crime. The goal of this chapter has been to document and describe key elements of these contributions. First, feminist scholars have provided important critiques of traditional criminological theories, challenging the generalizability of theories developed to explain male crime, and highlighting the importance of the gender-ratio of offending as a key issue in need of explanation in any theoretical accounts of crime. As a consequence of the efforts of feminist scholars, there is now widespread recognition that women and men lead gendered lives, and recognizing and accounting for this is a fundamental issue for criminology. Moreover, a particular strength of feminist criminology is its ability to incorporate and grapple with critiques of feminist works, in order to generate even more valuable scholarly insights into the impact of gender, race, and class inequalities in shaping women's and men's lives. As the theoretical and empirical contributions discussed in this chapter illustrate, the important contributions of feminist scholarship have led and will continue to contribute to the development of new theoretical insights that strengthen our understanding of the causes and consequences of crime.

Discussion Questions

1. What are the five aspects of feminist thought that distinguish it from traditional forms of inquiry?

2. Why do feminists argue that gender should be examined as interlocking with race and class oppression?

3. Describe the two critiques feminists raise against traditional criminological theories. What's the difference between ignoring *women* and ignoring *gender*?

4. What is the issue of generalizability? Why do feminists argue that a gender-neutral approach is insufficient for understanding crime?

5. What is the gender-ratio problem, and why is it important to take into account when theorizing about crime?

6. What does it mean to view gender as "situated accomplishment"? How has this perspective been used to explain crime?

7. What is the concept of "blurred boundaries" and how has it been used to theorize women's crime?

8. List and explain the three critiques raised against feminist criminology.

9. What are the four areas of inquiry within contemporary feminist scholarship?

10. Compare Heimer and DeCoster's "The Gendering of Violent Delinquency" with Maher's *Sexed Work* in terms of research methodology, and their application of a feminist approach. How do these works complement one another in attaining feminist goals?

CHAPTER 3

Left Realism on Inner-City Violence

Walter DeKeseredy

It was common in the 1990s to hear that "the economy has never been better" or that we "never had it so good, " with such supporting evidence as low official unemployment figures (Beauchesne, 1999), record profits accumulated by large corporations, a booming stock market, and a sharp increase in conspicuous consumption (e.g., buying cars, jewelry, etc.) (Hurtig, 1999). For many citizens, another good sign was an overall decrease in interpersonal violent crime. For example, the U.S. homicide rate had fallen to its lowest level in 30 years (Fox & Zawitz, 2000). Some people "credit the economy for a big drop in attacks" (Ellis, 2000:A13), while others, such as former New York City Mayor Rudolph Giuliani, attributed the decrease to aggressive policing and to increased sanction severity (Shapiro, 1999).

In response, an international community of critical criminologists say, "Get real!" They are left realists who empirically show that several major economic changes have led capitalist nations such as Canada and the United States towards a "dystopia of exclusion," where "[t]he poor are isolated in inner-city ghettos, in orbital estates, and in ghost towns where capital originally led them then left them stranded as it winged its way elsewhere, where labor was cheaper and expectations lower" (Young, 1999:20). Left realists also show that while the overall violent crime rate may have gone down, the following structural changes have fueled a considerable amount of violence in socially and economically disadvantaged inner-city communities: the rise of the "contingent" workforce; the outmigration of people who can afford to leave poor urban communities; the North American Free Trade Agreement (NAFTA); transnational corporations moving operations to developing countries to use cheap labor; the "suburbanization" of employment; the implementation of high technology in workplaces; and the shift from a manufacturing to a service-based economy (Alvi, DeKeseredy & Ellis, 2000; Jargowsky, 1997; Krivo, Peterson, Rizzo, & Reynolds, 1998; W. Wilson, 1987, 1996).

Consider the results of the Quality of Neighborhood Life Survey (QNLS), a study heavily influenced by two British left realist local crime surveys. The QNLS found that 19.3 percent of a sample of women (N = 216) who lived in six public housing estates in the west end of an urban center in Eastern Ontario, Canada stated that they were victimized by at least one of 12 types of intimate partner violence in the past year (DeKeseredy, Alvi, Schwartz & Perry, 1999). This figure is higher than most of the violence against women estimates uncovered by most of the larger North American surveys that used a similar measure of violence.[1] Similarly, Renzetti and Maier (2002) found that an alarmingly high number (33%) of poor female public housing residents in Camden, New Jersey were victimized by all varieties of violence.

It is not surprising that the rates of violence against women and other social groups (e.g., African-Americans) are so high in poor North American inner-city areas when you consider the above structural changes *and* that between 1970 and 1990, the number of U.S. people living urban ghettos, barrios, and slums grew from 4.1 million to eight million (Jargowsky, 1997). As described by Hatfield (1999) in Tables 1 and 2, things are not better in Canada even though it was ranked by the United Nations *Human Development Report* (2000) as the best nation in the world in which to live. Table 1 shows that except for Ottawa-Hull, the concentration of poor families in Canada's largest Census Metropolitan Areas (CMAs) has increased substantially between 1980 and 1995. Table 2 shows that a similar trend exists with neighborhood poverty rates. Thus, as in the United States, Canada is experiencing something similar to what Taylor (1999:31) refers to as "a distinctive new process of 'hyper-ghettoization'—the development of discrete urban territories where the mass of residents are permanently excluded from legitimate employment. . . ."

Table 1

The Increasing Concentration of Poor Families in Canada's Nine Largest CMAs, 1980 to 1995[2]

Census Metropolitan Area	Concentration of Poor, 1980	Concentration of Poor, 1990	Concentration of Poor, 1995
Montreal	30.1%	40.1%	40.2%
Winnipeg	23.5%	39.0%	36.1%
Toronto	14.7%	21.4%	29.8%
Ottawa-Hull	27.5%	24.1%	28.4%
Hamilton	21.6%	24.9%	27.9%
Quebec City	20.8%	26.6%	25.3%
Edmonton	4.1%	28.3%	18.8%
Vancouver	7.2%	15.5%	13.7%
Calgary	6.4%	20.3%	8.7%

Table 2
Increasing Neighborhood Poverty Rates in Canada's Nine Largest CMAs, 1980 to 1995[3]

Census Metropolitan Area	Neighborhood Poverty Rate, 1980	Neighborhood Poverty Rate, 1990	Neighborhood Poverty Rate, 1995
Montreal	14.0	20.4	21.3
Winnipeg	9.0	15.7	14.0
Toronto	4.7	7.9	13.6
Ottawa-Hull	10.0	8.4	10.4
Hamilton	8.1	7.9	10.8
Quebec City	9.0	11.2	11.2
Edmonton	1.6	12.8	7.8
Vancouver	2.5	6.1	6.7
Calgary	2.2	8.9	3.5

In sum, the reality is that despite rhetoric from politicians, academics, and others with a vested stake in maintaining the status quo, North American poverty has increased markedly over the past two decades and the poor are still highly vulnerable to violent victimization. On top of that, people located at the bottom of the socioeconomic ladder, especially those in inner-city areas, are subject to "a staggering degree of discrimination . . . at all levels of the criminal justice system" (National Council of Welfare, 2000:1). These are concrete problems taken seriously by left realists such as Jock Young, Elliott Currie, Brian MacLean, and William Julius Wilson. The main objective of this chapter is to describe and assess their scholarly and policy contributions. It is to their theoretical work that I turn first.

Left Realist Theory

Although there are variations in left realist theory, all versions start with the assertion that inner-city violence is a major problem for socially and economically disenfranchised people, regardless of their sex or ethnic/cultural background. This position is sharply attacked by those whom Currie (1992) refers to as "progressive minimalists." These are critical criminologists and liberals who downplay the seriousness and extent of such violence because of either the fear of pathologizing the poor, "whipping up" support for severe punishment, and supporting racist arguments or "because of a concern of being charged with 'racism' or with 'blaming the victim'. . . ." (W. Wilson, 1987:6). For minimalists, the criminal justice system is more problematic than is crime itself (Young, 1998), and the widespread fear of and concern about crime is a function of a moral panic fueled by a coalition of politicians, law enforcement personnel, and journalists used to obtain support for a social order detrimental to the disenfranchised and the construction of a socialist society (Chambliss, 1994; Reiman, 1998).

African-Americans are much more likely to be victims of "America's imprisonment binge" than are members of the dominant culture (Irwin & Austin, 1997). This does not mean, however, that crime victimization is not a serious problem for inner-city black communities. For example, despite a drop of about 36 percent in the past few years, homicide is the leading cause of death for African-American males aged 15 to 34 (Cook & Moore, 1999). African-American young men aged 18 to 24 had homicide victimization rates about eight times higher than that for the same aged white males or African-American females, and more than 34 times higher than that for white females (Fox & Zawitz, 2000). Obviously, homicide "is not a democratic crime" (Cook & Moore, 1999). No wonder some researchers define homicide within the African-American community as a major public health issue (e.g., O'Carroll & Mercy, 1986). Others, such as Mann (1993:46), refers to black homicide as "a form of black genocide, since the victim of homicide is most often another black person and the incidence of this crime is so pervasive."

Think about the frightening results of Schwartz, Grisso, and Miles' (1994) western Philadelphia study. Conducted over a four-year period (1987 through 1990) in 17 census tracts, it found that 40 percent of young African-American males suffered violent assaults that required them to go to a hospital emergency room. Surely such high rates of interpersonal violence must be a major concern for many inner-city residents in the United States. They certainly are from a European perspective, as left realist Jock Young (1998) correctly points out. Because most Canadians live within 200 miles of the U.S. border and frequently cross it for business and pleasure, they too are deeply concerned about the levels of violence that plague U.S. urban areas and other parts of the country. Who would not know that by the mid-1990s, a young U.S. male was 37 times more likely to be a victim of homicide than an English youth, 12 times more likely than a Canadian youth, 20 times more likely than a Swede, 26 more likely than a young French male, and over 60 times more likely than his Japanese counterpart (Currie, 1998)? Unfortunately, there are still "too many well-meaning progressives" who "simply do not get it when it comes" to the problem of violence and other serious criminal harms in U.S. cities (Currie, 1992:92). More concerned with crimes by the powerful, they refuse to acknowledge socially and economically disadvantaged people's legitimate fear of inner-city crime and their desire to end it.

Left realists, like other critical criminologists, also view poverty as a powerful determinant of muggings, armed robbery, sexual assault, wife-beating, and so on. However, most poor people do not commit these crimes. This is why left realist criminologists contend that relative poverty rather than absolute poverty is the key to understanding violent crime (Lea & Young, 1984; Young, 1999). Absolute poverty refers to a family or person's inability to buy basic necessities (e.g., food, shelter, clothing), while relative poverty is defined in relation to a society's mean or median income. Thus, if your income is at the bottom end of the income distribution, you are poor regardless of your absolute income (Devine & Wright, 1993).

According to left realists, it is not the inability to buy a DIRECTV satellite dish or other "glittering prizes of capitalism" that motivates people to commit crime. Rather, it is a "lethal combination" of relative deprivation and individualism (Young, 1999). For example, poverty experienced as unfair (relative deprivation when compared to someone else) breeds discontent (Lea & Young, 1984). Individualism leads such discontent to foster "Hobbesian jungles" of the urban poor (Young, 1999), a "universe where human beings live side by side but not as human beings" (Hobsbawm, 1994:341). Crime, then, is an unjust individualistic "solution" to the "experience of injustice" (Young, 1998). However, it is important to note that such experienced injustice, combined with an individualistic solution, occurs throughout society (Young, 1998). Crime is certainly not "ghetto-specific" (W. Wilson, 1996). After all, many affluent people use illicit drugs, beat their wives, and sexually assault their dating partners. Still, because of the structural changes described previously (e.g., deindustrialization), many poor ghetto residents cannot find work and thus have little reason to refrain from criminal activity. This is the key reason why interpersonal violence, drug dealing, illicit drug use, and other crimes occur with greater frequency in ghettos, barrios, and slums (W. Wilson, 1996).

Left realists also argue that people who lack legitimate means of solving the problem of relative deprivation may come into contact with other frustrated disenfranchised people and form subcultures, which, in turn, encourage and legitimate criminal behaviors. For example, receiving respect from peers is highly valued among ghetto adolescents who are denied status in mainstream, middle-class society. However, respect and status is often granted by inner-city subcultures when one is willing to be violent, such as using an assault rifle (Messerschmidt, 1993).

A cautionary note about ghetto-based criminal subcultures is required here. They should not be construed as "somehow alien to the wider culture" (Young, 1999:86), which is what culture of poverty theorists like Lewis (1966) and Banfield (1974) do. The truth is that they, like most North Americans, want to achieve the "American Dream" and its related status but lack the legitimate means of doing so (Messner & Rosenfeld, 1997). For example, the Puerto Rican drug dealers Bourgois (1995) studied in East Harlem, New York City are a core element of U.S. culture. In fact, criminal subcultures like this one are "based on all-American notions of work as an area of rugged individualism and competition and sanctioned by a film industry which carries the message of didactic violence. . . ." (Young, 1999:87).

According to Bourgois:

> Like most other people in the United States, drug dealers and street criminals are scrambling to obtain their piece of the pie as fast as possible. In fact, in their pursuit of success they are even fol-

lowing the minute details of the classical yankee model for upward mobility. They are aggressively pursuing careers as private entrepreneurs; they take risks, work hard, and pray for good luck. They are the ultimate rugged individualists braving an unpredictable frontier where fortune, fame, and destruction are all around the corner, and where the enemy is ruthlessly hunted down and shot (1995:326).

Criticisms of Left Realist Theory

Left realist theory is criticized on several grounds, especially by feminist scholars. For example, although left realism embraces elements of radical and socialist feminism, as evident in several local victimization surveys conducted in the United Kingdom (e.g., Jones, MacLean & Young, 1986), there is no attempt to theorize women's experiences of crime as suspects, offenders, defendants, and inmates (Carlen, 1992). The issues of why women's offenses are distinct from men's and the sexist nature of the criminal justice system are also given short shrift. These are valid criticisms because left realists' theoretical work on the relationship between gender and violence has focused mainly on male-to-female victimization in domestic/household settings and in public spaces. Still, their analysis of this major problem is deemed by some critics to be problematic because they have not developed and tested theories of male patriarchal domination and control over women (DeKeseredy & Schwartz, 1991). This is likely to change soon as we are seeing new left realist literature that addresses this concern.

Take, for example, Young's recent attempt to explain the relationship between relative deprivation, individualism, "macho" subcultural dynamics, and violence against women. Seen as a result of exclusion and inclusion, he (1999:13-14) argues that this form of woman abuse:

> can be caused by relative deprivation and by clashes among individuals demanding equality and others resisting them. Of course, where both relative deprivation and individualism occur together as in the macho-culture of lower class, young unemployed males when confronting the demands for equality of women, often in poorly paid yet steady employment, one would expect a particularly high rate of conflict, often resulting in the preference for setting up home separately and the preponderance of single mothers. Indeed this latter group have the highest rates of violence against them, usually from ex-partners.

Left realists have also been criticized for not explaining crimes of the powerful, such as corporate crime, white-collar crime, and political crime (Henry, 1999). In its current form, left realist theory cannot do so because it is restricted to interpersonal relations between economically and socially disenfranchised individuals (Pearce & Tombs, 1992). This is not to say, however, that left realists only advance what Henry (1999:138-139) refers to as a "narrow, common-sense concept of crime" that excludes "hidden victims of the structurally powerful." If this is the case, then why do British left realists John Lea and Jock Young (1984) contend that working class people are victimized from all directions and that a "double thrust" against both street crime and "suite crime" is necessary? Further, left realism "notes that the more vulnerable a person is economically and socially the more likely it is that both working class and white collar crime will occur against them; that one sort of crime tends to compound another as does one social problem another" (Young, 1986:23-24).

Although some criminologists have tried (e.g., Gottfredson & Hirschi, 1990), to the best of my knowledge no one has developed a theory that can adequately explain all types of crime. If this is a major shortcoming, then the theoretical work of many who attack left realists for devoting most of their attention to crimes of the powerless should also be considered flawed. For example, most of the people who criticize left realists for ignoring crimes of the powerful do exactly the opposite: only look at crimes of the structurally powerful but not crimes of the "truly disadvantaged" (W. Wilson, 1987). This, too, is a one-sided, narrow approach, and it inhibits the development of progressive alternative policies aimed at curbing predatory street crime, woman abuse, and other crimes that plague poor inner-city areas. Neglecting to deal with these harms allows right-wing politicians to manufacture ideological support for "get-tough" policies that will never make ghettos, barrios, and slums safer.

There are several other criticisms of left realist theory and because they are well documented elsewhere,[4] they will not be repeated here. Many more new ones are likely to emerge too, given that left realists are constantly modifying their theoretical contributions in accordance with rapid changes now occurring in societies such as Canada and the United States.

Left Realist Policy Proposals

Left realists based in Europe, Australia, Canada, the United States, and elsewhere offer many different crime control and prevention policies. Even so, all left realists have two things in common. First, although they would all like to see a major transformation from a society based on class, race/ethnic, and gender inequality to one that that is truly equitable and democratic, they realize that this will not happen in the immediate future. This view is well founded, given that there is massive public support for neo-conservative governments and their economic and social policies (e.g., government cuts to unemployment insurance),[5] a major anti-feminist backlash, widespread resistance to affirmative action programs, and other indicators that social injustice is deeply entrenched in North America. So, left realists seek short-term gains while remaining committed to long-term change. This is why they propose practical initiatives that can be implemented immediately and that "chip away" at patriarchal capitalism.

Second, all left realists are sharply opposed to policies heavily informed by what Young (1998) defines as "establishment criminology." Establishment criminologists see crime as a property of the individual rather than of broader social, cultural, economic, and political forces. Take Gottfredson and Hirschi (1990:90), two widely read and cited administrative criminologists who assert that people lacking self-control are more likely to commit crime because they "tend to be impulsive, insensitive, physical (as opposed to mental), risk taking, short-sighted, and non-verbal. . . ." Then there are more extreme others, such as the highly controversial J. Philippe Rushton (1999) who contends that African-Americans are more biologically predisposed to committing crime than are whites and Asians.

Once referred to by some critical criminologists as "right realists" (Young, 1996), another group of establishment criminologists (e.g., Dennis, 1997; Kelling & Coles, 1997; J. Wilson, 1985), while seeing crime as determined by forces within individuals (e.g., individuals choose to commit crime), view searching for causes of crime as a "distraction and a waste of their valuable time" (Platt & Takagi, 1981:45). According to them, energy and time would be better spent improving the ability of the criminal justice system to deter people from committing crimes, with the ultimate goal of decreasing the rewards of crime by increasing the costs.

Regardless of how they explain crime, all establishment criminologists call for policies aimed at deterring people from stealing, mugging, raping, etc. As you can imagine, this means such policies as bringing back chain gangs as was done in Arizona and Alabama, enacting "Three Strikes and You're Out" legislation for repeat offenders, implementing the "Broken Windows" approach to policing (Kelling & Coles, 1997),[6] and using other "get-tough" strategies. Such simplistic solutions are prime examples of "bad ideas," which are the key hurdles in the search for effective or sensible crime policies (Walker, 1998). For example, there is no conclusive evidence showing that incarcerating many people leads to major reductions in crime.[7] This is because solutions like this one disregard the broader structural aspects of society that create an atmosphere in which crimes are committed. In the case of violence, this includes high youth unemployment, extreme levels of social inequality and poverty, and the lack of meaningful jobs for many people.

Thus, left realists call for a "broader vision" (W. Wilson, 1996), which prioritizes social policy over criminal justice. This is not to say, however, that they are opposed to criminal justice reform. For example, British left realists call for strategies such as democratic control of policing and community participation in crime prevention and policy development (Kinsey, Lea & Young, 1986; Lea & Young, 1984). These initiatives can, to a small extent, help curb violence and other crimes, but they alone do little, if anything, to address the social causes of crime. It leaves criminal justice personnel as groundskeepers brought in to "clean up the mess" made by the rest of society (Currie, 1985).

This is why left realists emphasize the implementation of a broad range of short-term initiatives aimed at reducing poverty and unemployment, curbing violence against women, and building strong communities.

Below are some examples of progressive policies that can help lower poverty and unemployment rates:[8]

- Job creation and training programs, including publicly supported community-oriented job creation.

- A higher minimum wage level.

- Government sponsored day care so that poor single parents can work without the bulk of their paychecks going to pay for child care. Some unemployed single parents today do not look for work because they cannot afford child care.

- Housing assistance, which not only helps poor people in general, but also enables abused women and children to escape their environments without ending up destitute and on the streets. Consider Zorza's (1991) study, which suggests that 50 percent of homeless women and children ended up this way after escaping abuse.

- Introducing entrepreneurial skills into the high school curriculum.

- Creating linkages between schools, private business, and government agencies.

- Universal health care.

As expected, conservatives viciously attack strategies like these. For example, many agree with Charles Murray's (1984) assertion that social programs like universal day and health care increase poverty and crime by contributing to the development of a welfare-dependent and deviant subculture. There is no scientific evidence for this "theory," which is not surprising given that it is little more than conservative ideology "dressed up in social scientific regalia" (Devine & Wright, 1993:125). Still, Murray's (1984) arguments are strongly supported by conservative politicians and have been put into practice throughout North America.

Some progressives have also raised concerns about policies located in the welfare state. Tomaszewski (1999:242), for example, reminds us that in capitalist societies, state-sponsored social services (e.g., unemployment insurance) are not intended to eliminate inequality, but rather to "pacify the truly disadvantaged and prevent civil disorder." He urges left realists such as Wilson (1996) to think about the dangers associated with the complex relationship between governments and capitalist societies. For the most part, a capitalist state is there to buttress capitalism and will not threaten the gains made by corporate and political elites under the current unequal political economic order. This is a valid point. Nevertheless, again, something needs to be done now because the revolution is not around the corner. Further, there is evidence that some left realist work has made a major difference.

Consider Basran, Charan, and MacLean's (1995) local survey of corporate violence against Punjabi farmworkers and their children. This study influenced Kwantlen University College and the British Columbia government in Canada to provide suitable and affordable child care for Punjabi farmworkers. This is definitely not a means of strengthening inequality so that people can continue working under capitalism. Rather it is one of several "realistic solutions to distorted social conditions" (Devine & Wright, 1993).

Poverty is a key determinant of male-to-female violence against women and such violence pushes many women into poverty.[9] Violence against women is also one of the key factors associated with female crime, such as prostitution (Chesney-Lind, 1997; DeKeseredy, 2000b). Recognizing these problems, several North American left realists (e.g., DeKeseredy, Schwartz, & Alvi, 2000) are heavily informed by work done by members of the pro-feminist men's movement (e.g., Funk, 1993). Pro-feminist men collectively and individually confront expressions of sexism, support survivors of woman abuse, protest pornography, confront abusive men, and do a long list of other practical things aimed at making women's lives safer.

Do these strategies work? This is an empirical question that can only be answered empirically. So far, to the best of my knowledge, no one has systematically evaluated the effectiveness of pro-feminist men's efforts. Still, it is fair to assume that these initiatives alone will not do much. They have to be combined with other approaches, such as education, media campaigns, police intervention, and strategies aimed at curbing other forms of structured social inequality. The good news is, however, that a growing number of men are getting involved in the practical struggle to stop all forms of woman abuse, which is defined by some progressives as a major success and a sign of change (Thorne-Finch, 1992).

Crime cannot be solely attributed to one's position in the socioeconomic hierarchy or to an individual's terrifying experiences with intimate violence. Although these are two major determinants of inner-city violence, homicide, bank robbery, muggings, wife beating, and other serious aggressive acts are also functions of neighborhood or community social and organizational characteristics. For example, urban neighborhoods characterized by collective efficacy have lower crime rates than those that are not (Sampson, Raudenbush & Earls, 1997). Collective efficacy refers to "mutual trust among neighbors combined with a willingness to intervene on behalf of the common good, specifically to supervise children and maintain public order" (Sampson, Raudenbush & Earls 1998:1). A growing body of research on the relationship between collective efficacy and crime shows that the community—not the police or other social control agents—curbs crime. It is people who live in places where neighbors can depend on each other for social support and informal means of social control (DeLeon-Granados, 1999).

The above arguments and collective efficacy research were not developed by people who identify themselves as left realists. Nevertheless, their contributions are consistent with left realist views about the role of the community in crime prevention, which is why they are briefly reviewed here. Still, some inner-city communities are so shattered by poverty, joblessness, "market-generated geographic mobility" (Michalowski, 1991), and host of other social problems that it is highly unlikely that people living in these areas will work closely together to eliminate or reduce violence. For example, collective efficacy was low in Chicago communities with high levels of concentrated poverty (Sampson et al., 1998). This is why informal community-based means of social control should not be substitutes for economic strategies and help from the welfare state (Currie, 1985; Sampson et al., 1998). Collective efficacy will only exist when there are enough meaningful jobs and effective social programs.

Conclusion

Jock Young (1999) is correct to point out that North Americans and many Europeans now live in exclusive societies. These are societies where an alarming number of people are excluded from the formal labor market, where thousands of people have to live on the streets or in dilapidated public housing estates, and where inner-city violence is endemic. What is to be done about violence in poor urban areas characterized by social and economic exclusion? The first thing to do is to take it seriously, which is what many progressive criminologists are reluctant to do for reasons described previously. The second step is to provide short-term progressive solutions that prioritize social change over draconian criminal justice initiatives.

Left realists take these steps that not only help curb inner-city violence, but also enhance many people's economic, psychological, and physical well-being, as well as contribute to the development of strong, cohesive, and vibrant communities. Still, left realism has several pitfalls, as do all schools of criminological thought. Perhaps, however, left realists' biggest problem is convincing politicians and the general public that their policy proposals are effective and necessary. Unfortunately, the number of North Americans who support right-wing agendas is markedly higher than the number of progressives who embrace the alternative solutions advanced here. In addition to saying that left realist strategies will not work because crime is an individual—not a social—problem, supporters of neo-conservative policies (e.g., imprisonment) argue that left realist initiatives are expensive and the money would be better spent lowering the nation's deficit. But, if money has not been too tight to build new prisons, then money can be found to reduce poverty, unemployment, and a host of other social problems strongly related to crime if that is what people want. Government spending is always directly related to political priorities, and what we need now is a radical readjustment in thinking about our priorities.

Notes

[1] See Gelles (2000) and DeKeseredy (2000a) for descriptions of the data uncovered by these and other major violence against women surveys.

[2] Informed by Jargowsky (1997:20), Hatfield refers to the "concentration of the poor" as "the percentage of a metropolitan area's poor population that resides in high-poverty neighborhoods."

[3] Following Jargowsky (1997:20), Hatfield defined the "neighborhood poverty rate" as "the percentage of a metropolitan area's total population that resides in . . . high poverty census tracts." However, family rather than individual low-income rates were used because the latter are not available in the 1991 census, from which the some of the data presented in this table are drawn.

[4] For more detailed critiques of left realism, see DeKeseredy (1996), Henry (1999), Matthews and Young (1992), Michalowski, (1991), Ruggiero (1992), Schwartz and DeKeseredy (1991), Sim, Scraton, and Gordon (1987), and Taylor (1992).

[5] For example, in Canada, 61 percent of unemployed people do not receive unemployment insurance even though the federal government has accumulated a $26 billion Employment Insurance surplus that is growing by $5 billion a year (Beauchesne, 2000).

[6] Briefly, this involves police officers taking an aggressive response to relatively minor crimes, such as graffitti-spraying, panhandling, and public drunkenness. The idea is that such behavior left unattended gives the impression that no one cares, which leads to more serious crime.

[7] See Currie (1998) for a recent and powerful in-depth critique of incarceration.

[8] For more information on these strategies, see Alvi, DeKeseredy, and Ellis (2000), Currie (1985, 1993, 1998), DeKeseredy (2000b), and W. Wilson (1996).

[9] See DeKeseredy (2000b) and Ptacek (1999) for reviews of the literature on the relationship between poverty and violence against women.

Discussion Questions

1. What are the structural changes that have contributed to high rates of violence in socially and economically disadvantaged inner-city communities?

2. Why is homicide the leading cause of death for African-American males aged 15 to 24?

3. What is the difference between relative and absolute poverty?

4. What, according to left realists, motivates poor inner-city people to commit violent crime?

5. Why can left-realist theory not explain corporate crime?

6. Describe feminist criticisms of left-realist theory.

7. Provide some examples of policies proposed by establishment criminologists.

8. Provide some examples of left-realist policies aimed at lowering poverty and unemployment rates.

9. Why do neighborhoods characterized by collective efficacy have lower crime rates than those that are not?

10. Why are left realist policies not well received by politicians and the general public?

CHAPTER 4

Postmodern Justice and Critical Criminology: Positional, Relational, and Provisional Science

Bruce A. Arrigo

With the publication of *Time* magazine's last issue of the millennium (vol, 154, no.27), the weekly periodical proudly proclaimed that its "Person of the Century" was renowned theoretical physicist, Albert Einstein. The selection of Einstein is significant on a number of fronts and, as icon of the modernist age, he embodies the century's triumph of science and technology. Indeed, few would disagree that his many "thought experiments" forever changed our fundamental understanding of the cosmos.

However, Einstein's significance to the twentieth century, rests principally in the fact that his considerable discoveries helped solidify the scientific dawn of the *postmodern* age. As both symbol of and synonym for genius, Einstein's enduring legacy is that of scientific relativity. His investigations in quantum physics were the driving force behind such related discoveries as Werner Heisenberg's quantum theory of uncertainty (i.e., even at the level of sub-atomic particles, reality is affected by the one observing; thus, establishing some undecidability). From the geometry of Euclid, to the clock-work universe of Galileo, from the physics of Newton, to the biology of Darwin, it is Einstein who, seemingly in a breathless moment, discredited the sacred cows of science: cause and effect, mechanical order, rationalism, absolute truth. And it is Einstein to whom postmodernism owes a considerable debt of gratitude; from art to architecture, from culture to criticism, Einstein spawned a "social theology" (Isaacson, 1999:60) whose legacy lives on in the wake of the new millennium.

Criminology, particularly critical criminology, is no exception to the postmodern vision of Einstein. Although the discipline can hardly be said to have embraced the key beliefs of postmodernist thought (or likened itself to the principles of quantum physics for that matter), many of these notions find growing, although limited, respectability in the academy today. This chapter, then, represents a return to the "social theology" of postmodernism. It is specifically designed to lay out, in accessible, jargon-free format, the main features of postmodernist thought, mindful of the theory's practical limitations. Along the way, several related sub-disciplinary strains of thought will be discussed. These additional lines of analysis return us to the expanse of postmodern inquiry in the twenty-first century, and demonstrate the utility of this rich conceptual paradigm for ongoing critical criminological pursuits. Much like Einstein himself, postmodernist thought represents an elaborate web of complex and often confusing ideas. For purposes of simplicity and lucidity (often contradictions for strident postmodernists), relevant crime-law-justice examples will be employed throughout the ensuing commentary.

A Primer on Postmodern (Criminological) Theory

In a series of previously published articles (Arrigo, 1995, 1999, 2000; Arrigo & Friedrichs, 1997; Arrigo & Bernard, 1997; Arrigo, Milovanovic & Schehr, 2000), I explored, with several colleagues, a number of theoretical, methodological, and practical dimensions of postmodern thought in relation to law, crime, and justice studies. Readers are encouraged to review these articles as they represent both the evolution of my own thinking in this area of social theory as well as my general affinity for this unfamiliar, though provocative, strain of criminological discontent. In this section, I wish to rectify the shortcomings of my previous commentary. Individually and collectively the cited works either fail to communicate the pivotal questions that constitute the postmodernist challenge to modernist thinking, or embody them but lack sufficient reader-friendly prose for the average undergraduate reader. Given these preliminary remarks, I suggest that three (3) key issues principally inform the postmodern and critical criminological enterprise. The observations that follow are drawn from the work of Rosenau (1992) (among others) and form the basis of the postmodernist project I describe.

1. *The centrality of language*—If there is one thing that postmodernists agree upon, it is that language (i.e., written or spoken) always informs the reality we make and live. This understanding of language, however, is not akin to the representational interpretation of symbolic interactionism or the dramaturgic perspective of frame analysis. For postmodernists, language is neither an artifact of culture nor a prop by which we manage the impressions others have of us. Instead, language is both the source and product of our agency and the structural and organizational forces of which we are a part.

The "thought experiment" I use with my students to convey this point is quite simple. I ask them if they can think of something, anything, without first putting their notion into words? No matter how much my students try, they are at a loss to come up with an idea that is not always and already within some form of (unconscious) speech. What this means is that language shapes reality. Another way to convey this idea is that language *speaks* reality.

The fact that language is so integral to who we are and to what we do is of considerable consequence. It is particularly noteworthy in the field of criminology. If words define us, our interaction with others, and the institutions in which we work and play, what implicit values and/or hidden assumptions are contained in the language we use to convey our thoughts? In other words, whose values and/or assumptions are given preferred meaning or special consideration when we speak or write? Relatedly, whose values and/or assumptions are ignored, dismissed, or silenced when we speak or write?

If you have ever witnessed the unfolding of a trial (civil or criminal) the problem of language, specialized meaning, and values is readily apparent. Imagine a criminal case in which an indigent defendant, incarcerated for several long years, elects to represent himself in the courtroom. Assume further that as a "jailhouse lawyer" this individual has learned a great deal about the trial process, filing motions, rules of evidence, and examining witnesses. Indeed, one could say that, although not formally schooled in the practice of criminal litigation, this defendant has mastered both legal logic and the "legalese" associated with it.

Even if the indigent defendant wins his case, postmodernists seriously question the linguistic conditions under which this victory occurs (Milovanovic, 1988). Just as there is a unique language that constitutes the law (i.e., legalese), there is a unique grammar that represents prison life. In fact, there are a great number of language systems (e.g., computers, sports, advertising) that variably affect us. Each of these systems of communication relies on certain words or phrases to convey specialized meaning. For example, the phrase "tossing salad" is an unambiguous sexual reference in prison parlance whose meaning differs dramatically when used in every day, casual conversation. The expression "objection your honor, lack of foundation," means something quite specific within the courtroom setting but lacks the same specificity outside of that environment. In order to comprehend the full intent of what is being communicated in these and similar instances, one must insert oneself into or be situated within the language system in use.

This immersion into specialized discourses is fine if we are talking about fairly innocuous language systems. No one is personally harmed, for example, when failing to understand what a "ground rule double" means in baseball, or what a "formatted, high-density disk" means in computer-speak. However, there are entire fields of communication that require a careful adherence to their internal logic. The language of law is one such case in point. According to postmodernists, the problem is that by remaining faithful to how the legal system understands crime, criminals, and the criminal trial process, alternative understandings for such matters are dismissed. In addition, particularly in the instance of our indigent defendant, a more natural, true-to-self presentation of the case and the facts surrounding it are not possible. Legal language endorses only that speech that reaffirms its own legitimacy to settle disputes. Anything falling outside of the judicial sphere is declared inadmissable, irrelevant, immaterial. What this signifies is that all the shadings and nuances of meaning that might otherwise be conveyed if one were to speak his or her "true words" (Friere, 1972:57-65), are filtered through the lens of law-talk. Entire ways of knowing are denied expression and legitimacy in the courtroom. A fuller, more complete sense of being is silenced for our jailhouse lawyer, for other criminal defendants, and for anyone similarly disenfranchised.

2. *Partial knowledge and provisional truth*—The centrality of language in postmodern analysis gives rise to many understandings about society in general and to a host of practical comments about the nature of crime and justice in particular. If discourse structures thought in ways that are not neutral, then rationality, logic, and meaning (components of reality construction) are limited by the (dominant) language in use. Thus, not only are entire fields of understanding devalued or repudiated, but what we come to regard as meaningful is itself forever incomplete. The stories representing our lives, the narratives comprising the social order and human affairs, the stock of knowledge forming the basis of civilization are all partial, fragmented, unfinished projects. To some extent, this is because such "texts" are always evolving. More significantly, however, this incompleteness is a function of how privileged systems of communication (e.g., law, medicine, science) embrace certain understandings about the world and people in it, while resisting or dismissing others. As a result, what we take to be "truth," as an articulated expression of knowledge, can, at best, be defined merely as a provisional, relational, and/or positional reality.

Consider the example of law enforcement patrol work. The police stop, detain, and arrest suspects routinely as an expression of their "protect and serve," order-maintenance function. But how do officers understand police-citizen interaction? In other words, what are the linguistic forces that determine how patrol officers stop, detain, and make discretionary decisions about arresting suspects?

Students usually take for granted the manner in which police-citizen exchanges occur. However, when I question individuals in class about this interactional process, most admit how important it is to listen to what the police say and do what they are told, or else suffer the consequences. But in these telling comments we can begin to understand the power of language, partial knowledge, and positional truth to determine the fate of police-citizen encounters (Manning, 1988; Shon, 2000). One classic illustration is the case of Don Jackson, an African-American undercover surveillance officer in California.

During the 1980s, Jackson came to believe that the Long Beach police practiced and endorsed institutionalized racism in the department. In an effort to prove his point, Jackson engaged in a number of field experiments. For example, while typically wearing plain clothes and driving an unmarked car so as to not draw attention to his police officer status, he traveled late at night in communities known for their high rates of crime, reportedly perpetrated by black males. On one occasion, with video and audio equipment strategically and secretly stationed in his car, Jackson was pulled over by a white male cop who did not recognize him. There was no indication that Jackson was speeding or violating any other traffic laws.

Rather than remaining in the vehicle and saying nothing until approached by the officer, Jackson exited the car and repeatedly, but politely, asked the officer for an explanation. The officer insisted that Jackson remain still and quiet. Jackson continued to press the cop for an explanation and for more information on why he was being detained. The more that Jackson asked for clarification, the more the officer assumed that the "suspect" was potentially dangerous. The officer insisted that Jackson put his hands on his head, and face his vehicle. Jackson refused. The officer took out his billy club, demanding that the citizen-suspect comply. Jackson firmly but courteously continued to asked for an explanation. As the video footage discloses, Jackson eventually found himself thrown head-first threw a store-front, plate glass window. He was subsequently handcuffed and taken into custody for further questioning by the officer for resisting arrest.

What are we to make of this curious, if not tragic, event from a postmodern perspective? In part, the officer was responding to what he perceived to be a potential high-risk situation: it was late at night in an area known to be pocketed by violent crime perpetrated by black males. However, on closer inspection, the escalation of this police-citizen encounter was based on an exchange of different language systems and their corresponding values.

Jackson did not comport himself, through speech or behavior, consistent with what the officer understood to be a "good" citizen-suspect. The officer's knowledge of patrol work was circumscribed by his Academy training and field experience. As any rookie cop will tell you, controlling the situation (through words, gestures, and actions) is pivotal to avoiding potential conflict. But in the case of Don Jackson, did the officer's knowledge confirm an absolute truth about policing? No. In fact, Jackson embodied an alternative expression of knowledge (i.e., question police practices cordially but directly), yielding a different truth about patrol work (i.e., sometimes officers stop and detain black suspects without cause). The officer's rationality, logic, and meaning (control the situation) was incompatible with Jackson's (elicit information). By seeking an explanation for the officer's behavior, Jackson articulated a different set of citizen-suspect values than those harbored by the officer, leading to an atypical exchange that resulted, regrettably, in the officer's display of (excessive) force.

3. *Deconstruction, difference, and possibility*—Students often find unsettling the notion that truth is not absolute and that language is the culprit in this charade. Somehow it doesn't seem as if discourse could produce such devastating outcomes. Yet, the world "out there," once named as such, is value-laden. Certain expressions within the dominant language system in use (e.g., law, policing) filter the way in which people are to think, feel, act, and be. As postmodernists remind us, because our awareness of reality is circumscribed, constantly spawning fragmented knowledges, positional beliefs, and relational truths, there is a certain undeniable relativity to being human. This relativity returns us to Einstein and the uncertain, non-absolute, and random world in which he described the ordering of the cosmos.

One technique employed by many postmodernists to interpret this randomness is termed "deconstruction." Deconstruction or "trashing" entails a careful reading and de-coding of a text (written or spoken). The purpose of deconstructing the text is to unveil the implicit assumptions and hidden values (i.e., often inconsistent, contradictory beliefs about social phenomena) embedded within a particular narrative. Deconstruction shows us how certain truth claims are privileged within a given story while certain others are disguised or dismissed altogether. Because deconstruction focuses on the actual words people use to convey their thoughts, it attempts to uncover the unconscious intent behind the grammar people employ when writing or speaking. Thus, language or entire systems of communication are put under the microscope for closer inspection. In a sense, then, trashing a text entails reading between the lines to ascertain the meanings (i.e., ideology) given preferred status in a particular language system.

The "thought experiments" I entertain with students on this matter vary considerably. One example that they tend to appreciate, however, is sentencing mentally incompetent prisoners to death (Arrigo & Williams, 1999). Generally speaking, execution can only occur if one is psychiatrically competent. In other words, death row prisoners if incompetent, must be restored to competency before the execution can occur. Typically, some form of drug therapy is administered to restore to competency a psychiatrically disordered death row prisoner. Postmodern deconstructionists question what it means to receive such "treatment." One meaning of treatment is to confer upon another a gift or a reward. Medical intervention, then, represents the gift of reparation: it repairs, corrects, and remedies illness and disease. It intends the elimination of suffering and pain.

However, the reward of drug therapy for persons awaiting execution is built on faulty logic. Indeed, how can such a gift eliminate suffering if its obvious effect is the termination of one's life? What pain is eliminated that produces execution? Thus, following deconstructionism, drug therapy is not "treatment" or reward. It is the exercise of state-enforced power to regulate the mental state of prisoners. This regulation is particularly problematic when disordered prisoners receive forced drug therapy (i.e., treatment) over their constitutional right to object to it. Thus, competency restoration signifies a political and oppressive, rather than medical and humane, act to control the fate of death sentenced citizens. As a practical judicial matter, however, the United States Supreme Court continues to acknowledge the legitimacy (i.e., the value) of restoring to competency death row inmates so that they may be executed.

Deconstructionism allows us to see how certain ways of knowing are privileged while certain others are not. Therefore, the social theology of postmodernism seeks to include the voices of those whose understanding of the world would otherwise remain dormant and concealed. The postmodern challenge invites us to embrace articulated differences, making them a part of the social fabric of ongoing, civic interaction. This call to express one's authentic being and genuine humanity moves us beyond the modernist logic of tight, rigid control to the postmodernist sensibility of fluid, evolving possibilities.

In the realm of critical criminology, the language of possibility means that expressions of law, crime, and justice must reflect the multiple and disparate ways different people (or collectives) come to experience, know, and live reality. One illustration that poignantly captures this sentiment is the manner in which legal and psychiatric decision brokers civilly and/or criminally confine the mentally ill (Arrigo, 1996). Typically, in order to be released from custody, psychiatrically confined citizens must first turn to the very systems (i.e., the mental health and/or criminal justice apparatus) responsible for their institutionalization. Mentally ill persons must comport themselves in such a way that they convey "psychological wellness." In other words, their speech-thought-behavior must be devoid of deviant-oriented, disease-minded, or dangerousness-prone tendencies. In short, they must be made functionally well, corrected, and de-pathologized. But such cleansing often comes at a debilitating price. On the one hand, while ridding oneself of such predilections may stave off sustained confinement, forced compliance quashes a person's more natural, non-homogenous identity. On the other hand, refusing to comply, while affirming one's "right to be different," most assuredly results in protracted institutionalization.

The postmodern logic of difference, inclusivity, and possibility would acknowledge that neither of these options is particularly humane. Instead, creating enclaves of support or establishing zones of safety where expressions of nonviolent nonconformity are a welcome relief from the din of conventionality are integral to realizing a more just resolution to the dilemma of meaning (i.e., conformity) versus being (i.e., difference) described above. The challenge is in recognizing and accepting that different people express themselves differently and that ALL citizens (e.g., the chemically addicted, the frail elderly, the working poor, the mentally disabled, the homeless, adult and juvenile offenders), short of harming others, need a supportive space within which to articulate who they are, freed from the normalizing constraints imposed upon us first and foremost by disciplinary language systems.

The Limits of Postmodern Thought
for Critical Criminology

The precepts of postmodernist thought have been questioned on a number of fronts. Indeed, there are many, many criticisms. This notwithstanding, three particular challenges seem most problematic. In what follows, I summarize each criticism and offer a response to the identified limitation.

1. *Nihilistic, pessimistic, fatalistic science*—According to critics of the theory, postmodernism's refusal to accept absolute truths or foundational knowledge seriously undermines its legitimacy as a bonafide investigatory paradigm (Hunt, 1990; Schwartz & Friedrichs, 1994). Indeed, if everything is relative, as postmodernists most assuredly contend, how is it possible to make any statement about reality, events and people in the social order, and ongoing human interaction? If the world "out there" is forever incomplete, lacking any certainty, subject to randomness, isn't it impossible to speak about progress, knowledge, truth, and the like? Critics argue that this world view is too nihilistic, too pessimistic, too fatalistic, and too relativistic. Postmodernism, they conclude, is nothing more than subjectivism, masquerading as pseudo-science (Handler, 1992).

Much like Einstein witnessed, the notion that uncertainty pervades nature and the universe is uncomfortable, to say the least. When realizing the implications of such a scientific conclusion, the renowned physicist famously and frequently insisted, "God does not place dice." In his later years, Einstein unsuccessfully attempted to develop a unified theory that explained what appeared as random in the cosmos. It was not until the scientific breakthroughs wrought by chaos theory that such an explanation was possible (Gleick, 1987). The insights of chaos or complexity theory are significant to the modernist charge of relativism, subjectivism, and nihilism leveled against postmodernist thought.

Chaos theory or nonlinear dynamics argues that orderly disorder governs the behavior of all natural systems. Natural systems include such things as the movement of the stars, the regularity of snow fall, and the activity of the brain in humans. In each instance, there appears a certain randomness in behavior, making it difficult to predict how such systems will function with any certainty. The principle of orderly disorder, however, indicates that it is possible, over time, to plot the movement of natural systems. In brief, chaos theory tells us that all systems settle into or tend toward a certain patterned regularity. At the situational or micro-level there is considerable randomness, flux, and unpredictability. However, at the global or macro-level a pattern of behavior emerges that can be mapped out. This pattern can evolve over time; however, an identifiable configuration nonetheless exists. Thus, orderly disorder (i.e., chaos) governs the behavior of all natural systems.

Nonlinear dynamics confirms the postmodernist conviction that there is an appreciable degree of uncertainty underpinning the manner in which reality is constructed and lived. Where postmodernist thought relies on language to convey this point, chaos theory mathematically verifies the (dis)order in the universe. Social systems, too, are subject to the same logic. In the field of crime, law, and justice, research is now just beginning to emerge, applying the insights of chaos theory to concrete social problems (e.g., Milovanovic, 1997; Williams & Arrigo, 2001). What this means is that far from being nihilistic, pessimistic, or fatalistic, postmodernism represents an intellectual paradigm consistent with those scientific discoveries advancing the work of Albert Einstein. Moreover, as the critical criminological studies in this area suggest, alternative truth claims are possible, provided they are understood as positional, relational, and provisional.

An example of how chaos theory has been appropriated in the criminological literature is found in a study I conducted involving one single room occupancy (SRO) community for working poor and formerly homeless men and women (Arrigo, 1997). Over a seven-year period, I was able to demonstrate how orderly disorder was integral to the prosocial behavior of this vertical neighborhood. On a daily basis, when relying on a strength-focused approach to designing the SRO culture, there was a great deal of confusion, uncertainty, and unpredictability in tenant activity. Critics of the model warned that without greater control and structured interventions, crime and deviance rates would be high. However, when plotting out the behavior of the residence over time, a pattern of crime responses, measured by eviction notices and house rule infractions, emerged. When comparing these data against the previous SRO strategy which emphasized a needs-based approach with planned interaction, the level of crime in the community was considerably lower with the strength-focused model. Indeed, when principles of orderly disorder operated in the community, incidents of crime (e.g., destroying property, physically harming others) were nearly three times less likely to occur than during the building's more structured and organized phase (Arrigo, 1994). The more freedom SRO occupants had to shape, re-shape, change, modify, or eliminate various facets of their community, the more ownership they felt toward the facility and the more investment they described in making sure it was safe.

2. *Contradictory and elitist logic*—Critics of postmodernist theory contend that defining what the perspective "is," is inherently contradictory. Focusing on a singular or limited definition is a reduction in meaning that invalidates one of the theory's main principles; namely, resisting and renouncing all privileged points of view. To describe postmodernist thought one way, is to elevate that interpretation over and against all others. Thus, defining postmodernist theory and, more particularly, postmodernist criminology, is an inherent contradiction (Hunt, 1991). Relatedly, opponents of the perspective argue that much of the writing is idiosyncratic, abstruse, and incoherent (Schwartz & Friedrichs, 1994). The dense and cryptic prose not only fails to ingratiate postmodernist thought to a larger, relatively impartial, audience, it also suggests that the theory is fundamentally elitist. The delib-

erately obscure language undermines the perspective's notion of inclusivity and, accordingly, renders the theory nothing more than self-aggrandizing prattle (Cohen, 1993).

There are many strains of postmodernist thought and many ways to describe these perspectives. Postmodernists often qualify much of what they say for fear that their meanings will be regarded as dominant or privileged interpretations. The difficulty in conveying what the perspective signifies is that it calls for some reduction; a definable, tangible statement that the theory stands for some thing apart from what other theories represent. Moreover, in describing the perspective this way, it quickly transforms itself into a (post)modernist and, eventually, a modernist theory. Again, this is why there is such resistance to singularly defining the postmodern attitude, perspective, knowledge process, and the like. It is difficult to shed the baggage of modernist sense-making. Postmodern feminists (e.g., Irigaray, 1993), for example, have been particularly vocal on this point. They insist that the challenge women confront is to construct a contingent method of communicating feminine ways of knowing freed from the trappings of masculine logic, sensibility, and discourse. This project is still in the making.

In part, efforts to establish different modes of expression contribute to the often cumbersome, clumsy, and confusing postmodernist writing styles. There is something of a political statement embedded in the complexities of the prose. Creating a space within which meaning is not immediately recognizable or instantly grasped allows the reader to explore the subtleties of thought (e.g., ideology) that might otherwise be overlooked in the text. Typically, when we read something there is an expectation that coming to a period will produce *precise* meaning and *clear* intent. But this expectation leaves little room for different interpretations, different understandings of the same thought. The problem with this outlook is that certain views become "right" or "true" interpretations while other views, and the people who harbor them, are understood to have wrong explanations and are summarily dismissed because of them. Developing a writing style that slows the reader down compels one to study the text over and over again. This strategy fosters multiple and divergent interpretations, making possible the inclusion of many different ways of knowing without privileging any one of them.

Students often question whether it is possible to write or speak in such a way that allows different voices to be heard, without valuing one position over others. The "thought experiment" I rely upon centers around the experience of rape or domestic abuse (Manning, 1995). I ask individuals in class to imagine how they would articulate this harrowing event in a court of law without having opposing counsel object, claiming that such testimony was prejudicial, inflammatory, or misleading. Usually, several responses are offered, mostly dealing with the technicalities of direct testimony and trial procedure. I then ask them to consider whether words can fully convey the pain, trauma, devastation, or humiliation a rape survivor lives with daily. Often students are quiet; it is as if language escapes them, leaving *them* helpless. Then, in that long pause, someone finally says something that rescues the rest of the class: "words are all that we have." In that moment, students recognize that writing and speaking are both source and product of our identities. Language both constrains *and* liberates us. For the victim of domestic abuse, much like for the rest of us, the possibility of establishing a non-hierarchical, non-oppressive grammar that captures the felt experiences of people, resides in language and our evolving conceptions of it.

3. *Deconstruction as apolitical, ahistorical, non-humanitarian speech*—Opponents of postmodernist theory question how language helps us understand the problems posed by race, gender, and class disparities in any meaningful way (Lynch, Lynch & Milovanovic, 1995). In other words, the material or social forces that inform existing power relations wield effects that far surpass linguistic interpretations. What more can mere words tell us about the exercise of coercive power, corporate exploitation, worker alienation, brutalizing police practices, state-sponsored oppression, hegemonic legal decisions, and the like? It is hard to imagine how postmodern analyses can advance our knowledge of these very "real" experiences, much less change them. In short, postmodernist thought, especially in its reliance on deconstruction, represents an apolitical, ahistorical theory, fostering an anti-humanitarian "ideology of despair" (Melichar, 1988:366).

Postmodern deconstruction alone is not the answer to the social conditions that give rise to problems in crime and justice. Having said this, a critical deconstruction, grounded in materialist assumptions (i.e., race, gender, and class inequalities), directs our attention to the very structures of thought that create occasions for sociopolitical marginalization, victimization, and alienation. Thus, on a practical level, postmodernist thought can tell us "something more [than we presently know] about how jurists, criminologists, and criminal justicians view themselves in relation to their respective practice roles" (Arrigo, 1995:449). This form of understanding allows for a more reflective social criticism about police, court, and correctional personnel and the institutions in which they work. Perhaps more significantly, a critical deconstructive investigation, especially when combined with other strains of postmodernist thought not discussed here (e.g., semiotics, psychoanalytic, and post-structural), potentially creates a *reconstructive*, though contingent, vista from which to promote a more humane, transformative, praxis-oriented philosophy about social life and civic affairs. Meaning can be created from the depths of despair and postmodernist thought provides us with the necessary intellectual tools to accomplish this.

One facet of developing a reconstructive agenda entails replacement discourses (Henry & Milovanovic, 1996). Replacement discourses encourage us to resist the power others have to shape, through language, our identities in repressive, reductionistic ways, while affirming, in speech and behavior, the intrinsic humanity those others possess. The creative nonviolence movement of the 1960s led by Dr. Martin Luther King, Jr., and the peace protests that occur today around the country for economic, political, and social justice, exemplify the philosophy of replacement discourses. Becoming the change one seeks begins when people express their humanity and validate the humanity of others.

The entire restorative justice model, and its corresponding intervention of victim-offender mediation (VOM), is built on the premise that supportive healing, conveyed through words and action, makes meaningful reconciliation possible (Arrigo & Schehr, 1998). Talking openly about suffering and sadness for all parties in a criminal dispute and for the community affected by it, is the first step toward reconciliation and redemption. What these and similar initiatives (e.g., community policing and corrections) indicate is that making peace with crime and restoring justice to society entails a reconceptualization of how the criminal justice apparatus functions. Postmodernist theory simultaneously "subverts the comfortable structures of thought, images of reality, and certainty of thinking that underlie criminal justice science" (Arrigo, 1995:449), while challenging us to invent positional, relational, and provisional methods in which we retrieve and rediscover our unfolding humanity. Much like Einstein, the postmodernist project is a science built, in part, on the premise that we live in a world that is fundamentally disorganized, incomplete, and fragmented. The challenge for us all is to thrive in the face of this uncertainty.

Summary

Postmodernist thought, as a form of critical criminology, continues to evolve. This chapter examined several of the more prominently discussed features of the perspective, mindful of the theory's general limitations and practical problems in crime and justice research. In no way was this presentation exhaustive and readers are cautioned to understand that this objective was never intended nor pursued. The future viability of postmodernist thought, as a strain of critical criminological analysis, lies in its capacity to show, through ongoing application studies, where and how ideological forces saturate police, court, and correctional institutions, practices, and policies. In short, the sustainability of postmodernism, as both theory and method for conducting critical criminological inquiry, rests in its ability to show how language significantly shapes the identity of people and the organizational and structural forces of which they are a part. Beyond this, the postmodernist challenge is to develop multiple ways, through written and verbal texts, where the voices of the disenfranchised can find fuller, more complete expression within the very institutional arenas that define, reduce, and delimit their existences. This is an invitation to emancipate the subject and his/her meanings, borne of the despair that comes from oppression, exclusion, and silence.

Discussion Questions

1. Postmodernists (including postmodern criminologists) argue that language is pivotal to creating reality. In fact, they contend that we cannot think of a thought without first putting it in the form of a language. Please explain this statement. Can you think of a relevant criminal justice example to support your analysis? Be specific.

2. How does the language of law deny alternative or replacement readings of legal actors, institutions, procedures, and events? What are some of the limits of using legal language in a court of law, especially when addressing criminal issues like sexual assault, competency to stand trial, or a capital case?

3. Postmodernists contend that reality gives us partial knowledge and incomplete truths. Please explain this observation with reference to one specific criminal justice issue or controversy.

4. In this chapter, much was made of the case of Don Jackson, an African-American, former undercover surveillance officer in Long Beach, California. From a postmodernist perspective, what were some of the problems Jackson confronted?

5. What is deconstruction and how does it work? Please explain how the phenomenon of executing mentally incompetent prisoners can be deconstructed. What do we learn when we deconstruct this phenomenon?

6. What do postmodernist criminologists mean speaking about languages of possibility? Please give an example of how this notion operates in a criminal justice context.

7. One limitation of postmodernism is that it may be too nihilistic, pessimistic, and fatalistic. Please explain this. Use a crime and justice example to refute this claim.

8. One limitation of postmodernism is that it promotes contradictory and elitist logic. Please explain this. Use a crime and justice example to refute this claim.

9. One limitation of postmodernism is that deconstruction is a form of ahistorical, apolitical, and non-humanitarian speech. Please explain this. Use a crime and justice example to refute this claim.

10. As a student of criminal justice, what is the most significant strength and limit of postmodern criminology? Please explain your responses in detail.

CHAPTER 5

Constitutive Criminology

Stuart Henry & Dragan Milovanovic

Constitutive Criminology is a broad-sweeping, wide-ranging holistic perspective on crime, criminals, and criminal justice. Its roots lie in critical social
theory. Most influential in developing the perspective were the social theories of symbolic interactionism, social constructionism, phenomenology,
structural Marxism, structuration theory, Lacanian semiotics, chaos theory
and, generally, the "affirmative postmodern" approaches.[1] Constitutive criminology builds on the strengths of these critical theories and integrates more
recent theoretical advances to produce an alternative direction of critical
thought whose objective is to help build a less harmful society. In this chapter we will first outline some of the main ideas of the theory, go on to examine the key concepts in more detail, present some of the major criticisms
levied against it, and conclude with our own response to these criticisms.

Core Concepts

Coproduction Through Discourse

Constitutive criminology is founded on the proposition that humans are
responsible for actively creating their world with others. They do this by
transforming their surroundings through social interaction, not least via
discourse or language use. Through language and symbols humans identify
differences, construct categories, and share a belief in the reality of their
world that orders otherwise chaotic states. It is towards these social constructions of reality that humans act.

In the process of investing energy in their socially constructed categories
of order, humans not only shape their social world, but are also shaped by
it. They are co-producers and co-productions of their own and others'

agency. Constitutive criminology is about how some of this socially con-structed order, as well as the humans constituted within it, can be harmed, impaired and destroyed by both the process, and by what is built during that process: ultimately by each other as fellow humans.

Constitutive theorists argue that the co-production of harmful relations occurs through society's structure and culture, as these are energized by human actions. These actions come not only from offenders, but also from victims, criminal justice practitioners, academics, commentators, media reporters and producers of film and TV crime shows, and most generally, as investors, producers, and consumers in the crime business. Constitutive criminologists look at what it is about the psycho-social-cultural matrix (the cloth of crime) that provides the medium through which humans con-struct "meaningful" harms to others. The approach taken, therefore, shifts the criminological focus away from narrow dichotomized issues focusing either on the individual offender or on the social environment. Instead, con-stitutive criminology takes a holistic conception of the relationship between the "individual" and "society" which prioritizes neither one nor the other, but examines their mutuality and interrelationship. Humans are thus not discrete individual entities. They are integrally bound up with the social construc-tions they and others make. They act towards each other in terms of those constructions as if they were realities.

Harm as Crime and Crime as Harm

For constitutive criminologists a major source of harmful relations emanates from the nature of its power structure. Unequal power relations, built on the constructions of difference, provide the conditions that define crime as harm. Constitutive criminology defines crime as the harm resulting from humans investing energy in harm-producing relations of power. Humans suffering such "crimes" are in relations of inequality. Crimes are nothing less than people being disrespected by others who claim a position of dominance reflecting the structure of relations of inequality. People are disrespected in numerous ways, but all have to do with denying or pre-venting us becoming fully social beings. Being human is to make a difference to the world; to act on it, to interact with others and together to transform environment and ourselves. If this process is prevented or limited we become less than human; we are harmed. Thus constitutive criminologists define crime as "the power to deny others their ability to make a difference" (Henry & Milovanovic, 1996:116).

Constitutive criminological theory divides crimes into two types: "*crimes of reduction*" and "*crimes of repression.*" Harms of reduction occur when those offended experience a loss of some quality relative to their present standing. They could have property stolen from them, but they could also have dignity stripped from them as in acts of hate crimes. Harms of repression occur when people experience a limit, or restriction, preventing them from achieving a desired position or standing or realizing an accomplishment. For example, they could be prevented from achieving a career goal because of sexism or racism, or they might meet a promotional "glass ceiling." Considered along a continuum of deprivation, harms of reduction or repression may be based on an infinite number of constructed differences. This raises the question of whether it is *ever* legitimate to reduce or repress another. Here it is important to point out that actions and processes are not considered harms of repression when they limit the attempts by some person or social process to make a difference that *do not themselves limit others' attempt to do the same.* Where attempts to achieve a desired position or standing are themselves limiting to others, then the repression of these attempts might be more correctly called control. Such control also always a crime of repression, but the manner in which control is done can be more or less harmful and be more or less justified.

A Different View of Crime Causation: Criminals as "Excessive Investors"

Constitutive criminology's reconception of crime, offender, and victim locates criminality not in the person, nor in the structure or culture, but in the ongoing creation of socially harmful relations of power. This leads to a different notion of crime causation. To the constitutive criminologist, crime is not so much *caused* as *discursively constructed* through human processes of which it is one. In such a view we might consider that the focus on some people as "criminals" is merely an exaggeration of a condition of human existence that we are all subject to: the powerlessness to be free from our own constructions. Whether single human beings or human groups, constitutive criminology sees such people as "excessive investors" in the power to impose order (i.e., discursive constructions) on others. The offender is viewed as an "excessive investor" in the power to dominate others. Excessive investors put energy into creating and magnifying differences between themselves and others. This investment of energy disadvantages, disables and destroys others' human potentialities. The investor's "crime" is to limit others' freedom. Their crime is that they act toward others as objects for domination such that, in the process, the victim loses some of their humanity. Victims, from this perspective are disabled by the excessive investor and suffer loss. Victims "suffer the pain of being denied their own humanity, the power to make a difference. The victim of crime is thus rendered a non-person, a non-human, or less complete being" (Henry & Milovanovic, 1996:116).

A Different View of Criminal Justice

Constitutive criminology envisions criminal justice, as it is traditionally practiced, as part of the very problem it claims to control. Its practitioners act toward the discursively constructed categories of crime and crime control as if they were real. Criminal justice is an exercise in the investment of energy that perpetuates further harm. Criminal justice is a major excessive investor in harm. Both the discursive fear of the victimized and the system of criminal justice thus feed crime. Both fuel the energies that drive our notions of crime. Indeed, as indicated above, agencies of law and criminal justice, the official social control institutions of society, are themselves organizations that exercise power (and, therefore, harm). Agencies of justice and law not only accomplish both crimes of reduction (of liberty, of property, of life) and repression (incapacitation), they also deepen the problem by labeling and categorizing only some harmful behavior of power relationships as "crime," leaving other harmful behavior unlabeled, as though it were acceptable, legal, legitimate, or "not crime." In this process of societal social control, harmful behavior and those who produce it become colonized by criminal justice; they become subject to justice's own powerful relations. The result is amplification, concentration, and multiple layering of power relations and from this emerge multiple possibilities for harm.

Contributing further to the excessive investment in harm are crime shows, crime drama, crime documentaries, crime news, crime books, crime films, crime precautions, agencies of criminal justice, lawyers, and academic criminologists. Each contributes to the continuous co-production of crime by exploiting the relations of power and by perpetuating the discourse of crime.

Replacement Discourses

Given the continuous co-production of crime, and its compounding by the criminal justice process, and the mass media's discursive reproduction of the very relations of power that affirms their reality, what can be done? Constitutive criminology suggests that crime must be deconstructed as an ongoing discursive process, and that reconstruction must take place. The emphasis is on creating replacement discourses that provide the linguistic materials out of which new conceptualizations of being human in society may appear.

The new constructions are designed to displace crime as moments in the exercise of power and as control. They offer an alternative medium by which social constructions of reality can take place. Beyond resistance, the concept of replacement discourse offers a celebration of unofficial, informal, discounted, and ignored knowledge through its discursive diversity. In terms of diminishing the harm experienced from all types of crime (street, corporate, state, hate etc.), constitutive criminology talks of "liberating" replacement discourses that seek transformation of both the prevailing political economies and the associated practices of crime and social control. Constitutive criminology thus simultaneously argues for ideological as well as materialistic change; one without the other renders change only in part.

Replacement discourse can be implemented through attempts by constitutive criminologists to reconstruct popular images of crime in the mass media through engaging in "newsmaking criminology" (Barak, 1994). It can also be induced through "narrative therapy." Narrative therapy was developed as part of family therapy to enable offenders (excessive investors in power) to construct more liberating life narratives and through these reconstitute themselves. We have theorized how replacement discourse emerges (Henry & Milovanovic, 1996:203-211), especially in integrating Paulo Freire's more historically and socio-culturallly specific dialogical pedagogy, Jacque Lacan's psychoanalytic semiotics and chaos and catastrophe theory (Milovanovic, 1996a, 1996b).

Critics of Constitutive Criminology

Constitutive criminology has raised much discussion in recent literature (see, for example, Gibbons, 1994:160-164; Beirne & Messerschmidt, 1995:533-535; Einstadter & Henry, 1995:277-300; Naffine, 1996:75-77; DeKeseredy & Schwartz, 1996:275-276; Akers, 1997:176-179; Lanier & Henry, 199?:282-285; Deutschmann, 1998:378; Barak, 1998:219-234; Vold, Bernard & Snipes, 1998; Schmalleger, 1999). Several arguments have been levied against it, although most also share Thomson's (1997) view that this theory is stimulating, "raising issues that must be confronted by scholars in the empirical, romantic and Marxist traditions of modern theorising." In this section we will summarize some of the main critical arguments. At the outset, we note that many of the critics focus on parts of the project rather than the project as a whole. Indeed, it is somewhat disconcerting to us that, in spite of our urging that the harm of crime is a dialectical *coproduction* and that ceasing such production requires a holistic *response at multiple levels*, some commentators have sought to reduce the project to its component "parts." Here we address a variety of such partial evaluations, pointing out that by separating off aspects for analysis, without relating them to the whole project, critics undermine the integrational objective that we and others set out to achieve (see Barak, 1998 for a critique of such partial analyses in criminology).

Several of the criticisms of constitutive criminology relate to its postmodernist leanings. One central theme is that postmodern/constitutive prose is excessively complex, difficult and "esoteric." For example, Friedrichs (1996:125) says that this is "difficult work, dense and even bewildering in places, and especially likely to be challenging to those who come to it with no direct familiarity with the work of the various contemporary critical and postmodern writers cited" (See similar points made by Colvin, 1997:1450; Ruller, 1997:497; and Bohm, 1997:16).

A second issue is to challenge the value of using integrative methodology. The general charge here is that constitutive theorizing attempts artificial integration of incompatible theoretical positions. Howe (1997), for example, takes constitutive criminology to task for trying to integrate modernist and postmodernist ideas. She says, "criminology offers no insights into crime. Postmodern theories cannot be happily wedded with the modernist, positivistic paradigms of criminology" (1997:89). Indeed, she argues that any incorporation of modernist thought into postmodern thought is tantamount to sleeping with the enemy and must be avoided. Similarly, Naffine (1996) decries our attempt to integrate idealism and materialism, but then she argues that we come down on the side of materialism. This is very interesting because, more recently Thomson (1997) criticizes us for a lack of a political economic, materialistic analysis.

Third, some critics of the constitutive position not only object to its postmodernism, and its supposed prioritizing of idealism over materialism (a point which we dispute), but also disparage its embrace of social constructionist concepts. They assume that because of constitutive criminology's claim that crime is socially constructed, that we also believe crime does not have any real consequences (see a similar charge made by Schwartz, 1991:122, about postmodernism). Akers, for example, says that constitutive criminology seems to:

> take the extreme position that denies crime as such really exists. Crime exists only because it is a "discursive production," that is, a product not only of the interaction of offenders, control agents, criminologists, or other people, but also simply by their talking about it . . . This implies that there is no such thing as crime as an objective behavioral reality to be explained . . . Does this mean that criminal behavior would not exist if we did not talk about it? (1997:176-177).

Joel Henderson (2000) is concerned, too, about the problems of tying a definition of crime to an analysis of power. Indeed, he is puzzled by constitutive criminology's redefinition of crime:

> This seems to not be a redefinition of crime but the definition of a new field of study—the harm generated from differential power positions. Is constitutive theory providing an explanation of this harm? Is it providing an explanation of the differential power relations? And is there a simple set of propositions that explains whatever?

Thomson (1997) also has problems with the definition of crime, which he sees as inclusive of a wider range of harms, but failing to target the major offenders.

Other questions have been raised over whether a set of causal assumptions still really underlies the analysis, and if so whether this can be measured. For example, critiques have been levied against constitutive criminology's use of nonlinear logic, especially the use of chaos theory, rather than conventional causal analysis. Leading mainstream modernist theorists like Akers (1997:178) complain that "constitutive criminology has not yet offered a testable explanation of either crime or criminal justice."

Related to this issue Henderson (2000) further questions the validity of chaos theory as an analytical frame:

> Has constitutive theory taken the position of chaos? Does it move away from linear relationships and the other assumptions of chaos? . . . It appears that social scientists have bought into the physics and math models. I see two problems with doing that. First, it presumes very precise measurement, which is not the case in the social scientists. Second, it is based on the movement of physical objects yet the physical and the social worlds are different. Much like the arguments against the positivists, once again the physicists and mathematicians are operating in a different arena. The problems they encountered and addressed in the physical world were true for the social world but the examination and explanation I believe should be different (Henderson, 2000).

Given the various forms of repressive practices in society, the question of what to do about crime that we address above through replacement discourse has also led to significant amount of reaction. Here critics often feel that they have the last word against constitutive criminology claiming that such theorizing "can too easily lead toward nihilism, cynicism and conservatism" (Matthews & Young, 1992:13; see also Croall, 1997), even though this is more aptly directed at skeptical rather than affirmative postmodernism. Others challenge the policy of constitutive criminology for being naïve. For example, some point out that there is nothing sacrosanct about the idea of "replacement discourse" as a form of reconstruction that limits its strategic use to progressive and harm reducing objectives. Nor is replacement discourse the prerogative of one particular political persuasion. Indeed, even some sympathetic supporters indicate that replacement discourse may itself be harm producing, and that while affording a means of resistance it can also allow new negative constructions to occur (See Sanchez, 1999; Kappeler & Kraska, 1999). For example, hate speech could be seen as "replacement discourse," replacing that of multiculturalism and integration. This line of criticism leads to the question of "values" embedded in constitutive criminology ideology. Indeed, Joel Henderson posses a question about replacement discourse that captures this point well. He asks

"While, I have read the rationale for moving from deconstructionism to reconstructionism, I am not clear on how you avoid the basic argument of the deconstructionist. How is your construction not a cultural production coming from some particular point of view?" (Henderson, 2000). Finally, there are critics who believe that the constitutive approach to social change implies a vanguard of intellectuals rather than workers, which they claim, is likely to be ineffective against the powerful excessive investors.

Our Response

Constitutive theory must be understood as standing in contrast to more traditional mainstream theorizing which attempts to compartmentalize, dichotomize, and categorize, and divide the world into ever more specialized bodies of knowledge and disciplines. This is directly relevant to the issue of complex prose. In mainstream theorizing comprehension is divided, and since each discipline develops its own specialized jargonistic knowledge, crossovers to other disciplines become increasingly more difficult. Constitutive theorizing, as well as postmodern theorizing, attempts to cross-disciplinary borders. In doing so their prose more genuinely "captures" complexity and interconnectedness. Hence, prose becomes largely unfamiliar to the narrowly invested reader. Some of our critics already recognize this (Friedrichs, 1996:124-25). Critics of the "difficult prose" advocate a writing style of "saying it simply." This would be nice if life itself was so simple. Rather, the complexity that exists needs prose that can "capture" its complexity in movement. Often, consumeristic forms of reading demand that something be used (read) once then thrown away for yet more things to be used (read). Constitutive criminology, however, demands that "saying it simply" or demanding the ability of a single read to understand militates against the kind of prose that might momentarily "capture" complex phenomena in dialectical movement. In short, the call for "clarity" and "simplicity" assumes a singular form of writing and reading whose continued acquiescence fuels the politics of containment not liberation. At the outset, this wholehearted acquiescence to singular and essentialist arguments is troubling, as we have previously outlined.

With regard to the problem of integrative methodology, we find much work sympathetic to this approach. Recent theorizing in critical pedagogy, "border pedagogy," and "postmodern pedagogy" served as examples. Giroux (1992), for example, argues for activist intellectuals to become "border crossers." "Borderlands," he tells us, "should be seen as sites for both critical analysis and as a potential source of experimentation, creativity, and possibility" (1992:34). Similarly, Lippens (1998, 1999, 2000), applying this theme to criminology, asks: "who owns this discipline and who claims to police its borders?" He argues that border policing constitutes the discipline but in so doing limits our understanding of the issue. We believe that cross-fertilization should be encouraged in the "disciplines" (see for example, Norris, 2000; Barak, 1998). After all, Einstein was reading heavy philosophy as well as the usual stuff in physics when he came up with his dramatic formulations. Many theorists have crossed over. Many theorists come very close to philosophy in explaining the workings of subatomic matter. Consider quantum mechanics and such things as the "observer effect." Constitutive criminology finds that the disciplines have become overly compartmentalized and their community of scholars becomes resistant to crossing over. Indeed, when one does cross disciplinary borders, one is accused of engaging in esoteric, jargonistic discourse. Underlying this is an ideological commitment to the particular discipline in which one has invested energy. Constitutive criminology encourages movement beyond the confines of such boundaries.

Further, why is considering the relevant contributions of mutually interrelated events, activities, arrangements, structures, etc., considered contradictory? As we have repeatedly stated, the dialectical concept of causality, "interrelationships," or "coproduction," is preferable over the linear and deterministic concept of single or multiple causality. With regard to the politics of causality, Colvin's reading of *Constitutive Criminology* explains that:

> these processes comprise relationships that are not deterministic but dialectical, a dialectic that assumes nonlinear development and a movement, through human agency, toward instability of social forms . . . Whether a particular situation or interrelationship will result in criminality cannot be determined with any precision since the dynamics of human relations are indeterminate, can be altered by seemingly small events, and are part of an historically situated, on going process that is also in-determinate (1997:1449).

Unlike much of modernism's dualisms such as "free will versus determinism," "conflict versus consensus" and "order versus chaos," constitutive theory sees that each of these is operative. Indeed, according to the insights generated by chaos theory, we can have order and disorder in the same system. This does not mean despair, resignation, and nihilism. Rather it poses new challenges in the ways that we conceptualize complexity. The future challenge will be to further integrate chaos theory's ideas such as non-linearity, feedback, fractal geometry, attractors, phase space, self-similarity, indeterminacy, and iterations into our scholarly horizons. It is not, therefore, that complexity cannot be understood, but that it cannot be captured solely within the prevailing categories of much of modernist thought. Nor can the idealization of prediction be our goal. Constitutive criminology is an ongoing search for understanding complexity over time. Constitutive theory has not taken the place of chaos theory. Rather we have argued (Henry & Milovanovic, 1996, Chap. 6) that the notion of nonlinearity is more useful in understanding constitutive interrelational (COREL) sets, which are historically situated, complexes of coupled iterative loops in movement. This movement has dialectical components, and can be nonlinear in its effects.

Even in the best of modernist empiricism, sensitive scholars (Sampson & Laub, 1993) have recognized in self-criticism that non-linear effects (i.e., "feedback effects," "reciprocal effects," "dialectical processes," "reverse causality") could be at play. We have noted the notion of disproportional effects and sensitivity to initial conditions, such as in the "butterfly effect" which may produce unintended results (good and bad). So, in short, constitutive theory is derived from a number of threads developing in postmodern analysis as well as in critical theory of modernist analysis. Interestingly, with chaos theory (as in quantum mechanics which is a probability model), deterministic equations can produce indeterminate results. This appears in the notion of iteration. Empiricist methodology more often attempts linear analysis, and dismisses small "inconsequential" factors, usually after the third identified independent variable. We find "rounding" in empiricism to the one hundredth place as acceptable. This is not so for chaos theory. Even dismissing a point of difference of say .00001, upon a number of iterations can produce dramatically different results (graphs). The social scientists of the modernist persuasion try to convince themselves that precision is attainable and it will thereby lead to greener pastures. Chaos theory questions whether we can ever predict with certainty and that even small factors, upon iteration, can produce disproportionate effects.

The question of the politics of social constructionism that leads to the simplistic assumption that the social world is real, relates to what is meant by "talk" or more precisely "discursive practices." The realist critics of social constructionism assume there is a neat separation between reality and our talk about it. Our argument is that discursive practices are part of the process that produces what then seems to be a separate reality. However, the critical issue for criminology is not whether the discursively produced representations have some underlying and independent existence, but that people act toward them *as if* they possess this quality. As such, categories based on socially constructed difference become invested with energy from those who treat them as real. Investors then act toward these categories to either defend their interest in that reality or oppose others' notion of reality. It is human actions that produce harm. To be clear, it is not that the harm of crime is unreal, but that the constructions that lead to its effects are the outcome of discursive practices. Consider race, ethnicity, sexuality, gender, and class, all socially constructed, reified categories produced by the creation of distinctions based on perceived difference. Actions of people based on these differences (e.g., impositions, reductions, repressions, etc.), whether men against women, straights against gays, etc. (all themselves constructed categories) produces avoidable harms. Crime, as we have said, is the expression of the power to create harm based on socially constructed differences. The pain of that expression is real; its constitution is socially constructed. Thus, we are not arguing that crime (as harm) will disappear if we stop talking about it. Rather we argue that harm will cease to be the outcome of a world that does not invest in the realities of difference in ways that value some human subjects over others and that exploit difference as a means of domination. This leads directly to the problem of policy.

Given that the basis of crime (as harm) is the socially constructed and discursively constituted exercise of power through difference, it follows that human subjects whose investment in power relations harms others have the potential to reconstitute their use of human agency to be less harmful or have the potential to be reconstituted through interactive relations with the wider culture or structure. Such a perspective, as Colvin (1997:1450) comments: "opens the possibility for transformation of human subjects and the social structures we construct."

One of the means to achieve this reconstruction is through replacement discourse that fuels positive social constructions. Replacement discourse is designed to displace harmful moments in the exercise of power with discourses that tell different stories about the world. This is not simply saying that if we stop talking about crime it will go away. Rather it is to say that if human discursive practices cease to construct differences as a basis of power (see Cornell, 1991) the site for investment will be deconstructed, and investment and defense of it as a reality will be less possible. This is because the perception of people as less than fellow human subjects, as "others," will be dissipated. Harming others will be tantamount to harming oneself. This is why we advocate a policy of "social judo" in which the use of power is turned away from harm production, and toward reinvesting in positive connections with a relationally oriented community of fellow human subjects. As Bohm (1997:16) says, "The judo metaphor is apt here because, on the one hand . . . using power to reduce the power of others only replaces one excessive investor with another. On the other hand, when using judo as a means of self-defense, the power of the aggressor is turned back against the aggressor."

The problem of policy, then, is not one of merely applying strategies but of teaming deconstruction and reconstruction so that appreciation of difference rather than domination based on difference, pervades the spirit of social life. Difference without domination is to be celebrated (see Cornell's point about an "ethical feminism," 1999). Nor should the classical economic equivalency principle be quickly embraced, because subsuming difference within notions of formal equality is to deny the variability and polyvocality of the human condition and to ride roughshod over substantive inequality. The problem is not to remove existing institutional and social structures that reproduce these differences whose investment with power results in oppression and inequality. Instead, the problem is how to cease our unreflexive rebuilding of these social forms and structures while reinvesting energy in alternative, connective interrelational social forms. Fitting well with this direction is Laclau's (2000:306) recent analysis of how contingent "universalities" may develop (with alternative social imaginary) constructions which become the basis of political agendas and change (see also Cornell, 1999), and Butler's (2000:179) call for a "language between languages" in accommodating "competing universalities."

What we are suggesting, then, is that "dissipative structures," that is, structures that are extremely sensitive to their environment and its perturbations and consequently undergo continuous change while still providing provisionally stable horizons for social action, have much in common with the notion of "contingent universalities" (Butler, 1992). Here provisional truths may become the basis of political action and social policy, but these are always contingent; subject to change, refinement, substitution and deletion when faced with historical conditions and further reflective investigation. In short, in our view the problem of policy should remain a problem; there are no answers, only working solutions.

Note

[1]   We have developed the constitutive criminological perspective in several articles and two books (Henry & Milovanovic, 1991, 1993, 1994, 1996, 1999). This chapter draws substantially from these works.

Discussion Questions

1. One of constitutive criminology's core concepts is "coproduction." What do Henry and Milovanovic mean by this concept? How far does coproduction integrate the micro-level human actions with the broader level social structure and culture? What is the case for arguing that this theory explaining crime is holistic, rather than weighted toward individuals actions or society's forces?

2. What role does language play in relation to social structure and ultimately crime? Where does crime come from in constitutive criminology? Are words and phrases used in "crime talk" actually causing crimes to occur, or do Henry and Milovanovic have something different in mind when they talk about the importance of discourse as the "cloth of crime," and if so what?

3. What is distinctive about constitutive criminology's definition of crime as harm produced by the exercise of power? Using crime cases that you've read about, give an example of a crime of reduction and an example of a crime of repression. What are the implications of constitutive criminology's view of crime for relations of power that are a part of hierarchical societies like the United States?

4. What is meant by the constitutive criminological concept of the "excessive investor"? How does this translate into examples of cases of crime that you have read about? What makes this theory of crime causation radically different from the theories used by other mainstream criminologists?

5. If, according to constitutive criminology, crime is the power to deny others their own humanity, how is it possible for criminal justice to be exercised, since police, courts and corrections use power to control offenders? Does this make them offenders also? If constitutive criminology does not use power, how then does it envisage controlling those who do and what role does the concept of "replacement discourse" play in this process?

6. Because of its reliance on social constructionism, constitutive criminology is criticized, particularly by realist criminologists, for its failure to take crime seriously. How far is it possible to hold the view that crime is socially constructed yet still real in its consequences? What are the advantages and disadvantages of the constructionist position and why do these theorists consider deconstruction important?

7. Is there a danger, as critics like Henderson and Thompson argue, that constitutive criminology takes such a broad definition of crime as "harm" that it loses sight of the seriousness of some harms relative to others? Or are constitutive criminologists suggesting that the principle of harm production underlies all crimes? What are the implications of arguing that some harm production is acceptable, either because it is less serious, inflicted on categories that do not matter, or that it is justified under certain conditions?

8. Is replacement discourse simply describing politics? Is the key issue a process occurs that results in a particular institutional and structural formation, or is the issue about whether what is conveyed by the process is good rather than bad? If so, does the process or the outcome matter most?

9. What do constitutive criminologists mean by the "social judo" concept of crime control? How does this resolve the contradiction in their notion of power as harm? Consider once crime that you have read about and explore what harms the victim suffered, what power the offender (excessive investor) exercised and how a "social judo" approach would deal with and prevent or respond to this crime?

10. What does constitutive criminology contribute to the body of criminological theory? Why is it considered affirmative postmodernism rather than skeptical postmodernism? Why is it considered a peaceful response to the crime problem and how does it compare with draw on peacemaking criminology?

CHAPTER 6

Cultural Criminology

Jeff Ferrell

Cultural criminology critically investigates the ways in which the dynamics of media and popular culture, the lives and activities of criminals, and the operations of social control and criminal justice come together in everyday life. Cultural criminologists emphasize the role of image, style, and symbolic meaning among criminals and their subcultures, in the mass media's representation of crime and criminal justice, and in public conflicts over crime and crime control.

Originally, "cultural criminology" denoted a critical perspective on crime, criminal subcultures, and popular culture developed by Ferrell (1999) and Ferrell and Sanders (1995). The notion of cultural criminology now refers more broadly to the increasing attention that many critical criminologists give to popular culture constructions, and especially mass media constructions, of crime and crime control. Most broadly, the existence of a perspective such as "cultural criminology" reflects the growing influence of cultural and media analysis in the traditional domains of criminological inquiry, such that critical criminologists increasingly investigate, for example, not just domestic violence, but the mass media's gendered coverage of domestic violence; not just crimes committed by street gangs, but the everyday values, language, clothing styles, and graffiti that define the lives of gang members; not just illegal drug use, but the media campaigns and mediated "wars on drugs" that create public understandings of drug use and shape drug policy.

As a foundation for this sort of inquiry, cultural criminology imports the insights of cultural studies into criminology, building especially from the pioneering work of the British cultural studies movement regarding subcultural symbolism and mediated social control. Similarly, cultural criminology draws on the insights of postmodernism, operating from the postmodern propositions that style is substance, that meaning resides in representation, and that crime and crime control can therefore only be understood as an ongoing spiral of intertextual, image-driven "media loops" (Manning, 1998). From this view, the study of crime necessitates not simply the examination of individual criminals and criminal events, not even the straightforward examination of media "coverage" of criminals and criminal events, but rather a journey into the spectacle of crime, a walk down an infinite hall of mirrors where images created and consumed by criminals, criminal subcultures, control agents, media institutions, and audiences bounce endlessly off one another. Undergirding the use of these contemporary perspectives in cultural criminology is a more traditional intellectual projects as well: the expansion of existing sociological, social interactionist, and social constructionist understandings in criminology. Cultural criminologists attempt to develop the "symbolic" in "symbolic interaction" by exploring the stylized dynamics of illicit subcultures and the symbolic representations of crime and justice offered by the mass media. Similarly, they seek to explore the many ways in which perceptions and understandings of crime and crime control are constructed.

Most importantly, cultural criminology emerges out of the tradition of critical criminology, incorporating as it does a variety of critical perspectives on crime and crime control. Utilizing these perspectives, cultural criminologists attempt to unravel the politics of crime as played out through mediated anti-crime campaigns; through evocative images of deviance, crime, and marginality; and through criminalized subcultures and their resistance to legal control. To the extent that it integrates interactionist, constructionist, and critical perspectives, cultural criminology thus attempts to develop what Cohen (1988:68) has called "a structurally and politically informed version of labeling theory"—that is, an analysis that accounts for the complex circuitry through which the meaning of crime and deviance is constructed, enforced, and resisted. Put more simply, cultural criminology heeds Becker's (1963:183, 199) classic injunction—that we "look at all the people involved in any episode of alleged deviance . . . all the parties to a situation, and their relationships"—and includes in this collective examination and critique those cultural relationships, those contested webs of meaning and perception, in which all parties are entangled.

These theoretical orientations also inform the methodologies favored by cultural criminologists. As employed within cultural criminology, field research and ethnographic research investigate at close range the nuances of meaning and symbolism developed within particular situations and events, and explore the precise dynamics of various criminal subcultures. At its extreme, such research is designed to develop a form of criminological *verstehen* whereby the researcher approaches an empathic understanding of the meanings and emotions associated with crime and crime control. Alternatively, other cultural criminologists utilize methods of media and textual analysis to develop critical readings of mediated crime accounts. Such scholarship investigates both historical and contemporary texts, ranging from newspapers, film, and television to popular music, comic books, and cyberspace. Recently, cultural criminologists have also begun to integrate these two methodological frameworks in producing case studies that document the ways in which the workings of criminal subcultures, the operations of the mass media, and the fears and understandings of the public all shape and influence one another.

Subtopics

Framed by these theoretical and methodological orientations, cultural criminology has emerged within a number of substantive areas. As will be seen, some of these focus more on the mass media, others more on criminal and deviant subcultures. But as will also be seen, many of these areas expose the complex interplay of both media representations and subcultural dynamics.

Media Constructions of Crime and Criminal Justice

Cultural criminologists investigate the complex institutional interconnections between the criminal justice system and the mass media, documenting not only the mass media's heavy reliance on criminal justice sources for imagery and information on crime, but more importantly, the reciprocal relationship which undergirds this reliance. Working within organizational imperatives of efficiency and routinization, media institutions regularly rely on data selectively provided by policing and court agencies. In so doing, they highlight for the public issues chosen by criminal justice institutions and framed by criminal justice imperatives, and contribute to the political agendas of the criminal justice system and to the generation of public support for these agendas. In a relatively non-conspiratorial but nonetheless powerful fashion, media and criminal justice organizations thus coordinate their day-to-day operations, and cooperate in constructing circumscribed understandings of crime and crime control.

A large body of research in cultural criminology examines the nature of these understandings and the public dynamics of their production. Like cultural criminology generally, much of the research here builds on the classic analytic models of cultural studies and interactionist sociology, as embodied in concepts such as moral entrepreneurship and moral enterprise in the creation of crime and deviance (Becker, 1963), and the invention of folk devils as a means of generating moral panic (Cohen, 1972/1980) around issues of crime and deviance. Exploring everyday understandings of crime controversies, this research critiques taken-for-granted assumptions regarding the prevalence of criminality and the particular characteristics of criminals, and traces these assumptions to the interrelated workings of interest groups, media institutions, and criminal justice organizations.

Emerging scholarship in cultural criminology also offers useful reconceptualizations and refinements of existing analytic models. McRobbie and Thornton (1995), for example, argue that the essential concepts of "moral panic" and "folk devils" must be reconsidered in multi-mediated societies; with the proliferation of media channels and the saturation of media markets, moral panics have become both dangerous endeavors and marketable commodities, and folk devils now find themselves both stigmatized and lionized in mainstream media and alternative media alike. Similarly, Jenkins's (1999) recent work has begun to refine understandings of crime and justice issues as cultural constructions. He demonstrates that attention must be paid to the media and political dynamics underlying not only constructed crime but "unconstructed" crime as well. For example, Jenkins explores the failure to frame activities such as anti-abortion violence as criminal terrorism, and situates this failure within active media and political processes.

Through all of this, cultural criminologists emphasize that in the process of constructing crime and crime control as social concerns and political controversies, the media also construct them as entertainment. Intertwined with mediated moral panic over crime and crime waves is the pleasure found in consuming mediated crime imagery and drama, in "entertaining the crisis" (Sparks, 1995). Given this, cultural criminology focuses as much on popular film, popular music, and television entertainment programming as on the mediated manufacture of news and information, and investigates the collapsing boundaries between such categories. Recent work in this area targets especially the popularity of "reality" crime programs (Fishman & Cavender, 1998). With their mix of street footage, theatrical staging, and patrol-car sermonizing, reality-crime television programs like "COPS" generate conventional, though at times contradictory, images of crime and policing. They in turn spin off secondary merchandising schemes, legal suits over videotaped police chases and televised invasions of privacy, and criminal activities allegedly induced by the programs themselves.

Media Constructions of Popular Culture as Crime

The notion of "popular culture as crime" refers to the reconstruction of cultural activities as criminal endeavors—through, for example, the public labeling of popular culture products as criminogenic, or through the criminalization of cultural producers. Art photographers, for example, have faced public campaigns accusing them of producing obscene or pornographic images, and art centers exhibiting such images have been charged with criminal activity. Punk and heavy metal bands, and associated record companies, distributors, and retail outlets, have encountered obscenity rulings, civil and criminal suits, high-profile police raids, and police interference with concerts. Performers, producers, distributors, and retailers of rap and "gangsta rap" music have likewise faced arrest and conviction on obscenity charges; legal confiscation of recordings; highly publicized protests, boy-cotts, and political hearings; and ongoing media campaigns and legal pro-ceedings accusing them of promoting crime and delinquency. More broad-ly, a variety of television programs, films, and cartoons have been targeted by public campaigns alleging that they incite delinquency, spin off "copycat" crimes, and otherwise serve as criminogenic social forces.

These many cases certainly fall within the purview of cultural crimi-nology because the targets of criminalization—photographers, musicians, television writers, and their products—are "cultural" in nature, but equally so because their criminalization itself unfolds as a cultural process. When contemporary culture personas and performances are criminalized, they are primarily criminalized through the mass media, through their presentation and re-presentation as criminal in the realm of sound bites, shock images, news conferences, and newspaper headlines. In this way, media-produced popular culture forms and figures are, ironically, criminalized by means of the media. Given this, cultural criminologists have begun to widen the notion of "criminalization" to include more than the simple creation and application of criminal law. Increasingly, they investigate the larger process of "cultural criminalization" (Ferrell, 1998), the mediated reconstruction of meaning and perception around issues of culture and crime.

The mediated context of criminalization is a political one as well. The contemporary criminalization of popular culture has emerged as part of larg-er "culture wars" waged by political and cultural reactionaries; and contro-versies over the criminal or criminogenic characteristics of art photogra-phers and rap musicians have largely resulted from the sorts of well-funded, politically sophisticated campaigns that have similarly targeted feminist/gay/lesbian artists. In this light it is less than surprising that con-temporary cultural criminalization is aimed time and again at marginalized subcultures—progressive punk musicians, politically militant black rap groups, lesbian and gay artists—whose stylized confrontation with their mar-ginality threaten particular patterns of moral and legal control. And, as a process conducted largely in the public realm, cultural criminalization con-tributes to popular perceptions and panics, and thus to the further margin-alization of those who are its focus.

The Media and Culture of Policing

Today the production and consumption of mediated meaning frames not only the reality of crime, but of crime control as well. Contemporary polic-ing can in fact hardly be understood apart from its interpenetration with media at all levels. As "reality" crime and policing television programs shape public perceptions, serve as controversial tools of officer recruitment and suspect apprehension, and engender legal suits over their effects on street-level policing, citizens shoot video footage of police conduct and misconduct—some of which finds its way, full-circle, onto news and "reality" programs. Meanwhile, within the police subculture itself, surveillance cameras and on-board patrol car cameras capture the practices of police officers and citizens alike and, as Websdale (1999) documents, police crime files themselves take shape as "situated media substrates" that, like surveillance and patrol car footage, regularly become building blocks for subsequent mass media images of policing. The policing of a postmodern world emerges as a complex, expanding spiral of mediated social control.

From the view of cultural criminology, policing must in turn be understood as a set of practices situated, like criminal practices, within subcultural conventions of meaning, symbolism, and style. In this regard, Kraska and Kappeler (1995:85) explore the subcultural ideologies, situated dynamics, and broader "cultural and structural context" within which police deviance and police sexual violence against women develop. Perhaps most interesting here, in light of the ethnographic methodologies discussed above, is Kraska's (1996) investigation of police paramilitary units. Immersing himself and his emotions in a situation of police paramilitary violence, Kraska details the stylized subcultural status afforded by particular forms of weaponry and clothing, and documents the deep-seated ideological and affective states which define the collective meaning of such situations. With crime control as with crime, subcultural and media dynamics construct experience and perception.

Situated Media, Situated Audiences

Many cultural criminologists argue that the everyday notion of "media" must be expanded beyond the "mass media" to include those media that are situated within the various subcultures of crime, deviance, and crime control. Various illicit subcultures certainly come into regular contact with the mass media, but in so doing appropriate and reinvent mass media channels and products as part of their subcultural worlds. Further, illicit subcultures regularly invent their own media of communication; as McRobbie and Thornton (1995:559) point out, even the interests of "folk devils" are increasingly "defended by their own niche and micro-media." Thus, alternative and marginalized youth subcultures self-produce a wealth of zines and websites; street gang members construct elaborate edifices of communication out of particular clothing styles, colors, and hand signs; BASE jumpers videotape their own illegal jumps; and graffiti writers develop a continent-wide network of freight train graffiti that links distant subcultural members within a shared symbolic community. Further, multiple, fluid audiences witness efflorescences of crime and crime control in their everyday existence, consume a multitude of crime images packaged as news and entertainment, and in turn remake the meaning of these encounters within the symbolic interaction of their own lives. Investigating the linkages between "media" and crime, then, means investigating the many situations in which these linkages emerge, and moreover the situated place of media, audience, and meaning within criminal worlds. Ultimately, perhaps, this investigation suggests blurring the analytic boundary between producer and audience, and recognizing that a variety of groups both produce and consume contested images of crime.

Crime as Culture and Subculture

Much of what we label criminal behavior is at the same time subcultural behavior, collectively organized around networks of symbol, ritual, and shared meaning. While this general insight is hardly a new one, cultural criminology develops it in a number of directions. Bringing a postmodern sensibility to their understanding of deviant and criminal subcultures, cultural criminologists argue that such subcultures are defined by elaborate conventions of argot, appearance, and stylized presentation of self, and thus operate as repositories of collective meaning and representation for their members. Taken into a mediated world of increasingly dislocated communication and dispersed meaning, this insight further implies that illicit subcultures may now be exploding into universes of symbolic communication that in many ways transcend time and space. For computer hackers, graffiti writers, drug runners, and others, a mix of widespread spatial dislocation and precise normative organization implies subcultures defined less by face-to-face interaction than by shared, if second-hand, symbolic codes.

Much research in this area of cultural criminology has focused on the dispersed dynamics of subcultural style; cultural criminologists have investigated style as defining both the internal characteristics of deviant and criminal subcultures and external constructions of them. Miller (1995), for example, has documented the many ways in which gang symbolism and gang style exist as the medium of meaning for both street gang members and the probation officers who attempt to understand and control them. Ferrell (1996) has shown how contemporary hip hop graffiti exists essentially as a "crime of style" both for graffiti writers, who operate and evaluate one another within complex stylistic conventions, and for media institutions and political authorities who perceive graffiti as violating their ongoing control of urban environments. Lyng and Bracey (1995) have documented the multiply ironic process by which the style of the outlaw biker subculture came first to signify class-based cultural resistance, next to elicit the sorts of media reactions and legal controls that amplified and confirmed its meaning, and finally to be appropriated and commodified in such a way as to void its political potential. Significantly, these and other studies demonstrate that the importance of style resides in the tension between subcultural dynamics and external media and political constructions.

If subcultures of crime and deviance are defined by their stylistic organization, cultural criminology has also begun to show that they are defined by intensities of collective experience and emotion as well. Cultural criminologists like Lyng (1998) and Ferrell (1996) have utilized verstehen-oriented methodologies to document the experiences of "edgework" and "the adrenaline rush"—immediate moments of risk, danger, and skill—that shape participation in deviant and criminal subcultures. Discovered across a range of illicit subcultures, these intense, ritualized moments of pleasure and excitement define the experience of subcultural members and seduce them into continued subcultural participation. Significantly, research shows that these experiences of edgework and adrenaline are collectively constructed, and encased in shared vocabularies of motive and meaning. Thus, while these experiences certainly suggest a criminology of the body and the emotions, they also reveal the ways in which collective intensities of experience, like collective conventions of style, construct shared subcultural meaning.

Bodies and Emotions

Perhaps the most intimate of situations in which crime and crime control intersect are those in and around the physical and emotional self. The fleeting experience of edgework and adrenaline rushes, heightened by risk of legal apprehension; the evolution of subcultural style as marker of identity and criminalization; the utilization of researchers' own experiences and emotions in the study of crime and policing—all suggest the importance of the situated self. These also suggest that other moments merit the attention of cultural criminology as well, from gang girls' construction of identity through hair, makeup, and discourse (Mendoza-Denton, 1996) and phone fantasy workers' invocation of sexuality and emotion (Mattley, 1998) to the contested media and body politics of AIDS (Kane, 1998). Together, these and other situations in turn point to a cultural criminology that can account for crime and crime control in terms of pleasure, fear, and excitement, and that can confront the deformities of sexuality and power, control and resistance that emerge in these inside spaces. They also demand the ongoing refinement of the verstehen-oriented methodologies described above—of ways of investigating that are embodied and affective, always moving closer to the intimate meaning of crime and crime control.

Cultural Space, Crime, and Crime Control

Many of the everyday situations and everyday controversies in which crime and policing are played out involve the contesting of cultural space—that is, the contentious construction of meaning and identity in public domains (Ferrell, 1997). Homeless populations, for example, reveal by their public presence the scandal of inequality, and are in turn hounded and herded by a host of loitering, vagrancy, trespass, public lodging, and public nuisance statutes. "Gutter punks" invest downtown street corners with disheveled style, "skate punks" and skateboarders convert walkways and parking garages into playgrounds, Latino/a street "cruisers" create mobile subcultures out of dropped frames and polished chrome—and face in response aggressive enforcement of laws regarding trespass, curfew, public sleeping, even car stereo volume. Street gangs carve out collective cultural space from shared styles and public rituals; criminal justice officials prohibit and confiscate stylized clothing, enforce prohibitions against public gatherings by "known" gang members, and orchestrate public gang "round-ups." Graffiti writers remake the visual landscapes and symbolic codes of public life, but do so in the face of increasing criminal sanctions, high-tech surveillance systems, and nationally coordinated legal campaigns designed to remove them and their markings from public life.

As with mediated campaigns of cultural criminalization, these conflicts over crime and cultural space regularly emerge around the marginalized subcultures of young people and ethnic minorities, and thus raise essential issues of identity and justice. Such conflicts in turn incorporate a complex criminalization of these subcultures, as part of a systematic effort to erase their self-constructed public images, and to substitute in their place symbols of safety and commerce. Ultimately, these disparate conflicts over crime and cultural space reveal the prevalence of contested public meaning in contemporary society, and something of the work of control in the age of cultural reproduction.

Politics, Crime, and Cultural Criminology

Clearly, a common thread connects the many domains of cultural criminology: the presence of power relations, and the emergence of social control, at the intersections of culture and crime. The stylistic practices and symbolic codes of illicit subcultures are made the object of legal surveillance and control or, alternatively, are appropriated and commodified within a vast machinery of consumption. Sophisticated media and criminal justice "culture wars" are launched against alternative forms of art, music, and entertainment, thereby criminalizing those involved, marginalizing them from idealized notions of decency and community and, at the extreme, silencing the political critiques which they present. Ongoing media constructions of crime and crime control emerge out of an alliance of convenience between media institutions and criminal justice agencies, serve to promote political agendas regarding crime control, and in turn function to both trivialize and dramatize the meaning of crime. Increasingly, then, it is television crime shows and big budget detective movies, nightly newscasts and morning newspaper headlines, recurrent campaigns against the real and imagined crimes of the disenfranchised that must constitute the subject matter of critical criminology.

At the same time, cultural criminologists emphasize and explore the various forms which resistance to this complex web of social control may take. The audiences for media constructions of crime are diverse in both their composition and in their readings of these constructions; they recontextualize, remake, and even reverse mass media meanings as they incorporate them into their daily lives and interactions. Varieties of resistance also emerge among those groups more specifically targeted within the practice of mediated control. Artists and musicians caught up in contemporary "culture wars" refuse governmental awards, resign high-profile positions, win legal judgments, and organize alternative media outlets and performances. Within other marginalized subcultures, personal and group style exists as a stigmata, inviting outside surveillance and control, but at the same time as a valued badge of honor and resistance made all the more meaningful by its enduring defiance of outside authority. Likewise, those immersed in moments of illicit edgework and adrenaline construct resistance doubly. First, by combining high levels of risk with precise skills, those involved invent an identity, a sense of crafted self, that resists the usual degradations of subordinate status and deskilled labor. Second, as these moments become more dangerous because targeted by campaigns of criminalization and enforcement, participants in them find an enhancement of the edgy excitement they provide, and in so doing transform political pressure into personal and collective pleasure.

Moreover, cultural criminology itself operates as a sort of intellectual resistance, as a diverse counter-discourse on conventional constructions of crime. In deconstructing moments of mediated panic over crime, cultural criminologists work to expose the political processes behind seemingly spontaneous social concerns. Beyond this, Barak (1994) argues for an activist "newsmaking criminology" in which criminologists integrate themselves into the mediated construction of crime, and in so doing produce what constitutive criminologists (Henry & Milovanovic, 1996) call a "replacement discourse" regarding crime and crime control. Much of cultural criminology's ethnographic work in subcultural domains functions similarly, as a critical move away from conventional understandings produced by the media and the criminal justice system and reproduced by a "courthouse criminology" that relies on these sources. By attentively documenting the lived realities of groups whom conventional crime constructions have marginalized, and in turn documenting the politics of this marginalization process, cultural criminologists attempt to deconstruct the demonization of various outsiders and to produce alternative understandings of them. Approaching this task from the other direction, Hamm (1993) and others venture inside the worlds of particularly violent criminals to document dangerous nuances of meaning and style often invisible in official reporting on them. In its politics as in its theory and method, then, cultural criminology is designed to produce alternative images of crime.

Points Made by Opponents

Perhaps the broadest criticism of cultural criminology involves the charge that, like the cultural studies perspectives on which it draws, cultural criminology uncritically embraces an emerging postmodern world driven by the mass media and defined by image and style. From this view, cultural criminology is as shallow as the world it seeks to explain, never moving beyond surface appearances and stylized identities. And in this sense, cultural criminology focuses so intently on the cultural dimensions of contemporary society that it misses the politics and economy on which such cultural dimensions are predicated.

From the perspective of cultural criminologists, however, this focus on culture, media, and image constitutes an attempt to critically analyze emerging forms of power, control, and injustice. As critical historians of crime and justice have repeatedly shown, new arrangements of power and domination incorporate new forms of legal and social control; generate new forms of crime and criminalization; and at the same time foster new forms of resistance and insubordination. Thus, in a contemporary world whose politics and economy are increasingly defined by the mediated marketing of images and impressions, whose criminal justice policies are increasingly intertwined with mediated anti-crime campaigns and aimed at the stylized identities of marginalized groups, critical criminologists must pay close attention to matters of representation and meaning. In this world, cultural dynamics constitute the turf, the battlefield, on which issues of identity and community, justice and injustice, crime and crime control are decided.

Yet this is not to say that cultural criminology's focus of inquiry is without its limitations. To begin with, despite recent advances in integrating media and subcultural analysis, much of the work in cultural criminology has remained divided between the study of illicit subcultures on the one hand, and mass media texts on the other. As demonstrated in this chapter, such a sharp disjunction inevitably misses key dynamics regarding the complex interplay of culture, crime, and crime control. Also disturbing is the inability of cultural criminologists to address actual issues of audience and audience meanings; as is the case with much media analysis and criticism, the perspectives and understandings of various audiences often remain more imagined than investigated. Most importantly, cultural criminology is just beginning to move beyond the myopia of its British and U.S. roots to explore the contested convergence of cultural and criminal dynamics in a variety of world settings, and to investigate the migration of illicit meanings across real and imagined borders.

Beyond this, certainly the most pointed criticism directed at the work of cultural criminologists involves the issue of romanticism. Left realists and other criminologists often argue that cultural criminologists create overly sympathetic portraits of deviant and criminal subcultures, romanticizing the bad behavior of criminals, ignoring its destructive consequences, and imagining that everyday criminality somehow constitutes a form of political resistance. Embedded in this debate over romanticism, though, is a key issue for cultural criminologists. The charge of "romanticizing" crime implies a divergence from the reality, the true nature, of crime. But for cultural criminologists, that's just the point: what in fact is the reality of crime, and how would we know it apart from the mediated representations and stylized images that increasingly define it? Given the recurrent creation of folk devils and mediated moral panics, and the consistent public overdramatization of crime in the interest of television ratings, political careers, and prison construction, it seems likely that what appears "true" about crime is in fact fiction, and that what appears "romantic" results mostly from cultural criminologists' attempts to rediscover the humanity, the cultural complexity, of crime, criminals, and crime control.

Finally, as a nascent perspective, cultural criminology has been criticized for constituting less a completed, definitive paradigm than an eclectic constellation of critiques linked by sensitivities to image and meaning in the study of crime and crime control. Oriented as they are to the multiplicity of meanings and indeterminacy of images continually developing around crime and crime control, though, cultural criminologists themselves would likely embrace cultural criminology as an always unfinished project, open to emerging configurations of culture, crime, and crime control, and to emerging critiques of them.

Concluding Synthesis

As an emerging perspective within critical criminology, cultural criminology draws from a range of critical perspectives. Revisiting and perhaps reinventing existing paradigms, cultural criminology seeks less to synthesize or subsume these various paradigms than to engage them in a critical, multi-faceted exploration of culture and crime. Guiding this exploration is cultural criminology's overarching concern with the meaning of crime and crime control. Some three decades ago, Cohen (1988:68; 1971:19) wrote of "placing on the agenda" of a culturally informed critical criminology issues of "subjective meaning," and of deviance and crime as "meaningful action." Cultural criminology embraces and expands this agenda by exploring the complex, contested construction of meaning that occurs between media and legal institutions, illicit subcultures, and audiences around matters of crime and crime control. In so doing, cultural criminology likewise highlights the inevitability of the image in the practice of power and resistance, crime and crime control. Confronting the stylized politics of a criminal subculture, watching "COPS" or perusing the morning paper, lost in the panic and pleasure of crime, there is nothing so real as representation.

Discussion Questions

1. Where do you see images and symbolic representations of crime, criminals, and criminal justice in your everyday life?

2. How many of the television shows that you watch are focused on crime, criminals, or criminal justice? Why do you watch them? Do they have any effect on your attitudes about crime?

3. What image comes to mind when you hear the phrase "gang member?" What image comes to mind when you hear the word "prostitute?" What are the sources of these images?

4. How has the media image of cigarette smoking and cigarette smokers changed over the past few years? If cigarette smoking were to be outlawed completely, what images of cigarette smoking and cigarette smokers do you think might become popular?

5. As seen in this chapter, what role does style play in criminal or deviant subcultures?

6. Do you believe that "copycat crimes" occur—that is, that individuals commit crimes in imitation of what they have seen on television or in the movies? If so, what should be done about this form of criminality?

7. What does it mean to talk about the "culture of policing?" What are some positive and negative aspects of "police culture" in the United States?

8. Is it possible today for criminals to share membership in a subculture, even if they have never met face-to-face? In what way?

9. What concerns might cultural criminologists have about the trend toward crime and criminals increasingly being packaged as "entertainment" and presented to the public in popular "reality television" shows? What, if anything, about this trend would concern you?

10. What do cultural criminologists mean by "cultural space?" What are some of the significant cultural spaces in the city or town where you live? What laws regulate people or activities in these spaces?

11. What does it mean to be "critical" when focusing on images of crime, criminals, and criminal justice? How can understanding mediated images of crime and criminals lead to better criminal justice policy?

CHAPTER 7

Peacemaking Criminology

John Fuller

Peacemaking criminology is a very recent theoretical orientation in which to consider the problems of crime and the criminal justice system. Its strengths include its positive view of humankind and its faith that individuals are capable of forgiveness and change. Its weaknesses are a result of its nascent development resulting in an incomplete and untested theoretical foundation. It will be argued in this chapter that the strengths outweigh the weaknesses and that as more scholars become familiar with peacemaking criminology, it will become a more important contributor to criminological theory. We begin with an overview of peacemaking criminology that links it to previous strains of critical theory. Next, there is a discussion of that practical or policy-oriented side of peacemaking criminology, restorative justice. Then we address several issues that critics have leveled at peacemaking criminology. Finally, in answering the critics, the promise and potential of peacemaking criminology are promoted.

Like all critical criminology theories, peacemaking criminology takes issue with conventional criminology. Specifically, the separation of individuals into criminals and citizens is critiqued. The relegation of law violators into the "enemy" upon whom all manners of violence and punishment can be visited is a major concern with peacemaking criminology. The war-like mentality that promotes this dualism renders conventional criminology ineffective in addressing the real issues that underlie the problem of crime. Conventional criminology, with its emphasis on the deficiencies of the individual, does not take into account the contribution that society's institutional arrangements make in the production of crime. Peacemaking criminology attempts to bridge the gap between individual responsibility and societal influence. It requires that the offender take responsibility for his/her actions and rehabilitation while challenging the state to provide a system of justice that is fair to all and does not simply reinforce the power arrangement in society.

The history of peacemaking criminology is short. Even though the ideas espoused are as old as humankind, the term peacemaking criminology first appeared in 1991 as in a book of readings edited by Harold Pepinsky and Richard Quinney titled *Criminology as Peacemaking*. This is a significant book because it gathered the thoughts of a wide range of scholars who are concerned with the human suffering caused by crime and the response of society to crime. It is especially important because it showed the linkages among three intellectual traditions that contribute to peacemaking criminology. These three traditions—religious and humanist, feminist, and critical—each contribute to the philosophical underpinning of peacemaking criminology and each emphasizes the relationship between individual and societal responsibility. By organizing the book according to these traditions, Pepinsky and Quinney showed how a wide range of individuals concerned with justice and injustice are connected.

Inspired by the work in the Pepinsky and Quinney book, Fuller (1998) wrote *Criminal Justice: A Peacemaking Perspective* in an attempt to aid in the development of peacemaking criminology and to introduce the concept to an undergraduate audience. In this work, Fuller contrasted the peacemaking perspective with the war on crime perspective that so dominates contemporary criminal justice policy today. In addition to reinforcing the intellectual traditions identified by Pepinsky and Quinney, Fuller showed how peacemaking criminology was part of a larger intellectual enterprise that spanned the range from interpersonal issues to global concerns, thus demonstrating the connectedness of criminal justice to larger areas of social justice. Perhaps the greatest contribution of this work is the development of the Peacemaking Pyramid Paradigm in which Fuller took a first step in envisioning how all the disparate parts of peacemaking might be arranged so that a coherent theory could be developed. Fuller's Peacemaking Pyramid Paradigm included six stages that need to be considered when fashioning solutions to the problems of the criminal justice system.

1. *Nonviolence*. Peacemaking criminology is first and foremost concerned with the issue of violence. The best example of how peacemaking criminology looks at violence is to consider capital punishment. Peacemaking criminology argues against the death penalty as a criminal justice policy. The premeditated violence of the state is viewed as just as wrong as the violence of the offender.

2. *Social justice*. Any solution to a criminal justice case needs to include the concept of social justice. Social justice considers a broader concept of justice than criminal justice issues of sexism; racism and inequality are also part of the concern of social justice. For instance, in considering capital punishment cases, a pattern of racial bias has long been apparent. The race of the offender and the race of the victim have been shown to influence the death sentence. Minorities have been more likely to receive death penalties than whites. While there are other reasons to argue against the

death penalty, this obvious racial proclivity is a violation of the notion of social justice. The minority offender may be guilty of a heinous crime, but the peacemaking perspective argues against the death penalty on social justice grounds when there are such extralegal factors affecting the sentence.

3. *Inclusion.* The idea behind inclusion is simple. It suggests that the criminal justice system needs to be more inclusive of the stakeholders in the community. In our highly formalized concept of criminal justice, the offender is pitted against the state. There are others who have an interest in the case and who can offer legitimate perspectives and alternatives. Families of the victim and the offender as well as individuals from the neighborhood or from community resources are all interested parties who have valuable insights. When the state takes such total control of a case it deprives the affected parties of the opportunity to develop their own creative solution. The Norwegian criminologist, Nils Christie (1977), likens this to the state taking away the property of the offender and victim. Often the solution imposed by the state satisfies no one. The concept of inclusion also entails giving the offender an opportunity to negotiate the outcome. Rather than having a sentence imposed on the offender, the offender agrees to the conditions and takes ownership for the offense and his/her treatment. The peacemaking perspective argues that such conditions of inclusion will form more satisfactory and lasting solutions than conventional sentencing.

4. *Correct means.* There is an old saying that the ends don't justify the means. This is especially true in the criminal justice system. A whole area of procedural law has been developed to ensure that criminal justice practitioners do not violate the legal and civil rights of the offender. Peacemaking criminology suggests that correct means entails ensuring that offenders and victims are not coerced into settlements of their cases. The due process guarantees of the law need to be preserved even while we search for more creative and effective solutions to cases. Additionally, policies and procedures employed by the criminal justice system must not sacrifice correct means for effectiveness. An example of this point is the extensive racial profiling used by many law enforcement agencies. While targeting minorities may seem justified to the police based on their expectations and experience, such incorrect means are inherently unfair and quickly become a self-fulfilling prophecy. When minorities are disproportionally targeted, they become disproportionally arrested and this is used as evidence in developing suspect profiles. It becomes a vicious circle where incorrect means contribute to the violations of social justice.

5. *Ascertainable criteria.* In order for victims, offenders, and community members to fully participate in the criminal justice system, they must understand what is going on. There are two types of language barriers that inhibit equal access to the law. The first is the

inability of many recent immigrants to understand English. While many jurisdictions provide adequate translators, many do not. Some would argue that courts and police should become proficient in the language of the community, and, while the peacemaking perspective is sympathetic to this suggestion, it raises wider issues than we can consider at this time. It is sufficient to say here that when individuals cannot understand English, they cannot fully participate in the court proceedings. The second issue concerning ascertainable criteria has to do with the specialized parlance used in the criminal justice system. The language of the law is a highly specialized professional argot that is completely understood only by the lawyers. The peacemaking perspective's concepts of ascertainable criteria and inclusion argue that efforts to insure that all parties fully understand the procedures are desirable. This would include education efforts aimed at non-English speaking individuals as well as clearly-written legal guidelines aimed at educating victims and offenders.

6. *Categorical imperative.* When considering the problems of crime and the criminal justice system, the peacemaking perspective aims at developing a consistent and predictable viewpoint. Using Kant's concept of the categorical imperative, the peacemaking perspective argues that responses to crime should reflect an underlying philosophy of nonviolence and social justice that are extended throughout the criminal justice system. Victims and offenders, criminal justice practitioners, as well as the public, should all be treated with the respect and dignity we all deserve. To that end, criminal justice decisions should employ Kant's axiom: "Act only according to that maxim whereby you can at the same time will that it should become a universal law." Thus, the peacemaking perspective is not a haphazard and inconsistent policy guide. It aims at providing true equality under the law that is tempered by a positive view of humankind.

By employing this peacemaking perspective in the criminal justice system, it is suggested that the problems of crime will be reduced. As opposed to the war on crime perspective, the peacemaking perspective has the potential to provide lasting solutions to the problems that lead individuals to commit violations of the law. The war on crime perspective with its emphasis on punishment and retribution ensure that offenders will strive only to commit their crimes in a more efficient manner so as not to get caught. The peacemaking perspective on the other hand, seeks to address the conditions of society that foster crime and to address the problems of the individual offender. Additionally, the peacemaking perspective seeks to understand and respond to the concerns of victims. To that end, we now turn to restorative justice to see how the peacemaking perspective is translated from a theoretical perspective to a practical public policy.

Restorative Justice

Restorative justice programs are designed to repair the harm done by crime. Because many criminal interactions are between individuals who will continue to have some type of relationship, restorative justice attempts to mend the relationship so the same issues do not result in further crime. Restorative justice processes sometimes present the occasion to solve underlying dysfunction in families and communities. Rather than simply punishing an offender, restorative justice looks to understand the context of the crime and bring together the various stakeholders to craft a mutually agreeable solution. This is done in a variety of ways depending upon the circumstances (Van Ness & Strong, 1997).

Victim-Offender Reconciliation Programs (VORPs)

Victim-Offender reconciliation programs are an informal way to resolve the issues of crime. In many jurisdictions, the victim and offender are given the opportunity to resolve the conflict with the aid of a trained third party mediator prior to processing into the formal criminal justice system. This informal process has several advantages over the traditional criminal justice system. First, it is less expensive. Often the mediators are volunteers, and the case can be decided without the use of expensive attorneys. Precious courtroom time is thus freed up for other cases. Second, VORPs allow the victim and offender to talk to each other directly, which can facilitate the resolution of the conflict. In the traditional courtroom situation, the judge and attorneys buffer victims and offenders. They do not get the opportunity to share their views on the case and to agree upon solutions. Third, the offender is not put in such a defensive position that he/she feels like a victim. The offender is given the opportunity to take ownership for his/her actions and to see the pain, harm, and inconvenience experienced by the victim. In VORPs, the offender can appreciate, sometimes for the very first time, just how deleterious the crime has been. Finally, there is often the occasion for forgiveness between the offender and the victim. This process enables them to get on with their lives and build upon the conflict experience. As mentioned previously, sometimes this process solves more than just the particular crime. Sometimes it rectifies the underlying problems. With the guidance of the third-party mediators, victims and offenders are able to develop creative and long-lasting resolutions to their difficulties.

Family Group Conferencing

Sometimes it takes more than just the victim and offender to resolve the conflict behind a crime and to promote the healing of affected parties. Family group conferencing expands the number of interested parties in the negotiation to include members of the families of both the victim and offender as well as, in some cases, the attorney for the offender or the police. The idea is for everyone to tell not only their story about the crime but also to relate how the crime impacted on their lives. This input from all involved helps put the crime in the context of the actual harm done to the individuals and the greater community. The result of this greater involvement is predicated on the expanded input in crafting the solution. As the plan is formulated, it is easier to see where the implementation problems will come from because most of the interested parties are in the room. Likewise, because of the greater involvement, there are more people emotionally invested in the plan. It is this participation by everyone involved that makes family group conferencing a peacemaking perspective practice. It embodies the concepts of inclusion, ascertainable criteria, and nonviolence as it attempts to craft a resolution that involves social justice for the victim and offender as well as their families and the broader community. Family group conferencing is used in the juvenile justice system.

Victim-Offender Panels

It is not always possible or desirable to bring the victim and offender into contact. Sometimes the pain of the victim is too great to be assuaged by a victim-offender reconciliation meeting or a family group conference. There are still ways under the restorative justice umbrella to address some types of offenses. Victim-offender panels bring together offenders with victims of other crimes. For instance, those convicted of drunk driving may be required to meet with family members of drunk driving victims. While there is not a direct link between the victims and the offender (these individuals are not involved in the same case), it is possible for the offenders to see what impact their driving under the influence could have on others. Someone arrested for drunk driving may see how serious this behavior could become when confronted with families who have lost a loved one in an accident. The victim-offender panel helps put a human face on the crime. The difference between victim-offender panels and the other types of restorative justice programs we have discussed is that victim-offender panels are not linked to a specific crime and are not an alternative form of resolution. They are preventive in nature and may be ordered as part of a sentence, but they do not attempt to heal the relationship between offender and victim. It is easy to see how this might be the program of choice when the victim is traumatized by the offense such as in cases of rape. It is preferable to have rape victims who have been able to adjust to the pain confront the offender, rather than the actual victim.

Peacemaking and Public Policy

Peacemaking criminology and restorative justice practices offer a coherent and positive blueprint for addressing crime. They present a logical and life-affirming guide to reclaiming the lives lost to the criminal lifestyle and to addressing the suffering of victims and society. One strength of peacemaking criminology is that it is not simply a reactive policy. Peacemaking criminology speaks to the controversial crime policy issues of contemporary times.

Capital Punishment

Those who espouse the peacemaking perspective are opposed to capital punishment. While there may be problems with the way the death penalty demonstrates both race and social class bias, the opposition of peacemaking criminologists is much deeper (Bohm, 1999). The death penalty is inherently violent and violates the first stage of the peacemaking pyramid paradigm, nonviolence. Given the religious and humanist traditions of peacemaking criminology, giving the state the authority to kill offenders is unacceptable. While there may be popular support for capital punishment, there also are a substantial number of people who question it. One of the major concerns is the risk of executing an innocent person. Illinois suspended its executions because it found too many cases of inmates on death row who were proved innocent of their crimes. While peacemaking criminologists applaud such policies, they would argue there are more fundamental reasons to exclude capital punishment.

Gun Control

The level of gun violence in the United States is extremely high when compared to other western industrialized nations. Americans have a history and a mythology that surrounds gun ownership that makes it difficult to have reasonable conversations about how to stem gun violence. The National Rifle Association and other gun lobbying groups are successful in keeping guns available not only for their members, but also for just about anyone who wants a gun on short notice. Gun proponents contend that weapons are needed by citizens to protect their lives and property from criminals. Peacemaking criminologists view the national obsession with guns as part of the failed war on crime philosophy. More guns do not mean less crime. Gun violence violates the first stage of the peacemaking perspective, nonviolence. The peacemaking perspective would look to the causes of violent crime such as unemployment, racism, alienation and despair, to attempt to fashion solutions to gun violence. The unrestricted availability of guns ensures more rather than less violence. Those who oppose any sort of gun control point to the Second Amendment of the Constitution as a holy writ to justify guns. More reasonable individuals view the second amendment as pertaining to a particular time in history that required such citizen ownership of weapons. These circumstances that underlie the second amendment have not been present in the United States since before the Civil War (Spitzer, 1995:38). Because guns are such an emotional and political issue, it is difficult to find common ground. However, there already exists much that reasonable people could agree upon. There are some forms of weapons restrictions already in place that are supported by most citizens. While the Second Amendment speaks to "the right to bear arms," many types of weapons are prohibited. If we were to interpret the Second Amendment to mean that the right would not be "impinged" then ordinary citizens would be allowed to own missiles, rockets, nuclear bombs, and any other type of destructive weapon. Clearly we restrict the use of weapons of deadly force, and the real question has become exactly where do we draw the line? With the level of gun violence we now experience, the peacemaking perspective would restrict guns more.

Capital punishment and gun control are just two examples of how the peacemaking perspective has policy implications and real-world applicability. By using the peacemaking pyramid paradigm, it is possible to see how, as a theoretical perspective, peacemaking criminology offers an alternative to the get-tough-on-crime policies that dominate the speeches of our politicians and media. However, if peacemaking criminology is to receive a wide following, it will have to address the questions and concerns of its critics.

The Case Against Peacemaking Criminology

Peacemaking criminology is a very new theoretical development, so it needs to be examined and evaluated just as any other theory that attempts to explain the problems of crime and the criminal justice system. If we date the inception of peacemaking criminology to 1991 with the publication of Pepinsky and Quinney's *Criminology as Peacemaking*, we can understand why there has not been much published that addresses this new development. Perhaps the most damaging blow a new theory can receive is to be ignored. Peacemaking has its share of critics, but few have looked at it systematically and attempted to rigorously critique its ideas. As the peacemaking perspective matures, we can expect to see more scholars subjecting peacemaking to greater scrutiny. While many theory texts now acknowledge peacemaking they do not expose it to the analysis they do other theories. There is a reason for this. Peacemaking has not been developed into a testable theory, so there are no scientific studies that can be used to talk about its efficacy.

Perhaps the best discussion of the limitations of peacemaking criminology is found in Akers' (2000) widely adopted theory text, *Criminological Theories: Introduction, Evaluation, and Application*. In this book,

Akers reviews the major theories in criminology in terms of how well they have stood up to empirical evaluations and how well they inform crime policy. It should be noted that Akers is one of the primary architects of social learning theory, and, not surprisingly, he finds it to be the most powerful or useful in explaining crime (Akers, 2000:97). Akers is no friend of critical theories and peacemaking criminology does not escape his scrutiny. His major criticisms can be summarized as:

1. Peacemaking criminology does not offer a theory of crime or the criminal justice system that can be evaluated empirically.

2. It is contradictory to claim Marxist/critical theory as one of the main foundations for peacemaking because Marxist theory is based on class conflict and Marx's own endorsement of violent revolution.

3. Feminism also is not consistent with peacemaking. The nurturing role of women is, according to feminism, simply part of the patriarchal system of the oppression of women.

4. Almost all of the policies of peacemaking have long been mainstays of the policy recommendations of traditional criminology, so peacemaking is not really anything new or different.

5. Peacemaking does not provide a plan for getting past criminal justice policies to suggest how large-scale structural changes can be made to make society less violent.

There are problems with Aker's understanding of peacemaking criminology. First, it is based only on the Pepinsky and Quinney reader of 1991. Peacemaking as perspective has advanced since then, and, perhaps in future editions of his book, Aker's will incorporate some of the more recent reasoning. The second and more serious problem with Aker's criticisms is that he selects only small points to critique a larger issue. His selected use of evidence acts to obscure rather than illuminate the issue.

Akers is right that peacemaking does not offer a theory that can be tested empirically. It has not developed to the point that it has testable hypotheses. Presumably, as more scholars turn to peacemaking, this important theoretical development will take place. However, it also should be noted that critical theories do not embrace the idea that in order to be true, something has to be reduced to numbers and be empirically tested. Science is a powerful tool, but it too has limitations. Critical theories recognize there are alternatives to the positivism of traditional criminology.

Critical theory and Marxism do provide some of the intellectual foundation for peacemaking criminology. However, peacemaking is not Marxism. It does not adopt in total the principles that underlie Marxism. The ends of equality and community that peacemaking shares with Marxism do not extend to the means of revolutionary violence. The concept of nonviolence that is fundamental to peacemaking is a major distinction between peacemaking and Marxism. Just because peacemaking draws on the intellectual tradition of Marxism, does not mean it shares all concerns.

Akers likewise misses the relationship between peacemaking and feminism. He contends that because feminists recognize that men and women have different ways of thinking about relationships, that this simply represents patriarchy, and, as women become more powerful and enlightened, they will adopt the power processes of men. The goal of feminism is not to simply replace male power with female power but to transform the way power is acquired and used to benefit both women and men. There is nothing wrong with the nurturing role. It is only wrong if it is forced upon women exclusively. Peacemaking envisions a world where both men and women nurture their children and each other. Feminism has made a major contribution by showing how rigid gender roles structure society. Peacemaking criminology draws on this intellectual tradition to advance the humane treatment of offenders and victims in the criminal justice system.

Next, Akers is correct that the policies that flow from the peacemaking perspective, such as non-punitive treatment of offenders, mediation, restitution, offender reintegration, rehabilitation, and so on, have been advocated by traditional criminology. Unfortunately, with the war on crime mentality that dominates the criminal justice system today, these policies have fallen into disuse. Additionally, the peacemaking perspective provides a coherent web to weave together all of these progressive policies.

Finally, Akers reiterates a criticism that peacemaking criminology does not go beyond already-used policies to articulate the large-scale structural changes in society that would result in nonviolent and peaceful crime control. The answer to this concern is both simple and complex. To the extent that citizens practice peacemaking in their everyday lives, there will be less crime to control. Certainly, there will be those who choose to harm others, but this perspective provides a way of dealing with offenders that does not accelerate their path into the criminal lifestyle. Treating offenders as the enemy, apart from civilized society as the war on crime mentality does, contributes to, rather than alleviates, the conditions that cause crime.

Conclusion

As one of the emerging critical criminological theories, peacemaking shows a great deal of promise for increasing our understanding of crime and the problems of the criminal justice system. It draws from several intellectual traditions that are grounded in the concern for alleviating peoples' suffering. The strength of peacemaking criminology is as an antidote to the war on crime perspective that dominates the criminal justice system. Peacemaking criminology has long way to go before it can reach the status and acceptance of the more established and traditional criminology theories. At present, it represents more of a philosophy or perspective than it does a well-developed theory. As more work is done on theory-building and application, particularly in the area of restorative justice, we can expect peacemaking criminology to gain a wider following among academics and to guide the development of more programs aimed at improving the quality of justice.

Discussion Questions

1. In what ways is peacemaking criminology a critical perspective on crime and society's response to crime? How does it differ from other critical theories?

2. Hal Pepinsky and Richard Quinney suggest that peacemaking criminology is derived from three intellectual traditions: religious and humanist, feminist, and critical. Discuss how each of these traditions informs peacemaking criminology.

3. Discuss the six stages of Fuller's Peacemaking Pyramid paradigm. Which of these stages is most crucial to developing this perspective?

4. What is restorative justice? How is it related to peacemaking criminology?

5. Are Victim-Offender Reconciliation Programs (VORPs) useful tools for bringing about long-term solutions to the problems of interpersonal crime?

6. What is family group conferencing? Which stage of Fuller's Peacemaking Pyramid Paradigm does it reflect?

7. Victim-Offender Panels do not match up the victim with her/his specific offender. Why? What good can come from these panels?

8. How would a peacemaking criminologist address the issue of gun control? Do more guns mean less crime?

9. What would be a peacemaking criminologist's position on capital punishment?

10. Ron Akers contends that peacemaking criminology has several major limitations. Address Akers' criticisms and defend peacemaking criminology.

CHAPTER 8

Restorative Justice:
A Paradigm of Possibility

Rick Sarre

The criminal justice systems of modern common law countries are premised upon the fundamental notion that the state should take whatever official action is required against criminal offenders. While it is theoretically possible for a citizen to launch a private criminal action in the common law tradition, it is extremely rare. This has not always been the case. Prior to the eleventh century, victims, or their kin, were principally responsible for the legal pursuit of offenders in response to criminal violations of the victims' families or their property. The desire for compensation was probably at least as common as the urge to retaliate. Indeed, in Roman law—upon which much Anglo common law is based—if a guilty person accepted his or her guilt and made restitution, then the case was settled between the parties and no further punitive action was required. These principles, however, did not survive the Norman Conquest 1,000 years ago. Crime moved away from being a private or community affair and became an offense against the state, and victims were referred away from the criminal courts for their grievances to be heard elsewhere, if at all.

The upshot of this for latter day societies is that victims, their families, their supporters and communities in general have lost any crucial role that they may once have enjoyed in the penal process. Informal communities, such as religious, ethnic, social or geographical communities, have lost whatever power they may formerly have had to influence proceedings. As a corollary, and for all intents and purposes, modern criminal justice systems have lost what could, with the value of hindsight, have been described as their *restorative* edge. That is, they have sought to drive a wedge between offenders and their communities, rather than to allow reconciliation and restoration of relationships to occur.

It is the purpose of this chapter to reflect upon the possibilities presented by a renaissance of thought in respect of restorative principles. The reasons for the resurrection of these themes are many and varied, but one can locate them most readily within Mennonite activism (eg. Lederach, 1999) and victim groups (Sarre, 2000a). Be that as it may, it is useful to begin by reviewing restorative themes and then contrasting them with the more traditional "retributive" themes.

Restorative Principles

Restorative principles are expressed in different ways, but some clear themes emerge. In models of restorative justice there is:

1.   shared responsibility for resolving crime and for one another;

2.   the use of informal community mechanisms in addition to the involvement of criminal justice professionals;

3.   the inclusion of victims as parties in their own right;

4.   an understanding of crime as injury, not just lawbreaking;

5.   an understanding that a state monopoly over the response to crime is inappropriate (Justice Fellowship, 1989; Sarre, 1997a).

A restorative system of criminal justice endeavors to listen to, and appease, aggrieved parties to a conflict and to restore, as far as possible, right relationships between antagonists. In restorative models, crime is defined as a violation of one person by another, the focus is upon problem-solving, dialogue and restitution (where possible), mutuality, the repair of social injury and the possibilities of repentance and forgiveness. The offence is understood in a range of dimensions including its moral, social, and political implications (Ministry of Justice New Zealand, 1995; United Nations Alliance, 1995).

The Distinction Between Retributive and Restorative Models of Justice

Retributive justice, in contrast, presents the conflict as one between the offender and the state in an adversarial environment and seeks to ensure that offenders atone for their sins through receiving their "just deserts." Crime is thus defined as a violation of the state, the focus is on blame and punishment, and the offense is defined in purely legal terms, devoid of moral, social and political dimensions. Under retributive justice, a form of "atonement" must occur in the life of the offender by appropriate punishment, regardless of any deterrent effect or any rehabilitative counter-effect. Lest it be said that retribution is intrinsically harsh, however, it must be remembered that retribution provides a brake on the excesses of punishment; that is, it seeks to have punishment meted out only in direct proportion to the misdeed. The "eye for an eye" of the Judaic law in fact was a limiting feature in retribution. One could only take an eye for an eye, not two eyes or a life, for example (Bianchi, 1994).

It is not the case, of course, that our common law systems of criminal justice operate only upon retributive principles. There are clearly restorative notions in the concepts of rehabilitation, parole and probation, for example. But there is little doubt that the emphasis is on retributive, rather than restorative goals. Restorative principles play little part in the modern adversary systems of criminal justice. This has led and continues to lead to some problems. For crime is first and foremost a conflict between people. Yet under traditional models, crime is treated and deemed to be something that has happened only between the state and an offender. Such models ignore the fact that crime often occurs between people who may be in continuous contact, and may be in intimate relationships with each other. It often fails to take into account that many offenders are victims as well.

For example, cases of assault, theft, or damage between parties who are familiar with each other or who have an ongoing relationship with each other, are dealt with on the basis, largely, that only one party is legally culpable. That is rarely the case. The party singled out for attention may have been responding as part of an ongoing acrimonious relationship with the other party. While provocation associated with criminal acts may be a mitigating feature in sentencing, it cannot and does not exculpate the assailant.

Moreover, cultural and gender issues are, for the most part, officially irrelevant to traditional criminal proceedings although they may, in fact, be crucial both to the etiology of the incident and to the ultimate outcome. For example, a racist or sexist taunt may lead to an assault. Even though, legally speaking, the criminal conviction is recorded and the case is "concluded," the racism or sexism may persist. In fact, the taunts may continue given the trouble that the victim placed the offender in. Both parties to the conflict are no better off. Thus, at the end of the day, many parties tend to view the criminal justice system experience as one that leaves them embittered, burdened with costs and often determined to seek further action. This is a common experience amongst many victims, offenders, and their families alike (e.g., Rose, 1996:51; Bottoms, 1994).

If policymakers were to attempt to mediate hurt and restore parties to a right relationship with each other, then the retributive adversarial system would be the last choice they would make. More enduring solutions and satisfactory outcomes are likely to occur, say the renaissance theorists, in a restorative, non-adversarial environment. Not only that, adversarial encounters are criticized as contributing to costs, delays, over-servicing and poor accountability (ALRC, 1997:8).

Early Development of the Notion of Restorative Justice

The moves to engender a "restorative" milieu have thus been explored enthusiastically in the past 20 years, but most recently by American social scientists and policy-advisers (e.g., Zehr, 1985; Van Ness, 1990; Van Ness & Strong, 1997; Umbreit, 1994; Bazemore & Umbreit, 1994). Australia is able to boast one of the harbingers, the late John Freeman (1988) as well as some contemporary key thinkers in the field (e.g., Braithwaite, 1999; Moore, 1996; Strang, 2000).

The *concept* of restorative justice, however, finds its roots earlier in the twentieth century, and indeed earlier in ancient religious faiths if one were to delve into matters theological (Sarre, 1999a). In 1917, the American social psychologist George Herbert Mead highlighted the inadequacy of the punitive system of justice.

> The concentration of public sentiment upon the criminal which mobilizes the institution of justice, paralyses the undertaking to conceive our common goods in terms of their uses . . . [and] we see society almost helpless in the grip of the hostile attitude it has taken toward those who break its laws and contravene its institutions. Hostility toward the lawbreaker inevitably brings with it the attitudes of retribution, repression, and exclusion. These provide no principles for the eradication of crime, for returning the delinquent to normal social relations, nor for stating the transgressed rights and institutions in terms of their positive social functions (Mead, 1917:226-227).

In the 1970s, the Danish criminologist Nils Christie again explored the notion of putting "justice" in context, and returning criminal conflicts to their "rightful" owners, an evolution of people's sense of power over the legal process:

> [The current system is] a loss of opportunities for a continuous discussion of what represents the law of the land . . . Lawyers are . . . trained into agreement on what is relevant in a case. But that means a trained *incapacity* in letting the parties decide what they think is relevant (emphasis in the original) (Christie, 1977:8).

From this time on, the recognition that relationships are crucial to the criminal justice process began to gain some currency. In 1977, psychologist Albert Eglash coined the term "restorative justice," writing:

> The reparative effort does not stop at restoring a situation to its pre-offence condition, but goes beyond: Beyond what our own conscience requires of us, beyond what a court orders us to do,

beyond what family or friends expect of us, beyond what a victim demands of us, beyond any source of external or internal coercion, beyond any coercion into a creative act, where we seek to leave a situation better than it ever was (Eglash, 1977:95).

Restorative justice soon emerged as a legitimate justice model,

> . . . designed to provide the context for ensuring that social rather than legal goals are met. The expected end result is that communities and individuals are empowered in dealing with their problems and in influencing the direction of the criminal justice process, so formal punishment and incarceration become less relied upon sanctions (La Prairie, 1995:78).

The Reluctance to Embrace the Concept

There has been some resistance to the notion of restorative justice. There are probably seven main reasons one can identify.

1. *Rehabilitation by another name*
There are ongoing doubts about the success of the 1960s and 1970s "rehabilitation" models of punishment and correction, especially since Martinson's (1974) damning critique that has reified and persisted despite all attempts to clarify it (Sarre, 2000b). It is thought that perhaps restorative justice is just another name for rehabilitation, with its perceptions of failure, and its paternalistic overtones.

2. *Excuses*
Those on the political "left" are of the opinion that restorative models excuse too much men's violence against women and children. Those on the political "right" believe that proponents of restorative models are too keen to excuse offenders' behaviors, and are thus "soft" on crime.

3. *Private outcomes*
There are grave concerns that the privatization implicit in some restorative models, for example, the lack of publicity of "family conference" outcomes, are anathema to the concept of an open system of justice. There is a perceived danger that safeguards need to be in place to protect offenders and victims alike from the perils of so-called "informal" justice and the way in which it can co-opt unwilling participants to engage in dialogues they simply do not wish to have (Laster & Erez, 2000; Strang, 2000:31).

4. *Retributive public attitudes*

There is little doubt that the public in general sees the purpose of the criminal justice system first and foremost as an agent of retribution and deterrence, and anything that looks likely to undermine those concepts, and undermine a strong statement against criminal conduct, is likely to be viewed with suspicion.

5. *The traditional legal expectations*

The adversarial encounter is entrenched in the current style of legal education and thus expected by legal practitioners and clients alike. One is taught to think that disputes are best solved in an adversarial contest. There is still a strong assumption in the public domain that legal reasoning is distinct from ethical or political discourse in general, as a method for reaching "correct" results (ALRC, 1997:51).

6. *Certainty and consistency have deep appeal*

There is great power in the symbolic function of the law as being certain and consistent. Restorative models are, *ipso facto*, variable, based upon the players and stakeholders themselves reaching outcomes. Many people, however, prefer to live under a concept of legal (if not moral or philosophical) certainty even when it is said or suspected that such certainty may be ill-conceived (Sarre, 1994:29; 1999b).

7. *Restoration to a status quo may be inadequate or harmful*

There is an argument, put persuasively by Harry Blagg, that restorative models are not always readily assimilable into existing bureaucratic and administrative frameworks. For example, there may be an unwillingness on the part of indigenous peoples to be involved in a restorative justice practice that seeks to have an offender "restored" to an unsatisfactory status quo (Blagg, 1998:6). For this reason some theorists prefer the term "relational" justice (e.g., Burnside & Baker, 1994; Townsend, 1994). or "transformative" justice (e.g., Moore, 1996). These terms allow for relationships to become the focus of any transformations that need to occur.

Restorative Justice in Practice

Notwithstanding the above caveats, there is good reason to suspect that restorative models have great possibilities to enhance and improve the options available to criminal justice administrators. For a start, restorative options are usually potentially cheaper (cf Editorial, 1996:3). A trial costs the state a great deal more money than outcomes derived through mediation and private restitution, for example. Moreover, there is some evidence in the examples following that more lasting outcomes (and hence cheaper outcomes) are more likely where restorative principles are in place. Policymakers thus are inclined in a number of fields of justice practice to explore opportunities for the implementation of restorative goals.

The following examples are presented not as models of distinctly restorative practice, but as restorative-style alternatives to traditional models.

Family Conferencing

The well-researched "family group conference" juvenile justice model provides an ideal example of a restorative justice forum separate and apart from the formal system. It has shown encouraging evidence of success (e.g., Strang, 2000:24). Under this model, offender(s), their extended families and advocates (if appropriate), victim(s) and their supporters, and police are brought together with an independent facilitator. Offenders are required to confront their wrongdoing (for the most part the less serious offences) while being empowered to develop their own negotiated settlement. The aim of the process is to bring about reconciliation, not to exact punishment. Communities are thereby being asked to seek their own solutions to problems rather than relying upon the state to take center stage (Braithwaite & Mugford, 1994). In this respect, consistency is not as important as "democratic creativity" (Braithwaite, 1994:203). It has been found in evaluative studies that offenders are more likely to respond to their justice experience positively when they perceive it to be fair, and the evidence is clear that conferencing programs do give rise to favorable perceptions (Strang, 2000:27). The experiment of family group conferencing has been warmly embraced in Australia, and the subject of much research in its implementation (e.g., Alder & Wundersitz, 1994; Bargen, 1995; Fisher et al., 1992; La Prairie, 1996; Moore, 1993; Polk, 1994; Sarre, 1999c; Warner, 1994; Wundersitz, 1996).

Family Violence Court

The family violence court was piloted in 1997 in South Australia as an interventionist court designed to reduce violence in the home. Essentially, magistrates (all male, by design) in these courts use their powers under the *Bail Act (SA)* to ensure that recipients of bail orders or restraint orders are not inflamed into further acts of violence thereby. Police refer to the court all family matters that appear to have a family violence component. At the first hearing, guilt and innocence are irrelevant. Men who are a danger to their families are referred to an appropriate agency to deal with violence issues, such as anger management programs and substance abuse treatment. Final orders are made when the matter is returned to court, at which time the magistrate is better able to consider the alleged offender's future prospects in light of the immediate history of the matter. The aim is to minimize the possibilities of repeat victimization.

Mental Health Court

A joint initiative of the South Australian Department of Human Services and the Department of Justice, this court, which commenced operation in 2000, takes referrals from police, legal counsel, and magistrates. It is designed to, amongst other things, prevent persons who may border on being unfit to plead from being drawn inextricably into the legal system. In that sense, it is capable of being deemed "restorative." Matters are selected on the following criteria: the cases must be able to be finalized in the summary courts, the accused must admit the objective elements of the offense, and he or she must not be suffering from severe mental incapacitation nor be facing a serious charge. In the final analysis, a person is only given an order of the court if the magistrate is satisfied that the program set out for the accused can achieve something, and that he or she can cope with whatever regime is prescribed. Once the accused is admitted to a program, the matter is adjourned until called on again, if at all.

Drug Assessment and Aid Panels

The South Australian Drug Assessment and Aid Panel, established in 1985 under the auspices of the *Controlled Substances Act (SA) 1984*, is a pre-court diversionary program designed to divert people caught with possession of illicit drugs for personal use away from the courts and to the Panel, placing pre-eminence upon the medical, rather than criminal, nature of the problem. There has been, in this context, specific attention given to Aboriginal offenders (ADCA, 1996a:8). Unless offenders wish to defend the matter in court, fail to adhere to the requirements of the Panel or are found unsuitable by the Panel, their matters are not referred to the courts and no conviction is recorded (ADCA, 1996b:14). The continued operation of the Panel bears testimony to its practitioners' perceptions of its ability to reduce criminality through an offender-focused, restorative treatment regime.

Problem-Solving Policing

Western governments have, in the last two decades, adopted a notion of public policing which incorporates so-called "problem-solving" policing. This model encourages greater flexibility in policing, allowing greater levels of community involvement and input and thus has the potential to encourage non-adversarial policing to prevail. There is some reason to suspect that the transfer of power from authorities to communities has not happened in the manner often maintained in the rhetoric (Sarre, 1996:36). But academics who have reviewed the policing needs in the new South Africa (e.g., Brogden & Shearing, 1993) have highlighted the greater possibilities currently alive in that country for a police vision that places less emphasis upon police *forces* and greater emphasis upon the self-policing abilities of communities themselves.

Aboriginal Court Day (the "Nunga" court)

The $40 million Royal Commission into Aboriginal Deaths in Custody (Royal Commission, 1991) was a milestone down the continuing road of justice reform in Australia. The key conclusion to come out of this report was that too many Indigenous Australians were being drawn into the formal justice setting. Its key recommendation, therefore, was to encourage jurisdictions to consider ways to reduce Aboriginal rates of imprisonment (Cunneen & McDonald, 1997). The notion of a Nunga court day, while not mooted in the 1991 report specifically, is an example of a contemporary idea that would have received acclaim from the Commissioners as involving a significant degree of Indigenous input in its planning and execution (South Australia, 1999a). The court in South Australia, which commenced in 1999, sits one day per fortnight, for sentencing, not trials. The magistrate is guided by input from a range of sources, and sits not above the court but at the bar table, with an Aboriginal elder. Each of the matters is dealt with on a case by case basis, with the outcome firmly determined by what the magistrate considers is in the best interests of the offender, in order to ensure his or her rehabilitation in so far as it is not inconsistent with the interests of the community.

Likewise, a memorandum of understanding was signed in September 1999 between the South Australian State government and the elders of the Anangu Pitjantjatjara Lands. It is designed to enable the Umuwa community to self-supervise offenders on community service orders, parole, and probation. It is another example of the creation of a less formal justice setting designed to encourage attendance at court and to reduce re-offending (South Australia, 1999b).

The Recognition of Customary Law in Sentencing

In the Aboriginal Community Justice "scoping" document (South Australia, 1999b) is to be found a range of projects that are designed to build partnerships with the community, "that foster understanding, involvement and ownership in criminal justice system processes and programs" (South Australia, 1999b:i). The report encourages the use of tribal and customary law to solve justice issues within Indigenous communities. There is a good case to be made for the greater recognition of Indigenous law in sentencing:

> Recognition must be given . . . to the existence (and survival) of customary law. As Indigenous cultures are organic (rather than static), customary law may exist (albeit in an evolved/evolving format) in contemporary communities, as well as in their more traditionally orientated counterparts. As Australian society examines socially just ways of dealing with its Indigenous peoples, and as Aboriginal and Torres Strait Islander peoples continue to demand the right of more culturally appropriate responses, the importance of customary law cannot be underestimated (Social Justice Commissioner, 1995, ¶ 31). (See also ALRC, 1986; Royal Commission, 1991, ¶104; Sarre, 1997b).

What is crucial here is an understanding that for restorative justice to have any resonance in the administration of justice for indigenous peoples, it must be contextualized by any political and legal forces at play (Cunneen, 1998).

Offender and Victim Reconciliation

While this notion has attracted a good deal of attention in North America (e.g., Marshall & Merry, 1990) and Europe (e.g., Hartmann, 1996), it is still very much in a nascent form in Australia (cf. MacRae, 1994, Fisher, 1993). The concept is designed to put in place a mediation process to bring about "right" relationships, in contradistinction to the imposition of pain as a deterrent. It endeavors to repair social injury and encourage mutuality. Offenders are encouraged to understand the impact of the crime and to take responsibility for it. The work of Zehr (1985; 1990), outlining the Victim Offender Reconciliation Program (VORP) in the USA and Canada has been emulated in Australia to some degree. The Victorian Law Reform Committee (Victoria, 1993:137) supports both pre-court and post-conviction models for both adult and young offenders and has had a pilot program since October 1993. The Western Australian Department of Corrective Services (Western Australia, 1992) has explored a post-conviction model and has a pilot pre-sentence victim-offender (adult only) conciliation program operating. Queensland has a similar pilot project applying to both adults and juveniles (Murray, 1991).

Evaluating the Evidence

How does one test the success of a concept as broad as restorative justice, using examples of practices as varied as those above? The "success" of a justice system based upon restorative notions, say its adherents, is not necessarily measured by the final outcome or legal result, but rather by the degree to which people feel they have an impact, that they have been treated fairly, that they have understood each other, that they have better mechanisms for making decisions and handling their differences, and that their key issues have been addressed. In particular [is there] an enhanced level of participation in decision-making that affects people's lives. If successful, the participants feel that they are a valued part of their community (Lederach & Kraybill, 1995:368).

The dilemma for those hoping to find concrete evidence of the "successes" of restorative options, however, is that there is a lack of definition and a lack of data, for example, on the manner in which communities value participation and the way that victims may feel that they are included. Evaluations of these sorts of criteria in the manifestations of some of the ideas presented above are only now becoming available, and their conclusions remain guarded and tentative (e.g., Braithwaite, 1999). As theoretical developments occur, and as the literature grows, there is, however, good reason to hope that a better picture of the practical realities of restorative justice may soon begin to emerge and that its strengths and weaknesses may eventually become more apparent.

Summary

The current themes of criminal justice that place great store on retribution and adversarial encounters have not provided an environment that is conducive to the possibilities of better relationships between offenders, victims, and their communities. The possibilities will exist more often, claim the proponents of restorative options, if policymakers can enjoin communities, prosecutors, judges and governments to embrace more life-affirming themes and choose restorative means, where they are available, rather than retributive ends. Of course, we need to find out a lot more about the performance of each restorative model in order to determine whether it can "support the hopes of its proponents or . . . succumb to the criticisms of its detractors" (Strang, 2000:31).

To the extent that, at the very least, thinking about restorative options can draw us away from an assumption that the only workable and effective systems of criminal justice are based upon retributive and adversarial notions, restorative justice is worth further exploration. Evaluations of its practical manifestations and applications should continue apace.

Discussion Questions

1. Distinguish between restorative and retributive justice. Are these terms mutually exclusive?

2. In the context of restorative justice, examine the strengths and weaknesses of family group conferences.

3. Could/should conferences be extended to the adult justice system?

4. Are the traditional institutions of law so steeped in their own self-importance that they impede restorative justice?

5. Can restorative practices achieve restoration, or are there limits?

6. What may be the difficulties associated with a criminal justice system embracing restorative justice entirely to the exclusion of retributive themes?

7. If the difficulties seen in the previous question appear insurmountable, is there some preferred middle ground for policymakers?

8. "Although the law is created and enforced to ensure that justice is done, very often the opposite occurs. For example, just ask any victim, or member of any marginalized group." Comment on the ability of restorative themes to overcome this anomaly.

9. Is the term "restorative justice" to be preferred to, say, "relational justice"?

10. Find out what you can about the differences between restorative justice and "transformative justice."

CHAPTER 9

Crimes of the State

David Kauzlarich & David O. Friedrichs

Surely when most people think of crime, and criminals, they most readily think of murder, rape, burglary, assault, and the like, and those who commit these crimes. We have all been socialized—at home, at school, through the media and so on—to think of crime and criminals principally in such conventional terms. In the more recent era, the concept of white-collar crime, and corporate executives, businessmen, professionals or other respectable members of society who commit financially driven illegalities in the context of their organization or occupation, has become somewhat more familiar as well. But what about states, and state officials or political figures? What about state crime, state-organized crime, and the state officials who authorize or carry out harmful or illegal actions on behalf of the state? This chapter provides an overview of the phenomenon of state crime, its significance, and its connection to critical criminology. We also examine controversies surrounding the concept of state crime and explore why so little attention has been given to the problem.

What Is State Crime?

Critical criminologists have conceptualized and researched a number of events, processes, policies, actions, and inactions as state crime. One formal definition of state crime reads:

> State crime is an illegal or socially injurious act, process, or policy of omission or commission by an individual or group of individuals in an institution of legitimate governance which is executed for the consummation of the operative goals of that institution of governance (Kauzlarich, 1995:39).

There are two critical parts to the definition. First, the term state crime is best applied to harmful acts carried out by state officials *on behalf of the state,* not for the benefit of the individual state official. Even though it is obviously true that any state crimes must be carried out by people—state officials or their underlings—if the crimes are carried out to advance state interests, or in the name of the state, are only possible through use of the resources of the state, and reflect norms and values that have developed within the state (or some branch of the state), then we have state crime. Society is more than the sum total of its parts. This is also true of state organizations; they have cultures and structures which shape decisionmaking. It is therefore instructive to view state crime within its larger social contexts. To speak of state crime, then, is certainly not to deny or downplay the personal responsibility of individual state officials; rather, it acknowledges that such crime cannot be fully understood solely in terms of the actions of humans.

The second critical part of the definition is that there is no requirement that a "law" be broken in order to identify a state crime. One of the hallmarks of critical criminology is its rejection of a purely legalistic definition of crime. Indeed, most critical criminologists subscribe to the view that the violation of domestic criminal law is but *one way* to define crime. Other ways to define state crime include the violation of human rights, principles of self-determination, international law, and regulatory and administrative laws. States can also be said to be engaged in crime if they refuse to alleviate avoidable human suffering, pain, and exclusion. As we shall discuss later, this dimension of the definition of state crime is especially controversial.

Several types of state crime can be identified. A *criminal state* is one whose central purpose is a criminal enterprise, such as a state policy of genocidal action. In the twentieth century it was arguably most widely applied to Nazi Germany (as we discuss later), although many other states have been characterized as criminal states as well (e.g., Hussein's Iraq and Milosevic's Serbia). There is also the *repressive state*, which engages in a fundamental denial of basic human rights (e.g., totalitarian dictatorships in many parts of the world, and the apartheid South Africa as a classic, historical case); the *corrupt state*, where the state is used as an instrument to enrich its leadership (e.g., the Phillipines under Marcos, or Indonesia under Suharto); and the *negligent state*, which willfully fails to act to prevent unnecessary tragedies (e.g., the United States, in its response to work-related diseases, injuries, and deaths, AIDS, black infancy mortality, and homelessness) (Friedrichs, 1996a).

Critical criminology has also influenced the study of state crime at a higher level of abstraction. For example, Marxist analysis continues to be invoked to expose class biases of the capitalist state, and its desire to facilitate the concentrated accumulation of capital rather than to protect the well-being of its citizens (Aulette & Michalowski, 1993; Lynch & Stretesky, 1999; Matthews & Kauzlarich, 2000). Left realism, while it has been concerned with effectively addressing conventional form of crime, has also exposed the hypocritical and countrerproductive dimensions of many existing policies of the capitalist state in responding to such crime (DeKeseredy, MacLean & Schwartz, 1997). Feminist criminology has exposed patriarchal attitudes of contemporary states, and their complicity in on-going forms of discrimination and abuse of women, although state crime has not been its principal concern (Jurik, 1999; Wonders, 1999). In a parallel vein, critical race theory has exposed the state's complicity in the exploitation and oppression of racial minorities (Russell, 1999), and queer theory exposes the state's role in the exploitation and oppression of gay people (Stockdill, 1999). Peacemaking criminology quite specifically treats many aspects of "the war on crime" as both inhumane and ineffective strategies of the state, and at least implicitly as forms of state crime; alternative, community-based peacemaking strategies are proposed (Pepinsky, 1999). Prophetic criminology delineates the contrast between oppressive forms of justice linked with the capitalist state, and a more liberated, humane form of justice (Quinney, 1999). Anarchist criminology by definition views the state as an inherently oppressive entity, and calls for the abolition of state law and state authority (Ferrell, 1999). Each of these critical criminological perspectives, as well as other perspectives such as constitutive criminological, chaos/topological criminology, postmodern and semiotic criminology, and cultural criminology, provide a basis for exposing claims made on behalf of the capitalist state, and for revealing the state's complicity in criminal and harmful activities (Friedrichs, 1998a).

Critical criminologists and others have recently made significant advances in the understanding of the causes and consequences of state crime. However, the victimology of state crime has been slow to develop. As a relatively new area of study within criminology, it is to be expected that little in the way of comprehensive theory and rigorous research would exist on the victimology of state crime. Beyond brief descriptions and sometimes anecdote, there has been no real criminological attempt to establish the nature, extent, and distribution of the victimology of state crime. On one level the avoidance of the victimology of state crime makes sense because victimology (and the victims' rights movement) has deep political roots in conservatism. However, critical criminologists have always been concerned with understanding and correcting harms caused by powerful agents and organizations, both governmental and private. A radical or critical victimology calls for more attention to the victims of state and corporations (Friedrichs, 1983). To date, state crime scholars have not deeply explored the harmful consequences to people victimized by state actions, inactions, and policies (Kauzlarich, Matthews & Miller, 2001). Nevertheless, critical criminologists have treated the following groups as actual or potential victims of state crime: Civilians and soldiers in war, peoples targeted for genocide, research subjects, countries and nations oppressed by powerful states, workers, union organizers, prisoners, citizens victimized by environmental degradation, suspects in criminal cases, passengers on planes, and those suffering from racism, sexism, and classism (Kauzlarich, Matthews & Miller, 2000).

Very few categories of crime match the depth and breadth of injury which can be caused by state crime. We believe that the greatest threat to the well-being and survival of human beings, through the twenty-first century, comes from state crime. In stating such a premise it does not follow that one is belittling the scope of the threat posed by other forms of crime, including conventional predatory crime, organized crime, white-collar crime, and anti-state terrorism. But the state continues to have the largest measure of resources, the most potent capacity to mobilize, and control over the most formidable coercive or destructive forces and weapons, relative to any other entity. Arguably the single greatest threat to the survival of humanity is the threat of nuclear war. Of course the state is also complicit in other large-scale threats, including ecocide, over-population, and the spread of infectious disease. In terms of intensity, magnitude and severity, the deliberate actions of state officials would appear to represent the largest threat of all. In this regard, it is instructive to consider two manifest cases of state crime, genocide and U.S. nuclear weapons related crimes.

Genocide and U.S. Nuclear Crimes

The term genocide was introduced in 1944 by Raphael Lemkin, who applied it to the destruction of a nation or ethnic group. In subsequent decades the term has been invoked in quite different ways: broadly—e.g., the nonlethal destruction of indigenous cultures—and narrowly—e.g., intentional mass killing with the purpose of exterminating an identifiable group of human beings. The destruction of the Hittites and of Carthage in the ancient world, the Albigensian Crusades, and the witch hunts in medieval Europe, have all been identified as historical cases of genocide. In the twentieth century genocides have occurred in many different parts of the world, and have involved many different nationalities and ethnic groups. Fairly or not, the German involvement in genocide has been highlighted in most accounts on the subject. The massacre of some 65,000 Southwest African Herero tribesmen by German colonial forces, beginning in 1904, may be the first significant case of genocide in the twentieth century.

With the end of the twentieth century many lists were compiled, including lists of "crime of the century." Such lists typically feature very high profile homicides such as the kidnapping/murder of the Lindbergh baby, and the O.J. Simpson murder case. But if any event merits the designation of "crime of the century" it is the Holocaust perpetrated by the Nazis in the early 1940s. The combination of the events of the Holocaust, the response to them, the massive literature and analysis, its role as metaphor, the impact and influence of the event—that is, the totality of the event itself and its aftermath—renders the Holocaust a criminal event apart from all others.

That humans are capable of murder has always been disturbing, but that murders on a monumental scale have been carried out on behalf of states is still more disturbing. It has been credibly estimated that between five and six million Jews died at the hands of the Nazis, and many others (e.g., the mentally ill, homosexuals, and gypsies) were also systematically murdered by them. In addition to these crimes against humanity, the Nazi regime launched unprovoked attacks on other countries, committed numerous assassinations, acts of plunder, and many other subversions of human rights (Friedrichs, 1996b). It should be quite evident that it was a crime of the Nazi state, and not simply of Hitler, high-level Nazi officials, bureaucrats, and police or extermination camp personnel. The Holocaust was carried out on behalf of the Nazi state, with the immense resources of the state, and reflected the ideology of Nazism. It is often invoked as the paradigmatic case of genocide in the modern world.

Perhaps the single worst case scenario in the realm of state crime is this: One or more states launch a nuclear attack, a nuclear holocaust occurs, and a resulting "nuclear winter" brings about the "death of death," and the end of humanity and life on earth. It is difficult for us to even contemplate such an event, but who clearly foresaw in the nineteenth century the total wars and massive genocidal campaigns that plagued the twentieth century? Who, indeed, foresaw the development and deployment of nuclear weapons in the twentieth century? These questions are not as distant as one might think, for nuclear weapons and nuclear energy have already been associated with major forms of state crime in the twentieth century.

While easily dwarfed by the horrors of the Holocaust, the U.S. government has committed numerous state crimes through its involvement with nuclear weapons. As most people know, nuclear weapons were only exploded on a population in the context of war by the United States, against Japan, in 1945. But in addition, the U.S. government has *threatened to use* atomic and nuclear weapons on at least 17 different occasions since World War II. The most dangerous threats occurred in the contexts of the Korean and Vietnam Wars, the Cuban Missile crisis, and the Persian Gulf War. Why should these threats be considered state crime? It is clear that even a limited use of nuclear weapons would sacrifice thousands (perhaps hundreds of thousands) of innocent people's lives. It would also compromise their overall health (in some cases directly causing cancer and leukemia) and raise their rates of birth defects and infant mortality to extraordinary levels. The use of nuclear weapons would also make the area's water undrinkable, the food inedible, and the air unbreathable. Even people living thousands of miles away from a nuclear detonation could suffer similar fates, since winds can carry poisonous nuclear particles and debris over very long distances (Kauzlarich & Kramer, 1998). Quite simply, nuclear weapons have inherently murderous consequences, and this why their use could hypothetically dwarf the injury and suffering of the Holocaust. The International Court of Justice has recently recognized the great danger that nuclear weapons present to all living things and have ruled that the use or threat to use nuclear weapons by states *is illegal under international law* (Kramer & Kauzlarich, 1999).

Another state crime related to nuclear and atomic energy is human radiation experimentation. The U.S. Department of Energy and a host of other federal agencies have funded or otherwise managed thousands of human radiation experiments. Several of these experiments have been conducted in violation of the Nuremberg Code, which outlaws non-consensual, reckless, deceptive and coercive experiments. Two sets of studies have been found to be particularly unethical and illegal (Kauzlarich & Kramer, 1998). From 1945 to 1947, a series of Manhattan Project and Atomic Energy Commission (AEC) supported plutonium injection studies were conducted on 18 people. The subjects were expressly deceived into participating in the study. They were told that they were being *treated* for a life-threatening disease when in fact the studies were designed to help the state understand the effects of plutonium on the human body, in the case of nuclear war. The second series of experiments conducted in violation of the Nuremberg Code were the 1963-1973 prison radiation experiments. One hundred and thirty one prisoners at the Oregon State Prison in Salem and the Washington State Prison in Walla Walla were subjects in a study to determine the effects of irradiation on the function of testes. Prisoners were given $25 per irradiation and informed of only some of the possible risks associated with the experiments. Prisoners are not in a position to exercise the type of free will envisioned by the Nuremberg Code.

The production, manufacture, and testing of atomic and nuclear weapons by the U.S. Department of Energy have also resulted in massive injury. At least seventeen areas in the U.S. have been substantially damaged and polluted in violation of U.S. EPA laws, the Clean Water Act, and the Resource Conservation and Recovery Act. In Hanford, Washington, one hundred square miles of groundwater were contaminated with extremely high levels of tritium, iodine, and other toxic chemicals. Near the Savannah River Plant in the Carolinas, massive releases of mercury into the air and tritium, strontium, and iodine into the soil occurred (Kauzlarich & Kramer, 1998). Evidence shows that higher rates of miscarriages, leukemia, and other health related problems have occurred in the areas where nuclear weapons have been produced, stored, or tested.

The human effects of environmental degradation as a result of the hundreds of nuclear weapons tests in the Western part of the U.S. are also examples of state crime. A recent study by the National Cancer Institute estimates that tens of thousands of people have developed thyroid cancer as a result of nuclear tests (Kauzlarich & Kramer, 1998). The victims of these environmental crimes were not only the unknowing civilians who simply happened to be living near the test sites, but also military personnel who were forced to witness nuclear blasts and then tested for any negative side effects (Kauzlarich & Kramer, 1998).

Even this brief review of two major forms of state crime is enough to suggest that the harms caused by states can easily dwarf the injuries caused by other types of crimes. We are now living in the wake of massive state crimes involving the qualitites of genocide in Rwanda, the former Yugoslavia, Cambodia, and East Timor. All told, millions of people in these countries have been killed, physically assaulted, rendered homeless and hungry, raped, or emotionally abused by organizations, groups, and individuals representing the state or a state organization. We are also living at a time where nuclear weapons have been developed by a growing number of countries. At least a dozen countries either possess or are working to achieve a military use of nuclear weapons. State sponsored genocide, "ethnic cleansing," and the threat of omnicide are clearly not just ghosts of the past, but frighteningly contemporary problems as well (Kauzlarich, Matthews & Miller, 2001).

Controversies Surrounding the Concept of State Crime

The concept of state crime has not been attacked by mainstream criminologists so much as it has been ignored, but both the rejection and the neglect of the phenomenon have common sources. Most of the controversies surrounding the concept are related to the very definition of state crime.

First, insofar as the state is the primary source of both the laws that define crime and the institutions of enforcement and adjudication, the concept of state crime is especially open to challenge. Luis Molina (1995) and Ira Sharkansky (1995) have published critiques of the concept of state crime. Molina (1995:349) questions the very possibility of the existence of state crime: "In a strict sense," he argues, "the term *state crime* is almost, but not quite, an oxymoron, a legal absurdity" (author's emphasis). But Molina does not completely dismiss the idea of state crime. Sharkansky (1995), however, maintains that only the state can control the definition of crime. Obviously, we find both claims quite short-sighted, as we explain below.

How does one distinguish between "bad governmental policy" or "bad government," and real state complicity in facilitating and engineering harm? One way is to more clearly distinguish between crimes of commission and crimes of omission. There is no doubt that there is a difference between states that contribute, reinforce, or support harmful social process and structures and those that commit explicit acts of genocide or human rights violations. But both are engaged in state crime. Clarifying these forms of state crime in more meaningful ways is perhaps the next greatest challenge for state crime scholars. It is also important to make clearer distinctions because at least a few critics of the concept of state crime have used this issue to dismiss its very existence. For example, Sharkansky (1995:36) believes that the term crime "implies an action that invites an authoritative response." We take this to mean that if a system of criminal justice (i.e., police, courts, and corrections) is not in place to process an act as criminal, the act cannot be criminal in the first place. This is certainly a way of look-

ing at crime with a long history, and is a dimension of the social constructionist claim of the fundamental relativity of crime. Sharkansky's charge,
however, seems to be based on a highly legalistic notion that the state is the
only credible source of criminal definitions. No doubt state crime is both an
objective condition and a social construction, like virtually everything else
in the social world. It does not follow, however, that the state's position
should be privileged simply because it comes from the state. No scholarly
discipline should be so passive as to allow the state to reserve the exclusive
right to define its subject matter.

Sharkansky (1995:40) also believes that the concept of state crime has
been so overused that it has been rendered meaningless: "If everything can
be a state crime, then nothing is a state crime." This charge is motivated from
the claims of some state crime scholars' that a state can be considered
criminal if it fails to alleviate human suffering (so called negligent states). As
we noted earlier, this is contentious indeed, for it means that if a state
refuses to promote the well being of the people, or conversely, contributes
to harm or suffering, it is criminal in some way. So, if the state refuses to take
reasonable measures to stop racism, sexism, homelessness, the hidden economy, poverty, and so on, it can be said to be engaging in a crime of omission.
Turk (1995) has also noted the potentially problematic nature of such a
broad definition of state crime. In Sharkansky's view, this problem is so
important that it would be better to call undesirable state acts by other "con-
demnatory adjectives," and he lists over a dozen words to replace the term
state crime, including nasty, mean, odious, repugnant, terrible, and dis-
graceful. Note that he is not arguing that states do not do "bad" things, but
that these things should not be called criminal. In a related critique, Molina
(1995) also appears to accept a definition of state crime that is exclusively
dependent on the violation of law. Other definitions, he and some other critics imply, are too subjective. Let us investigate such claims more fully.

Radical or critical criminological attention to state crime has been specifically criticized as polemical or political partisanship. Many mainstream criminologists believe that criminologists should function as scientists engaged in
objective, value-free study and analysis. This type of positivist reasoning
holds that any intrusion of ideology or personal interest either voids or
diminishes the credibility of research or theory. In response, critical criminologists typically regard the claim of objectivity and neutrality as an illusion.
Indeed, by failing to define and interpret the immense harms carried out on
behalf of the state as forms of crime mainstream criminologists, however
unwittingly, may be criticized as advancing a political agenda of their own
(Schwendinger & Schwendinger, 1970). Jeffrey Reiman (1997), for example,
puts forth the provocative thesis that the American power elite does far less
than it could about conventional street crime because, as long as such crime
exists, middle-class anger is focused on this form of crime and attention is
deflected from the far more consequential crime committed by the powerful and the privileged. In a similar vein, as Richard Quinney (1977) pointed

out years ago, one might suggest that mainstream criminologists, by focusing so much attention on conventional crime, help deflect attention from crimes of the state, and therefore act as ancillary agents of the state.

State crime is more clearly visible from the perspective of critical criminology than from the perspective of mainstream criminology. Mainstream criminology has traditionally emphasized the role of the state as the legitimate source of law and the principal force for combating and controlling crime. Certainly many studies carried out within the mainstream perspective have recognized and analyzed abusive or corrupt practices by the police, the court system, and the correctional system, but the state itself as a major perpetrator of crime has been little acknowledged. However, critical criminology adopts as one fundamental premise a profound skepticism toward claims made on behalf of the state and those in power, and a recognition that the state and those in power are the source of much of the worst harms, as Tifft & Sullivan (1980:51) splendidly illustrate:

> . . . it is not the social harms punishable by law which cause the greatest misery in the world. It is the lawful harms, those unpunishable crimes justified and protected by law, the state, the ruling elites, that fill the world with misery, want, strife, conflict slaughter, and destruction.

Another manifestation of the controversy surrounding state crime is that it has traditionally been regarded as an inappropriate focus for graduate education in criminology and criminal justice. Few academics and researchers are likely to have received any significant exposure to the topic or encouragement to pursue it. Furthermore, it is hardly surprising that it has typically been more difficult to obtain research funding for state crime from state entities (in some cases, raising the prospect of biting the hand you hope will feed you). And for those who surmount the various hurdles just described the challenges of obtaining access to research venues and credible data tend to exceed those facing the researcher of more conventional criminological and criminal justice topics (Ross et al., 1999).

Finally, we should note that there is some controversy about how to control state crime. Should the United Nations and its bodies such as the International Court of Justice play a larger role in controlling state crime? Should international agreements such as the Declaration of Human Rights, the International Convention of Political and Civil Rights, and the Convention of Elimination of All Forms of Racial Discrimination be better policed? We would argue in the affirmative, but it is clear that many people, especially in the United States, view international agreements and bodies with skepticism, partly out of fears about losing sovereignty. The recently proposed International Criminal Court (ICC) has met with significant resistance because of such concerns. But there is an additional problem. While this new court will be a permanent rather than temporary institution devoted to prosecuting people who have violated human rights, the ICC will only tap into one dimension of state crime, the *individuals* who have criminally pursued state interests. There is no indication that the ICC would involve taking a broader approach to the control of state crime by defining state agencies or states themselves as criminological subjects (Kramer & Kauzlarich, 1999). After all, acknowledging the organizational genesis and persistence of state crime is crucial for identifying the causes of state crime and for diminishing its harmful consequences. It follows, then, that any attempt to control state crime which ignores the institutional nature of the phenomenon is too narrow and probably doomed to failure. Simply "throwing the bums out" is not sufficient (Michalowski, 1998:xiii), for it ignores the fact that organizational goals, norms, and interests persist even in the face of substantial personnel changes.

A Post-9/11 Postscript on Crimes of the State

The attack on September 11, 2001, on the World Trade Center towers and the Pentagon, was unquestionably a shock to the American people. The subsequent American military attack on Taliban Afghanistan was justified primarily on the grounds that the Taliban-run state was sheltering and supporting Osama bin Laden and his terrorist Al Qaeda organization, and in this sense was engaged in a form of state crime. Other states—characterized by President George W. Bush as an "axis of evil"—were also regarded as criminal states in some sense. On the other side, the 9/11 attack on America was widely celebrated in many parts of the Arab world by people who clearly regarded the United States as a criminal state, for—among other reasons— its support for Israel, which is viewed as a criminal state by many people in the Arab world.

The American invasion of Taliban Afghanistan was another dramatic illustration of its willingness to take strong measures in response to the perception of state crime. The proposed preemptive strike (as of February, 2003) against Iraq, and the call for replacing the regime of Saddam Hussein with another regime, was another illustration of this policy. The prevention of an anticipated state crime on a monumental scale—the broader use of weapons of mass destruction (including nuclear weapons) by Saddam Hussein—was at the core of President Bush's rationale for his call for support for this form of military action. However, any such military action would surely be viewed as criminal not only by many Iraqis, Islamic fundamentalists, Arab states and citizens of Arab states, but by many other countries and many of their citizens as well. At the same time North Korea—another "axis of evil" state—was taking a belligerent stance with regard to its nuclear arms. The status of unilateral American military action in international law, in these circumstances, was a matter of some debate, although we doubt such a preemptive military action by the U.S. could be consistent with the standards set by international law. At the same time, the United Nations had not achieved the status of an institution universally supported as the entity which alone should respond to state crime, or threats of state crime. The United States—widely described as the only remaining superpower in the world—was seeking immunity from prosecution of its nationals by the newly established International Criminal Court. Early in the twenty-first century, then, the world was confronted with large-scale issues relating to state crime and its control.

Conclusion

Crimes of the state are immensely consequential. Indeed, the loss of life and the destruction or expropriation of property traceable to state crime may well exceed that due to all other forms of crime. Critical criminology has provided one important framework for understanding state crime, and has played a key role in directing criminological attention to state crime. But even within the critical criminological tradition, state crime has not been the principal focus of criminological study. Various controversies about the very definition of state crime, along with assorted disciplinary, political, ideological, and practical difficulties, have inhibited the growth of state crime research and theory.

It is easy enough to experience a sense of impotence and futility in the face of large-scale state crimes carried out by immensely powerful persons and agencies. But critical criminologists have always taken on these kinds of challenges. And while there are many controversies surrounding the study of state crime, if we consider what is at stake, we should feel morally obligated to take on the challenge of understanding state crime and its victims.

Discussion Questions

1. Do you think the designation "state crime" is defensible, or do you believe that only people can commit crimes? Do you regard the terms "state crime" and "criminal state" as useful, or not? Why?

2. Do you agree with the broad application of the term crime adopted by critical criminologists, or do you favor restricting the term crime to specific violations of the criminal law? Defend your position on this issue.

3. What are the possible benefits—or drawbacks—of differentiating between a criminal state, a repressive state, a corrupt state, and a negligent state?

4. Which—if any—of the above labels can be applied to the United States? Why or why not?

5. Which of the many varieties of critical criminology identified here—i.e., Marxist, left realist, feminist, critical race, queer, peacemaking, prophetic, and anarchist—do you find most promising for more fully understanding state crime? Provide rationales for your answer.

6. What are some of the reasons—good or bad—that account for a traditional neglect of state crime by criminologists? Do you agree with the proposition that criminologists should devote significantly more attention to state crime?

7. What do victims of state crime have in common with victims of conventional crime? How do they differ? What are the benefits and drawbacks of encompassing victims of state crimes into the subject matter of victimology?

8. Do you agree or disagree that it is useful to frame issues of genocide and the misuse of nuclear power as criminological issues? What is gained or lost by taking such an approach?

9. What do the "crimes of the nuclear state" that are discussed in this chapter have in common with other, more conventional forms of crime? How significant are differences of intention with regard to uses of nuclear power and the commission of conventional forms of crime?

10. Which approach—if any—to the control of state crime seems most feasible to you? Are you generally optimistic or pessimistic on the possibility of controlling state crime as we move through the twenty-first century? Why?

CHAPTER 10

Crime and Embodiment

Victoria L. Pitts

In a British police operation called "Spanner," 16 gay, middle-aged men were arrested and prosecuted for engaging in consensual sado-masochistic acts. Even though in their defense the Spanner men argued that the so-called victims (themselves) were consenting adults, the men were convicted of assault charges. These convictions were upheld in the appellate court, and some of the men were sentenced to prison terms of up to three years (Bibbings & Alldridge, 1993). In their ruling (*R. v. Brown, Laskey, Lucas, Jaggard, and Carter*), the judges determined that:

> . . . it is not in the public interest that people should try to cause, or should cause, each other actual bodily harm for no good reason . . . Sado-masochistic homosexual activity cannot be regarded as conducive to the enhancement or enjoyment of family life or conducive to the welfare of society (cited in Bibbings & Alldridge, 1993:357).

As a result of Operation Spanner, a well-known body piercer and tattooist, Alan Oversby, was charged with a number of counts of causing bodily harm to his clients in his London clinic. While some of these charges were dropped when a judge ruled that body piercing for the purpose of decoration does not constitute an offense, Oversby was convicted of assault for piercing his lover's penis. The court found that decorative body modification was legal, but that body modification performed erotically was illegal.

These cases highlight the body as a significant space of public interest. Bodies, from the viewpoint of the judges in the *R. v. Brown* case, ought to be governed in ways "conducive to the welfare of society." But who determines what constitutes the welfare of society and its "enjoyment of family

121

life," and according to what standards do we decide that bodies are proper, healthy and "in the public interest?" The social control and regulation of embodiment, which are informed by assumptions about gender, sexuality, health, perversion and other bodily issues, highlight the ways in which bodies are saturated with sociality, politics, and ideology.

In this chapter, I describe classical assumptions of the body as natural, universal, and socially and politically neutral. In contrast, I describe how contemporary theories, influenced in part by the work of Michel Foucault and also by feminism, present the body as having a deep and complex relationship to power and the social order. This point of view can be applied to help illuminate the social, political, and ideological aspects of bodies, especially in relation to the social treatment of bodily deviance. In the second half of the chapter, as a way of illuminating the body's social, political, and ideological significance, I outline the recent debates surrounding deviant body art. The debates over body art reflect the contemporary recognition of the body as a site of social control and social contest. While the body was not for a long time explicitly theorized as such, its deeply political and social character is now increasingly hard to ignore.

The Body in Social Thought

Anthropologists have long considered the body to be socially significant, because in pre-modern societies, the body was seen as a "more important and ubiquitous target for public symbolism" (Turner, 1993:6) through indigenous body marks such as tattoos and scars and through public rituals. Anthropologists understood the body as a classificatory system; it was both the surface upon which social hierarchies—such as age, status, clan—were inscribed and, as Mary Douglas argued, it provided a symbolic model for broader social order. For much of the history of social theory, though, the body was not understood as a classificatory system in modern industrialized cultures. Even though modern societies also adorn the body and invest it with social importance, the body did not figure prominently in analyses of the social order, of power, and of social change until recently.

Modern social thought has long dismissed the body, and at the same time, assumed its naturalness and universality. The Enlightenment affirmed a mind/body binary that privileged the former and rejected the latter as a hindrance to *res cogitans*, Descartes' term for the intellect and selfhood (Shildrick & Price, 1999). Since then, the body has been largely perceived as fixed in its corporeality, a material fact of being to be transcended. In a dualistic paradigm, the mind is the realm of reason and logic, while the body can only be the source of (irrational) desires and (primitive) needs. Classical sociology, which developed partly in tension with biological explanations for social action, emphasized rational social structures and laws and for the most part left the body to other disciplines. To the extent that modern thought assumed and embraced rationality on the part of social actors and perceived the body only as an environmental constraint to rational decisionmaking, it neglected the social role of the body (Turner, 1993). Through its neglect of the body, social theorists have implicitly affirmed a notion of the body as solely biological or "natural," as fixed or unchanging, and as universal.

In contrast, contemporary theories of the body now identify it as a space of social control and social order as well as a site of social stratification in relation to class, gender, sexuality, and race. Conceptions of the body as fixed, natural and universal have been challenged, and bodies which do not fit dominant models have been reconsidered. The explosion of interest in bodies in the last decade or so, inaugurated by the work of Michel Foucault (see Foucault, 1978), has generated a theoretical recovery of the body in classical theory, encouraged the development of the social history of the body in the West, and served as a theme for the exploration of new feminist, postmodern, postcolonial and queer theories. Given recent developments in political culture and body theory, the body can no longer be taken as an uncomplicated, natural materiality that stands in clear contrast to culture.

So, what is the body then? Michel Foucault has famously insisted that it is socially inscribed, normalized, and socially produced, a point of view contemporary theorists such as social constructionists, feminists, queer theorists, and poststructuralists have advocated. Rather than fixed and universal, our norms influence how we produce, control and experience bodies. Further, bodies play a role in the production of social norms and hierarchies. The human body itself, then, cannot be conceived as existing outside of social influence. As Elizabeth Grosz writes,

> The body is, so to speak, organically, biologically 'incomplete'; it is indeterminate, amorphous, a series of uncoordinated intentionalities that require social triggering, ordering, and long-term 'administration'. . . . Among the key structuring principles of this produced body is its inscription and encoding by (familially ordered) sexual desires . . . its inscription by a set of socially coded meanings and significances . . . [and] its production and development through various regimes of discipline and training . . . (Grosz, 1999:382).

This means that the body is socially constructed, and also that it is not socially or politically neutral. As the histories of colonialism, misogyny and homophobia bear out, bodies are differentiated, encoded, inscribed, and disciplined through racial, sexual, gender, and class configurations.

The Deviant Body

Classical views of the natural, proper body conflated it with a functional, smooth, pristine and orderly one, and deviations from norms surrounding the body were perceived and represented as socially threatening. The nineteenth and early twentieth century practice of exhibiting "freaks" in circuses, fairs, and anthropological exhibits revealed how aberrant or different bodies were represented as frightening mistakes of nature (in the case of individual differences), or as the unfortunate outcome of the lack of civilizing influences (in the case of cultural ones). Sometimes, notions of cultural difference and fears about sexuality were conflated. A famous example of this was the display of the "Hottentot" on the streets of London in the early nineteenth century. The "Hottentot" was an African woman who was exhibited for spectacle and entertainment, but more importantly as evidence of the heightened, excessive sexuality of racial Others: her supposedly large clitoris was compared to the genitalia of apes. Colonial racism toward indigenous bodies linked notions of primitivism to uncontrolled sexuality. As Anthony Shelton (1996) points out, both European and colonized women in the Victorian era faced sexual constrictions which were couched in racist and misogynist logic about the uncivilized, savage nature of uncontrolled female sexuality. Deviant European women and colonized subjects were both regulated, albeit to different degrees, through discourses that linked the non-conforming or non-Western body to the female, the sexual, and the "primitive."

The Hottentot example shows not only an egregious racism on the part of colonialist men, but also a more general degradation of all female bodies, female sexuality, and of embodiment itself. The linking of women, and all degraded groups, to nature and sexuality situates them against and outside reason, government and the social order. It pits the body (especially the female body, which is somehow more bodily and less self-contained) against culture and imbues it with danger. Woman's association with reproduction—menstruation, breast-feeding, pregnancy—ties her biologically to the opened, leaking, classically improper body and makes her "volatile" (Grosz, 1994). Her embodiment, conceived as marginal and deviant compared to the universalized model of male embodiment, has long been cited as the reason and justification for her subjugation.

In the twentieth-century, non-mainstream bodily practices related to sexuality and gender roles have continued to be characterized variously as criminal and sick (Wilkerson, 1998; Medhurst & Munt, 1998; Murphy, 1992). Homosexuality, sodomy, female promiscuity, sex work, cross dressing, sadomasochism, abortion and many other aspects of the body and sexuality have faced modern forms of social control. This policing has accomplished the physical control of bodies, especially those of women and homosexuals, through incarceration, hospitalization, shock therapy and drugs, to name a few methods. The moral and ideological regulation of gender and sexuality has also been accomplished with the help all major social institutions, including the criminal justice system and medicine but also public welfare, education, and the culture industries. Specialists are now privileged to define bodies as normal or not, and those which challenge the social order may be stigmatized or pathologized.

Rethinking Deviant Bodies

In the late twentieth century, though, social theorists have challenged the legitimacy of traditional authorities to police and morally regulate bodies. In contrast to earlier depictions of the body as natural and fixed, social constructionist, feminist and cultural approaches to the body have identified the body as a social product interimplicated with the social order and its (often racist, misogynist, homophobic) configuring of social/bodily relations. It is crucial to the functioning of modern institutions of social control, socialization and social production. This perspective points out the ways in which the body is coded by culture as normal or deviant, and the ways such codes serve relations of power such as colonialism and patriarchy. Further, to the extent that power relations are multiple and continually challenged and reconstituted, bodies appear also as spaces of social contest.

Marginalized bodies are not only capable of "generating deep ontological anxiety" (Shildrick & Price, 1999:3), as they clearly did on the streets of London in the nineteenth century and in the body piercing studios and SM clubs of the same city in the late twentieth century, but they are also now seen as possible sites of subversion and resistance. In postmodern culture, universal notions of truth and naturalness, including those surrounding the body, are challenged. Subjectivity and bodies seem less fixed, at least to some, and multiple knowledges compete to define the meaning, place, and truth of bodies. From this perspective, the body appears not only as a space of social control but, potentially, a medium for self-expression, identity work, and even rebellion. In recent years, bodily spectacle has become recognized as a resource for marginalized groups and subcultures to attract attention and challenge norms. Subcultural, anti-fashion body alterations in the late twentieth century West, for example, such as hair sculpture and piercing by punks, tattooing among middle-class youth and women, scarification, branding and SM fashion and other deviant body modifications, are now attracting public attention and raising debates over the meanings and significance of bodily deviance.

New Deviant Bodies: Body Art

The body modification subculture, or subcultural 'movement' as it is sometimes understood, surfaced on the cultural landscape in the last decade, although its origins are decades older. Body modifiers have invented new and borrowed old body technologies and imbued them with personal and social meaning. Recent studies and essays have investigated, among other topics, the subculture's creation of the anomalous female body (Pitts, 1998; Hewitt, 1997), its 'technophilia,' (MacKendrick, 1998), its link to neotribalism (Klesse, 1999; Rosenblatt, 1997; Eubanks, 1996) and its association with SM and fetish subculture (Jones, 1998; Steele, 1996; Myers, 1992). This emerging literature reflects new theories of the body, recent interest in the "sociology of body marks in cool societies" (Turner, 1999), and the increasing visibility of anomalous body practices in contemporary culture.

The subculture is really a network of groups sharing an interest in non-mainstream body alterations. While some of the practices have been embraced by popular culture, they were pioneered by fetish club cultures, West Coast gay and lesbian SM communities, performance artists, neotribalists, and other marginalized groups. Since the 1960s, performance art has highlighted the body's social character by challenging conventional bodily behavior and adornment. Some performance artists, including a number of feminists, have focused on exploring sexuality and on undermining traditional sexual norms through creating spectacular, deviant bodies. Gay and lesbian SM groups in California pioneered the Western use of body piercing and scarification, linking them both to SM and later, to neotribalism. Neotribalism, or 'modern primitivism', links body modifications to non-Western rituals, including scarification, tribal tattooing, and other practices used in indigenous cultures. Its discourse, which surfaced in films and subcultural texts in the late 1980s and 1990s, presents indigenous practices as alternatives to normative Western embodiment (which is perceived as alienated from the body's spiritual, sexual, and communal potential), and articulates disaffection with mainstream Western cultural values. Most recently, radical body modification has embraced more high-tech methods of body alteration.

Today, many people use new forms of body modification, and "hard core" subcultural membership in body modification, to use Sweetman's term (1999), is diffuse, diverse, and links individuals from multiple communities, including youth, cyberpunks, fetishists, leathermen and SM women, and 'modern primitives'. The shared meanings of body modification, proliferated throughout its magazines, ezines, and marginal gathering spaces, emphasize bodily self-ownership, the body's capacity for illicit pleasures, self-expression through the body, and new possibilities for identity.

Body Art Debates

Deviant body art, and the debates which surround it, illuminate the body's social, political, and ideological nature. Some mainstream commentators, including journalists and therapists, have pathologized anomalous body art and framed the rise in tattooing, scarring, and piercing as a new social problem of delinquency, sickness and perversion. Liberal and postmodern writers, however, have argued a relativist position that sees deviant body art as fulfilling identity needs. Postmodern and poststructural feminists have emphasized how the practices highlight the power relations that surround the body.

Deviant body art is portrayed as an attack upon the body that reflects both self-abuse and social disaffection. Because the practices are sometimes painful, and because they often create permanent inscriptions that work against beauty norms, they are even considered by some to be self-mutilative (Favazza, 1996). Youthful, gay and female body modifications are especially likely to be framed as socially problematic in the mainstream media, which have relied on therapists and radical feminists as authorities on the practices (Pitts, 1999). Youths' body modifications raise fears of social delinquency; sensationalized media accounts that raise 'moral panic' associate children's tattoos and body piercings with drugs, homelessness, and other social problems (Pitts, 1999). That the practices are perceived to reflect cultural disaffection appears to be one reason for concern. That the practices are associated with fetishism and sadomasochism seems also to be a primary source of contention.

Gay and SM body modification has especially faced pathologization, censorship and criminalization. In addition to the cases in Britain of the Spanner men and Alan Oversby, there have been a number of controversies the United States surrounding gay body modification. Included among these are two National Endowment for the Arts controversies. In 1990, a National Endowment for the Arts ' porn ' controversy in Congress was sparked by a gallery's photographs of gay body modifiers (Vale & Juno, 1990). In 1994, the public scarification of gay, HIV+ performance artist Ron Athey, which was partially funded by the NEA, also caused national controversy (Abbe, 1994). This performance art sparked a wide public discussion of AIDS transmission, outrage from a number of both Republican and Democratic senators, and has been attributed as the cause of the two percent cut in funding the NEA received in its 1995 budget (Breslauer, 1994).

Women's body modification has also been pathologized. Because the practices appear to some to violate the body, some radical feminists have joined in the criticism of deviant body projects. Like other issues in relation to the body, sexuality, and perceived violence (pornography, sado-masochism), body modification places radical feminists and social conservatives in the same camp. Radical feminists argue that the practices harm the body's integrity and constitute self-attack (Jeffries, 1994). They also link tattoos, scars and piercings, even though they generally deviate from beauty norms, with anti-feminist backlash. Karmen MacKendrick (1998:5) puts the question this way:

> Can we in fact read body modification and its increasing popularity . . . as an intensification of sadistic patriarchal demands for conformity to discomfort in the name of beauty? . . . Are these relatively extreme styles inherently misogynist?

MacKendrick thinks not. She points out that the practices engender bodies that violate beauty norms. Rather than giving into pressures of normalization, they expand our uses of adornment and technology, explore diverse pleasures, and promote bodily diversity. She is one of a number of writers who have defended and celebrated body modification. Because in much contemporary theory, the "natural" body is perceived to be a social and ideological construct, and the "actual" body appears as culturally diverse and relative, arguments that such practices are either morally improper or inherently self-harming appear deeply problematic. In particular, much of the criticism of body modification problematically assumes and "naturalizes" classical notions of the proper body as smooth, closed, and self-contained. Further, it seems that such critiques are rather uncritical about the role of modern institutions in regulating the body's appearance and its experience of pleasure and sexuality.

In fact, in both United States and Britain, diverse groups of body modifiers appear unified as supporters of free speech and of the repeal of repressive sex laws (Shelton, 1996; Califia, 1994). This is reflected in the defense of body modification *itself* as free speech and free self-expression through the body. A number of liberal and postmodern academics have argued a relativist perspective, suggesting that the rise in spectacular body art, like more accepted body practices, expresses a sense of the body as a project of self-expression and identity creation. Their arguments rest upon recent understandings of the natural body as a social construct. The body is seen not as a fixed, mechanistic vehicle for the self, but rather as a flexible resource for pleasure and identity work. Also implied is a view of power that sees the breakdown of modern power's traditional authority over the body and identity, and suggests that new symbols, meanings and options for the body are possible.

Why body modification now? For some of these writers, the rise of postmodern culture, the expansion of leisure practices, consumer culture, technology, and globalization all increase interest in bodily intervention and expand the marketplace of available symbols and styles for embodiment. Body modification is one aesthetic among many that reflect views of the body as a "project which should be worked out and accomplished as part of an individual's self-identity" (Shilling, 1993:5). Writers like Chris Shilling (1993) and Bryan Turner (1999) suggest that the body is now widely perceived in contemporary cultures as a space of self-expression. Body projects are undertaken by many people, as the rise in popularity of keep-fit practices, yoga, and cosmetic surgery, among other practices, suggests. The postmodern condition of social life, which includes ontological insecurity about the ' truth ' of human subjectivity, the erosion of tradition (and with it, a sense of rootedness), nostalgia, and an expanding array of cultural and technological possibilities with which to identify, creates both pressures and opportunities for body work. In this scenario, cosmetic surgery and scarification are examples of the same process of self-creation through the body, except that one buttresses mainstream Western ideals and the other extends beyond them, looking to non-Western cultures for inspiration. There is no singular ideal; rather, the body is a "plastic space onto which the sense of self is projected" (Sweetman, 1999:15). Body modifications such as scarring, tattooing and piercing are, in this view, like other adornment practices: "narcissistic, playful signs to self" (Turner, 1999:42), forms of self-expression that deserve protection as free speech.

The relativist point of view denaturalizes dominant body ideals. However, while consistent with an understanding of the body as unfixed and 'unfinished,' it may not emphasize enough the political nature of embodiment, the social control of bodies and the normalizing pressures that are negotiated and sometimes contested in deviant body projects. This perspective is complicated by with a feminist understanding of how selves and bodies are symbolically differentiated by power relations.

Although the relativist point of view of body modifications as identity-oriented self-expressions avoids universal and essentializing conceptions of the body, it does not wholly account for the appeal of deviant practices and the symbolic significance of them. In our culture, cosmetic surgery that removes wrinkles is not only acceptable, but it is almost expected of people of a certain gender and class status. Conversely, scarifications and brandings can create horror, abjection, and revulsion. The social consequences of each are radically different, in particular for women and marginalized groups. Some body modifications, such as cosmetic surgery, spa practices, and keep-fit practices are linked to the economy and institutions such as medicine and the culture industries in ways subcultural body modifications are not. Even though at some level subcultural practices are commodified and fashionalized, they still have a "more than just a little problematic" relationship to fashion (Shelton, 1996:99). In subcultural body modification, "we find here an ironic distance from the 'natural' body *and* normalizing technology" (MacKendrick, 1998:21-22, emphasis mine).

Moreover, to the extent that the relativist perspective implies a liberal, fixed subject who freely and willfully shops in the supermarket of style, it does not adequately address the many ways in which identities and meanings of bodies are *not* choices. Even in postmodern culture, expectations for gender, ethnicity, and sexuality are imposed on individuals, and bodies are marked by race, class and gender. Because body-subjects are symbolically differentiated (they are marked as female, white or black, Western, homosexual, etc.), identity work takes place within the matrix of difference. Identities (and therefore bodies), as Stuart Hall argues, are not "unities" that are freely chosen, but are "constructed within the play of power and exclusion" (Hall, 1996:5). In this sense, body modifications are negotiations of power. Body modifications by women are inherently situated in the larger context of beauty norms. Their projects must be read in connection to gendered relations of power, and they must be compared critically with practices such as cosmetic surgery. Gay men and lesbians as well as straight women who use body modification must negotiate pathologization, a particularly powerful form of power facing these groups. Further, pleasure is normalized and regulated, even in postmodern culture, and so the visibility of fetishized body modifications must be seen in this context. White people who use non-

Western, indigenous practices express cultural privilege in their ability to appropriate the symbols and rituals of non-Western Others, even if they are in other ways marginal or disadvantaged.

From the point of view of feminist cultural theories which argue that bodies are inscribed and socially constructed through power relations, deviant body modifications appear not as inherently 'unnatural' or pathological, nor do they illustrate how individuals can freely shape their own bodies and identities. Rather, body projects suggest the ways individuals and groups negotiate the ways power is already inscribed on their bodies. Body projects can uncritically reproduce or critically challenge body ideals, and they are both symbolically significant and symbolically differentiated. Deviant body projects provoke debates that reveal the ideological underpinnings of body ideals, and the significant role of the body in supporting and reproducing the social order.

Discussion Questions

1. The British case, *R. v. Brown, Laskey, Lucas, Jaggard and Carter*, is illustrative of the way in which our bodies are "saturated with sociality, politics, and ideology." Explain this statement.

2. Describe the ways in which our bodies are "governed" in society. Think of the limits placed upon the deployment (and enjoyment) of the body as you prepare your answer.

3. Why was the body neglected in social theory? What position did classical sociology adopt with regard to the body?

4. Outline, in brief, the contemporary view of the body put forward by Michel Foucault. Contrast this view with the traditional concept of the body incorporated into classical sociology.

5. What does the historical practice of exhibiting "freak" bodies in circuses, fairs, and anthropological exhibits tell us about the importance of body norms?

6. How were sexuality and anatomical difference conflated in ideas of body deviance? Give specific examples in your answer.

7. What does it mean when we talk about crime as "embodied"? Give examples to support your explanation.

8. Describe the ways in which non-mainstream body modification practices have been regulated. Which social institutions have played a role in policing body practices defined as "criminal" or "sick"?

9. How might we rethink the coding of the body—as "normal," as "deviant," and so on—in order to avoid stigmatizing and pathologizing others?

10. Describe how fashion, or the practices of body modification, confirm or confront the dominant assumptions about bodies, power, and social control. In what ways is your own body a medium for self-expression or social rebellion?

CHAPTER 11

Masculinities, Femininities, and Homicide: Competing Explanations for Male Violence

Kenneth Polk

Despite the fact that, virtually since the first empirical studies of crime, it was clear that one of the major factors in crime was sex, it is only in recent years that criminologists have begun to take the data seriously and treat sex or gender as central theoretical issues in accounting for crime. Put simply, across many different countries and in many research studies, official crime, especially violent crime, involves mostly male offenders. In the case of homicide, for example, typically males make up between 85 and 95 percent of the known offenders (Wallace, 1986; Polk, 1994). In fact, closer examination will reveal that in over half the cases of homicide, males are involved as both offender and victim. While early studies of homicide might note such distributions, they would give little attention to the obviously important question of why it is that these crimes are committed by males, and the equally important theoretical issue of why females are much less likely to be involved.

In the last decade or so, this situation has altered dramatically. Social analysts have moved the factor of sex onto the center of the stage. In the case of homicide they have specifically addressed the question of why it is that males feature so predominantly in the offense. Two somewhat different pathways have been followed, one seeking to understand better the data of male offending, the other elaborating theoretical frameworks which address issues of masculinity, or more properly masculinities, and crime.

The Multiple Scenarios of Male Violence

Regarding the first of these, important research work has been done which examines the multiplicity of ways that masculinity plays out in the data of violence. There is, in other words, no single pattern of male violence. Looking specifically at the issue of homicide, for example, there are quite a number of different patterns, or scenarios of masculine violence that can be identified (Polk, 1994).

One that will come to the minds of many quite quickly is that where a male directs the violence toward a female, most often a sexual partner (Dobash & Dobash, 1992). Even here, however, it is significant that there are distinct patterns. A common form of male violence toward women is that which has its source in the readiness of males to use violence toward women sexual partners when the male feels that his control over the woman is slipping away. There is a pattern whereby males come to view their female partner as a form of sexual property, and the use of violence, including lethal violence, is a way that the male expresses his control over the woman. Often jealousy is an explicit part of this violence, and time and again the phrase "if I can't have you, no one will" echoes through the data of male violence toward women. This pattern can be described as distinctively male since it is empirically the case that women rarely kill their male partners out of jealousy.

As important as this theme of jealousy and sexual control is, there are others that involve male violence toward females. One that is common in homicide files is that where the male becomes extremely depressed and overwhelmed as he comes to feel the meaning of life creeping away, and he then decides to commit suicide. Such depressive males, if they have a wife, often will include the wife in the suicide plan, so that they wife is killed just before the male takes his own life. As in the previous scenario, the issue of violence is distinctively male, because very rarely are examples found where it is the wife who decides to commit suicide, and then dictates that the husband must also die. The common theme in both of these scenarios is that the male is likely to view the woman as a form of "property" over which the male exerts rights, including the right to terminate the life of the woman.

There are other patterns that, while rare, stir up considerable public controversy and concern. There are those occasional and isolated cases where males, out of a poorly understood personal history that leads to a deep antagonism toward women, become involved in a pattern of "serial killing." While it may be difficult to provide adequate theoretical explanations for why offenders engage in such extreme violence, it is clear that most such violence, consistent with the general pattern, is committed by males (while exceptions have been noted, few serial or other mass killers are female).

Most violence involving male offenders has as its victim other males. Even here, however, there are a number of important sub-themes that need to be distinguished (Polk, 1994). One of the commonest of the male-on-male patterns involves the typical pub fight, or what might better be termed "honor contests." These are events, which often escalate rapidly in such leisure scenes as pubs, parties, beach outings, or other public settings, frequently involving a combination of the use of alcohol in a setting of primarily young males. What sparks the violence often appears to the outsider to be "trivial" (while it is obviously not so to those involved), including a minor jostle, an insult, a comment to a woman companion, or in some cases simply challenging eye contact. The participants are often provoked by what is seen as a challenge to their standing as males, in a word, to their honor. The initial intent of those involved is to argue and to fight, and the lethal consequences, when they occur, are not what was initially intended. In addition to being male, the participants in such disputes over honor are likely to come from the lower rungs of the economic ladder, they are young, and there is some evidence that they have histories of trouble and violence. This latter fact suggests that for some young males, violence has become a way of responding to social situations that allows them to control and direct social encounters. Others have pointed out that the honor contest functions within a clear set of social rules, involving an "opening move" on the part of one of the participants which sets up the initial challenge, which is then responded to by a "counter-move" by another which sets the encounter off in the direction of escalating violence.

Another rather different pattern involves the planned use of violence as a device for resolving a dispute that has extended over time. In this pattern, those involved have known each other for some time; in many cases they have even been close friends and shared resources. Something happens and the relationship unravels. Lethal violence becomes possible when the social circumstances of the males closes off legitimate forms of dispute resolution, as is the case of those deeply enmeshed in criminal ways of life and thus are unable to call upon the police or courts as a way of resolving their differences. Persons involved in dealing of drugs, for example, may be partners in crime for a period of time, and then one might lend money to the other for a drug deal. If the second person refuses to pay back the debt, the offended partner may feel he has little option but to use violence as a way to resolve the matter. This pattern, of course, can take other forms when the criminal activities are more tightly organized, and lead to a whole range of behaviors under the rubric of "offers that can not be refused."

A final male pattern involves the use of violence during the course of another crime, such as armed robbery or burglary. Here, as is the case with the dispute resolution scenario, at issue is the offender's willingness to engage in the very risky behavior of taking weapons into the scene of a crime (because, as a matter of fact, it is the offender who often ends up being the victim of the lethal violence).

Feminine Violence?

But what of violence involving women? Women, certainly, can be violent, and at times their violence takes lethal form. Feminine violence, however, is much less frequent (especially serious violence), it has different targets, and it is generally based in very different motivations than male lethal violence. Women are rarely involved in the above male scenarios of violence. Women rarely kill their male partners out of jealousy, despite the imagery encountered in detective fiction. Women almost never feel that they must use exceptional violence to defend their sense of honor. And, while women may have disputes with close associates, they rarely employ lethal violence as a way of resolving such personal conflicts, and they rarely are involved in deaths which occur in the course of such crimes as armed robbery or burglary (although occasionally a woman may be a co-defendant in such circumstances).

Women do engage in lethal violence, but that violence has a whole different feel to it than masculine violence. This difference is seen perhaps most clearly in homicides where the woman kills her male sexual partner. In a great majority of such cases, the woman is reacting to the precipitating violence of the male. In some of these cases, there is a physical confrontation between the man and the woman. The man employs some violence toward the woman, and the woman retaliates immediately with some form of defensive violence. In such cases, the woman may be able to plead successfully that either her acts constituted legitimate self-defense, or that because of the precipitating violence of the male, she experienced some form of diminished responsibility that lowers the level of criminal culpability for the violence. There are many other circumstances, however, where the capacity of the male for violence is large, and the resources available to the woman are slight. Here the woman may bide her time and concoct some form of plot to pull off the killing successfully, such as waiting until the male is drunk to the point of incapacitation, and then taking advantage of that moment to carry out the killing. While it may be the violence of the male that is the provoking feature of both of these forms of killing, in the second scenario the woman may find herself facing a charge of murder in its most serious form, since she used "malice aforethought" as part of the killing.

A second major overarching scenario of feminine violence is directed at children, nearly always the natural children of the women involved (Alder & Polk, 2001). Proportionally, women are much more likely to kill children than are men, and in fact this is the one form of violence where some investigations will report that there are as many female as male offenders. Care must be taken with this assertion, however, because women and men tend to have very different patterns involving lethal violence toward children. When women kill children they are the natural mothers of their victims. The most common patterns involve neonaticide (where the child dies in the first 24 hours after birth), homicide involving children as part of a suicide of the mother (often where the mother's motives appear to be "altruistic": because she expresses the view that they children are better off not being left behind without their mother's care), or situations where the mother suffers from some exceptional psychiatric disorder (for example, where her "voices" tell her that she must kill her child). The situations where children are victims of lethal violence makes a strong contribution to the need to differentiate gender in the analysis of violence, because while mothers are likely to feature in homicides of younger children (under the age of 6), when the victims are older, especially over the age of ten, the killer is virtually always a male.

In short, while women can be violent, and in fact women occasionally kill, most serious violence is emphatically male behavior. Women rarely are involved in honor contest violence, or feel the need to take up violence as a way of resolving a long-standing dispute, and they (despite what might be encountered in detective fiction) almost never kill their husband or sexual partner out of jealousy. The empirical data lead us, in other words, to the conclusion that not only are males more likely to engage in serious violence, but that there are systematic themes or "scenarios" within which the violence occurs.

It needs to be noted that there are some situations where both men and women exhibit some amount of violence. Family violence surveys have found persistently that when it comes to low levels of violence, such as pushing, shoving, slapping or verbal abuse, women may be as violent at men (Straus & Gelles, 1990). While such findings have provoked considerable controversy, it is important to be clear about at two components of features of this research. First, the findings often refer to levels of violence that are well below the point of producing serious physical injury, and there is little doubt that the systematic use of extreme levels of violence is distinctively masculine in character. As discussed above, homicide as an example is a crime that rarely involves female offenders being violent toward their male partner, and even where this is the case, in most instances that female violence is a reaction to prior violence of the male. Second, one should not be surprised if one finds violent males and then observes as well that there are violent family environments (where women, too, are part of the violent pattern). If one assumes that violence, like other social behavior is learned, then it makes sense that some boys and girls learn from an early age that violence is an accepted device for coping with stressful situations (by observing, for example, their mother striking them or their siblings). For the males, this learning can become more focused as the child moves into adolescence, and some may learn that for them violence "works" as a device for negotiating their social world. That violence may become progressively more directed to issues of control and competition, and more extreme as early adulthood is reached. Further, this learning of violence may evolve most readily in family environments where both mothers and fathers engage in some level of violence (recognizing that life-threatening violence is likely to be male initiated), because such settings clearly convey the message that violence is acceptable as a process for coping with situations of stress and conflict.

Controversies Regarding the Social Origins of Violence: A Biological/Evolutionary Perspective?

What is it about masculinity that provokes such violence? Here there are profound disagreements regarding where the answer might be found. One vector of disagreement concerns the social origins of violence. One current view, derived from evolutionary psychology, argues that men are violent because of evolutionary processes that select for violence (Daly & Wilson, 1988). In the human ancestral environment, according to this position, male aggressiveness and violence contributed to the successful emergence of the species, and can be found today in the tendencies for males to employ violence both to control the reproductive capacities of their sexual partners (hence the violence of males toward women as an expression of the "proprietariness" over them), and the violence between males, especially younger males, is a continuation of violence as a way of addressing the ever present problem of competition between males. This view, especially as expressed by Daly and Wilson (1988), is logically well crafted, and is immediately appealing in the way it recognizes the distinct patterns of violence, for example, the sexual proprietariness that is an essential feature of jealousy violence, and the centrality of honor and competition in many of the male-on-male scenes of violence.

Countering such assertions, sociologists are likely to point out that whatever may have held for early human environments, certainly over recent decades the nature of human competition and cooperation has changed profoundly. The humans currently who are the most successfully in the competition for resources in fact are the least likely to employ serious forms of violence as a tactic in their interpersonal negotiations, including dealing with competitors either for economic resources or in terms of the reproductive capacities of women. As such, the sociologists observe that it is those with the least amount of economic resources (that is, those less successful in the competition for these goods) who are the most violent, and they then turn to the task of assessing why this should be so. Put another way, the sharp differentials in the level of violence among and between cultural groups raises questions about any simple assertion that masculine violence across the board is to be accounted for with some form of genetic reasoning (Polk, 1994).

For those inclined toward sociological reasoning, a counter argument is that while there is a persistent problem of competition between males that each male must address, how that competition is negotiated is in large part shaped by the resources that are available. Some from an early age have access to a number of economic and social supports that help assure an easy movement through the important scenes of competition that males (or females) face as they age. Resources such as wealth, class and status position, and power assure that some from an early age negotiate their way through highly competitive school and professional training settings, which lead to successful entry into adulthood. The more empowerment that one has from such resources, the less likely that risky strategies of competition need to be considered, including the use of violence. Complex male and female successful identities can be shaped and forged for such individuals, without needing to back up their sense of self through the use of violence. For those less empowered, however, there is the constant struggle with the problem of status failure in school and the onset of adulthood with looming unemployment that may trigger for the extremely marginalized virtually a life on the edges of the society. Unsuccessful in other ways, one method of asserting one's manliness is through violence, by letting people know that you are not a wimp, nor a person that others can push around.

One recent line of thinking has argued that in some respects violence among young, lower-class males is one of the ways that such individuals are able to engage successfully in the business of "doing gender," that is, making a clear and public statement that they are emphatically males, and stand ready to respond, with violence if necessary, to any person who attempts the challenge their manhood. Some such challenges, of course, might come from other males, and here we see the playing out of the male-on-male pattern of violence that makes up the honor contest. Another form of competition concerns the male's relationship with a female partner, and here the actions may take the form of violence toward the woman as a device for exerting control over her, or perhaps violence directed at the sexual rival. Violence, in short, for some becomes a device for assertion of manhood, for sending the message that they are not persons to be trifled with (Messerschmidt, 1993). In this view it is the social context, not biology, which is responsible for shaping the violence.

Gender and the Instrumental Character of Violence

There is considerable controversy currently about how such patterns of violence fit into general notions of "masculinity" and "femininity." One line of research has argued that masculine violence and criminality tends to be viewed as rational and purposive, with the violence then serving "instrumental" ends, while in contrast feminine violence is more likely to be perceived as spontaneous, emotive and reactive in character (Campbell, 1993). In addition to fitting well with common public views of gender, it is possible to enter the data of violence and find verification for such arguments. Certainly those in the area of domestic violence have underscored the idea that much of male violence toward women, in contrast to a perception of such actions as being immediate outgrowths of arguments that escalate suddenly, is in fact a deep, purpose pattern of behavior that the male evolves as a persistent and willful mechanism of control. Put another way, the male uses violence deliberately to achieve his end of exerting successful control over his female partner. Similarly, much of domestic homicides where men kill their wives or sexual partners are far from being arguments which go out of control. Instead they show such elements as careful tracing of the woman's routine movements (so that she can be overtaken in a moment of maximum vulnerability), and planning which might include obtaining a lethal weapon. In contrast, much of women's violence toward men is highly reactive, with the woman striking back during the course of a violent episode that in fact has been initiated by the male.

While there are numerous cases of violence that demonstrate the apparent instrumental character of male violence, and the emotive and spontaneous character of female violence, there are important exceptions that raise questions about this hypothesis of gender difference. It is precisely this planned character that in some cases has created the need for the "battered woman syndrome" as a legal defense against a charge of criminal homicide. This issue arises in cases where the woman has planned the homicide, often because of her fear of the male capacity for violence, and her planning contains elements of intentional behavior that are central material elements in charge of murder. The battered woman syndrome defense has been introduced as a way of bringing into consideration the long pattern of physical abuse in these cases (which is argued to be the actual precipitating cause of the lethal violence), either as a way of lowering the level of culpability (to a charge of manslaughter, for example), or even in some cases to a plea of self-defense which, if successful, would mean that violence would be determined to be justifiable. Whatever the turmoil that lies behind the violence, the particular act is in the eyes of the law clearly "instrumental" and as such has the potential to attract maximum criminal sanctions.

A close inspection of a complete file of homicides is likely to show that, in addition to these cases, there are those where for a number of reasons the woman has decided that she wishes to terminate the relationship with her male partner, and she then enlists the help of either female or male associates (or both) to use homicide as the device for achieving the separation. While far from the most common cases of female spousal killing, the presence of some such violence, as well as the cases of battered women who kill their husbands, demonstrate that in some circumstances women, too, are capable of instrumental violence.

Further, sexual partners are not the only victims of the lethal violence of women. In fact, women in general are as likely to kill their natural child as they are their spouse. In some forms of child killing, the woman carefully plans her actions. This is particularly the case when a central goal of the violence is the suicide of the woman. Having made the decision to take her own life, it is common for the woman to kill the children so that they will not have to suffer being left in a world without their mother. The woman often leaves tragic suicide notes behind, providing detailed instructions for the funerals, including how the children should be dressed (Wallace, 1986; Alder & Polk, 2001).

These exceptions require that we refine Campbell's hypothesis to recognize that at least some of the violence of women can be highly intentional, rational, and instrumental. In addition, consideration of the themes which run through the distinctive scenarios of male violence require further refinement because the nature of the elements of intentionality, that is the component elements of instrumentality, are quite different across the different forms of male homicide. When violence is chosen as a mechanism for resolving a long simmering dispute, its "instrumental" feature is manifest. In the situation of honor contests, the situation is more complicated, since the violence may be quite spontaneous, and the death far from what was intended by either party at the beginning of the interaction. There is a further problem, of course, because in the Campbell formulation, it is hard to see a place for the obvious emotional and expressive actions that are present in the accounts of at least some masculine violence. While Campbell's formulation provides the valuable contribution of a language within which male and female violence might be described, ultimately it may be important to go beyond the terms "instrumental" and "expressive" to account for gender differences in violence, especially in terms of addressing the theoretical forces at work which lead to such differences by sex in the meanings attached to violence.

The Utility of the Concept of "Masculinity"

There is, in fact, considerable turmoil in the current discussions regarding masculinity and crime. The more crafted analyses have pointed out that there are not patterns of "masculinity," but "masculinities" that must be considered (Messerschmidt, 1993). There is no single cluster of ideas that defines a masculine ideal of violence; rather, as the above patterns show, there are a number of patterned ways, much like scripts, that men become involved in violence. One can argue, of course, that there are dominant patterns that hold out principles of "manhood" which are understood as being general scenarios that guide male behavior. It is only relatively recently that there has been a challenge to the idea of the sexual attractiveness of the dark powerful barbarian, whom we are told to expect that quivering females hope will choose them for sexual coupling. Such stories run so deep in the culture, as illustrated by legends, drama, fiction and films, that one can see the ready appeal of the psychological evolutionists and their reference to masculine patterns of dominance and aggression emerging out of ancestral environments.

What is also clear, however, is that there are many such patterns of idealized manhood that are available is guides to behavior, and often the directions taken in one direction (for example, avoidance of violence) will be in conflict with another (where violence in a particular scene, as in the honor contest, may be seen as an imperative). Given this complexity, it should come as no surprise that there are those who argue that, in fact, the concept of "masculinity" as currently understood contributes little but confusion to an understanding of the behavior of males (Collier, 1998). If it is understood that what at least some of these arguments are addressing is the multitude of choices that confront a young male as he moves from childhood through adolescence into adulthood, then there may be some merit in what is being suggested. That is, young males as they move through these very complicated years will be confronted with a wide-ranging set of expectations, and these expectations often will be in conflict. There is no simple or single ideal of "each on of us as a real man" which operates to define and guide youthful male behavior, including violence. If the theoretical issue being addressed is how does a diverse group of individual young males move through these important years, the very diversity of their behavior indicates that there is no single standard of "masculinity" by which the behavior of emergent adults is being shaped.

Nonetheless, when it comes to violence, it is emphatically male conduct that we are addressing, both in terms of its character and it numbers. Furthermore, there are persistent patterns to the violence that can be identified. While much more empirical work needs to be done, these patterns often take the form of "scripts" or scenarios of behavior. The steps of the honor contest, from the opening move, counter-move, and then the mutual agreement to engage in violence, serve as culturally defined patterns which individuals know about, and draw upon, as they become swept up in such violence. What is important here is that the young males who engage in these exchanges do not themselves "invent" the steps involved in the honor contest. They, and the friends that make up the social audience in such encounters, "know the moves" that are expected as the violence unfolds. There certainly may be unique and innovative features to any honor contest, but what the general notions of maleness and masculinity provide are the basic scripts which establish for the participants the expected social rules by which the participants know and understand what each step means, what choices are available, which choices are those that "real men" might follow, and where the interaction is headed.

Within contemporary cultures, in other words, there are available as masculine ideals a variety of these scenarios that are understood as constituting the "rules of the game." Clearly, we may understand these rules even if we do not engage in an honor contest. In fact, both men and women are likely to have very clear ideas about such social scenes, and one of the pressures that may operate on some males is that the encounter evolves in front of potential or actual sexual partners, who will then "judge" the "manliness" of the male by virtue of how he negotiates his way through the interactions.

In a similar way, there are some clear expectations held by some males about what they should do in situations of jealousy. While some males, in fact hopefully a very large proportion, respond to the loss of the affections of a woman partner they value highly by some form of hurt withdrawal, others are provoked into a pattern of attempts at obsessive control which will in extreme forms lead to lethal violence. Here, again, however, the pattern seems to function much like a "script" which guides the male behavior. One indication of this can be found in the language so common in jealousy homicides. In Australia, Canada, Great Britain, and the United States over and over one hears the phrase: "if I can't have you, no one will.": chilling, deadly, but repetitive. As with the honor contest, the males are drawing upon a scripted vocabulary that guides their actions, and, find expression in their very words.

There are, in other words, persistent and repeated patterns of masculine violence that are played out in ways that indicate that the males are drawing upon their understandings of these as they proceed into the violence encounters. It follows that one reasonable line for research is to understand the nature of the scripts, their elements, and how the fit into wider understanding of masculinity (or masculinities), and different males negotiate their way through the complicated expectations represented by these scenarios.

But such scripted patterns are not exclusively male. While much less common, there are distinctive feminine patterns of violence, including lethal violence. The battered woman syndrome is obviously one such pattern, but there are others, especially in terms of women's violence toward children. One important fact here is that overwhelmingly violence toward children is a result of actions by the natural mother of the child. One especially disturbing patterns involves mothers (mostly young) whose actions (or inactions) result in the death of their baby within a few minutes of its birth. This pattern, known as "neonaticide" again has been observed in Australia, Canada, Great Britain, and the United States, and involves most frequently women who simply cannot and will not face the reality of their impending birth. Their denial is so strong that it even persists when the infant is born (not infrequently in a bathroom of a household that does not suspect either the pregnancy, or the birth when it occurs). When confronted afterward, the young woman is likely to say "I just hoped it would go away" or something like "I just could not face what people would say."

The position taken here is that while it is important to recognize that there are problems in conceptions and definitions of masculinity and femininity, these difficulties should not lead to the abandonment of these terms as guides either to understanding violence, or to carrying out future research. It is certainly the case that young men and women as they move through adolescence and into adulthood will be presented with myriad and at times conflicting definitions of idealized masculine or feminine behavior. There are, however, clearly patterned expectations about the way males, and females, ought to position themselves with respect to violence and the social scenes that produce it. Some of the most important questions, in fact, involve the issue of how and why most young people avoid violence, especially violence that might take lethal form. This avoidance is not because males are unaware of the expectations held out in the various scripts of violence, such as the honor contest. One does not have to be Conan the Barbarian to know what is expected of a "real man" when confronted with a challenge to masculine honor. Most males, however they might know the script, chose to conduct their existence such that they are not placed in situations where they are expected to be violent, or they find ways of withdrawing should they somehow find themselves in such scenes. One important line for future research, it could be argued, is precisely how these protective and restraining behaviors are deemed the desirable choice in encounters with a potential for violence. Included in such research would be a focus on the social audience, including the role of women, who often are critical in directing the flow of the behavior either away from, or toward, escalating violence.

Summary

In summary, the data of crime indicate that overwhelming serious risk taking, as reflected in violence, is the behavior of males. This raises important questions about what it is about males, and masculinity, that triggers these higher levels of violence. While some have suggested, perhaps correctly, that there is considerable confusion in current discussions of both masculinity and femininity as these relate to the question of violence, nonetheless there appear to be important and repeated patterns of both masculine and feminine violence (although of course feminine violence is much less common). Understanding both the elements of these patterns, as reflected in what appear to be the highly scripted scenarios within which these encounters evolve, and their social origins, is an important and continuing task for contemporary criminology.

Discussion Questions

1. What do we mean by the terms "masculinities" and "femininities"? How do these terms relate to the concept of crime? What are the differences between "masculine" and "feminine" violence? Give examples in your answer.

2. Explain why "masculinities" have been overlooked by criminologists until recently. In other words, why has analysis of crime (and offenders) neglected "masculinities" as an explanatory construct?

3. What difference does it make—to both the analysis and response to crime—if we place gender (especially "masculinities") at the forefront of our theorizing? Explain how our thinking about crime and offenders might be transformed.

4. Identify the two theoretical pathways, or explanations, that have been suggested to account for the predominance of males in homicide offending.

5. Describe some of the scenarios of masculine violence. What are some of the major motivational themes that accompany these scenarios, or patterns, of homicide?

6. How are youth, and social class, implicated in patterns of masculine violence? How would you explain this phenomenon?

7. What is the relationship between masculinity/femininity and the function or purpose of the violence? Relate you answer to the character of the violence: instrumental versus expressive. Give examples of specific scenarios in which this dichotomy might play out.

8. In what ways might it be necessary to modify Campbell's hypothesis regarding the link between gender and the function or purpose of violence? Provide a rationale for your answer.

9. What are "cultures of masculinity"? How might these cultures be embedded in the organizational practices and behaviors of police and other agents of the criminal justice system?

10. How do men and women come to acquire the "rules of the game" concerning appropriate gender behavior? How might we begin to change or at least modify these rules so as to reduce the level of violence in society?

CHAPTER 12

Accounting for Hate Crime

Barbara Perry

A 19-year-old junior at Harvard paints a Swastika on the dormitory room of a Jewish classmate. A 35-year-old construction worker beats his black co-worker. A 50-year-old supervisor verbally harasses her lesbian receptionist. A 16-year-old high school drop-out shoots the East Indian owner of a local restaurant.

The discipline of criminology has failed to provide a coherent framework for understanding the diverse phenomenon—such as those noted above—which we refer to as "hate crimes." The discipline has not seriously addressed the sociocultural underpinnings of the violent oppression of subordinate communities. As the following brief critique will reveal, traditional criminological theories lack sufficient explantory power in the context of hate crime. However, the contemporary framework referred to as structured action theory provides a valuable corrective to the limitations of criminological theory in helping us to understand the subjective and structural underpinnings of hate crime. Specifically, it allows us to conceptualize hate crime as a mechanism for the relational construction of difference.

Strain Theory

The majority of scholarly (and journalistic) accounts of hate crime and hate groups to have emerged in recent years are at least implicitly driven by strain theory. There is a tendency to argue that hate crime is symptomatic of the general malaise, the sense of threat felt by those who see themselves as "victims of affirmative action." From this perspective, hate crime (illegitimate means) is an outgrowth of enhanced economic competition for jobs (legitimate means). Hate offenders are said to blame their economic instability or lack of job security on the immigration of "foreigners" or the global financial conspiracy of the Jews, for example. Levin and McDevitt (1993) draw attention to such resentment as a possible motive in hate crime. Similarly, Kelly (1993:4) introduces his collected edition on hate crime with the assertion that hate crimes are "occasioned by systematic unemployment and poverty that live side by side with colossal affluence."

There is no doubt that hate crime occuring in the historical (recession) and sociogeographical (inner city) context of economic instability may be in part a response to perceived strain. Those facing downward mobility may indeed lash out against scapegoats whom they hold to be responsible for their displacement—women, immigrants, African-Americans, etc. However, not the least of the inconsistencies here is that if strain accounted for hate crimes, then those most prevalent among the victims would instead be perpetrators. Who is more disadvantaged—economically, socially and politically—than women and racial minorities? Yet these groups are much more likely to be victims than offenders.

In relative terms, it is apparent that hate crime offenders are not all "powerless," or alienated, deprived youth. Richard Girnt Butler, a recent leader of Aryan Nations, was an aerospace engineer; Robert Miles, who has played leadership roles in many white supremacist groups (e.g., Grand Dragon of the KKK) was a manager for an insurance company. Hamm's investigation of U.S. skinheads, for example, reveals that they are in fact "working class conformists with a hyperactive commitment to the goals and means of the dominant American culture. They are often multi-talented; they seem to be dedicated workers and responsible students" (Hamm, 1994a:130).

The most damning counter-evidence is that concerning secondary victimization of minorities. As legitimate agents of social control, police officers are the very embodiment of social power in our culture. Yet with all their available legitimate means and instruments of control, police often resort to the exercise of harassment and brute force, against not just criminals but also against those deemed unworthy of their protection—e.g., gays, black youths, etc. Comstock (1989), Rosen (1992), and Herek (1992) are among those who have documented the tendency of police officers (not to mention prosecutors and judges) to harass and even physically assault gay men or lesbians. Documentation of secondary victimization—and outright brutality—against racial minorities is even more readily available. The 1994 Mollen Commission on police corruption in New York City revealed some telling findings with respect to police violence against minorities, as did the Christopher Commission with respect to Los Angeles police officers.

In sum, strain theory fails as a satisfactory account of hate crime, since it acknowledges neither the cultural diffusion of prejudice and bigotry, nor the use of hate violence as an exercise of power by both the powerless and, especially, the empowered. In this sense, it shares the primary weakness of control theory, discussed below: an inability to account for the inclusion of otherwise conformist and integrated individuals in the ranks of hate offenders.

Social Control Theory

According to Hirschi's variant of control theory, criminal offenders are those for whom the "bonds" to conventional society have been loosened. That is, the constraints which ordinarily inhibit deviant behavior have, by some unidentified process, deteriorated to an extent that the perpetrator lacks the incentive to abide by the law. In Hirschi's (1969:16) words, "delinquent acts result when an individual's bond to society is weak or broken."

It is unlikely that we can make sense of hate crime within this framework. In fact, some of the most heinous and brutal acts of violence have been carried out in the name of religion and religious beliefs—central elements of "conventional" society. For example, some of the most violent and militant of the right-wing extremist groups (e.g., Aryan Nation; Covenant, Sword and Arm of the Lord; the Order) are saturated in the principles of Christian Conservatism and Christian Identity. Their readings of scripture identify a hierarchy of race and gender which serves to explicity justify their assaults on the "other."

Similarly, while hate crime offenders can be said to be violating the criminal code, it is not so apparent that they are violating normative standards in the United States. For Hirschi, it is the internalization of norms that inhibits criminal activity. In the case of hate crime, it is the internalization of norms which encourages criminal activity. In a generally racist, sexist, homophobic culture, violence motivated by hatred conforms to what is a normatively unjust value system. Moreover, as implied above, social control theory shares with strain theory the failure to address the cultural meaning of hate crime. That is, neither considers the role that hate crimes play in assigning meaning and identity to social beings. In this respect, labelling theory appears at first glance to hold some promise.

Labelling Theory

According to labelling theory, deviance is a social construct arising out of a process of "tagging" or labelling those deemed—by the audience—in some way defective or deviant. The resultant negative identity might also be understood as a stigma, a sign of disrepute—"an attribute that is deeply discrediting" (Goffman, 1963:3). According to Goffman (1963:3), those who have been stigmatized as "different" in some socially relevent way are reduced to a "tainted and discounted" image. One might "stretch" this and thereby conclude that it is their deviant designation—the stigma—which makes some individuals and groups vulnerable to official and unofficial acts of oppression.

But this is less than satisfying, since it generally explains only the "secondary deviance" of the victims, not the offenders. Moreover, hate crime offenders may meet with less negative censure than the victims of their violence. The "criminality" of those motivated by hatred of the "other" often inspires acclaim rather than condemnation, as when the secondary victimization of gays is supported by a homophobic police department, or when a neo-Nazi executes a Jew. Even on a more basic level, it is apparent that in a culture as chauvinistic as that of the United States, persecution of minority victims often goes unpunished. Ultimately, then there is often no process of stigmatization, or of negative identification applied to hate crime offenders.

Labelling theory also suffers from a failure to explicitly concretize the context in which crime occurs. What are the structural and cultural inhibitors and facilitators of hate crime? While labelling theory does address the issue of power, it often does so from a pluralist stand-point. That is it implies that "society is composed of a variety of interest groups or segments, and that power is spread among a number of groups or segments" (Lynch & Groves, 1989:46). Thus, it fails to address the impact of the carefully constructed hierarchies of race, class and gender which are so crucial to an understanging of hate crime. Empirically, labelling theorists have been much more interested in examining the social construction of "sensational" deviants, rather than their victimization.

These short-comings notwithstanding, there is yet a glimmer of hope to be derived from the interactionist perspective of which labelling theory is a part. Such approaches turn our attention to the importance of the construction of meaning and identity through interaction—this is a useful insight to bear in mind when examining hate crime. This particular crime, does in fact assert the hegemonic identity of the offender, at the same time that it reaffirms the subordination of the victim.

Critical Criminology

Critical criminology is a useful corrective to the theoretical tendencies to neglect the structural underpinnings of crime. And, it explicitly confronts at least two of the primary conceptual "facts" associated with hate crime specifically: marginalization and power. Both themes are crucial to a fully political understanding of hate crimes, given that they are themselves exercises of power intended to assert the marginal status of victims, and simultaneously, the relatively privileged status of the offenders. Moreover, the understanding of hate crime requires consideration of the specific socio-historical context in which it emerges—an approach which is also a hallmark of recent critical theorizing.

However, critical analyses of minorities and crime remain relatively underdeveloped. There is still a stubborn tendency to prioritize class and economic relations as determinant of crime and criminalization. This is an inadequate account, especially when dealing with hate crime. In many ways, critical criminology suffers from the same flaws as strain theory. It too, is unable to account for the relative lack of hate crime offending by those who are most marginalized—people of color, women, and gays. Conversely, it also fails to make sense of hate crimes perpetrated by the least marginalized—white, middle-class males, police officers, criminal justice officials, etc.

Critical criminology is most concerned with the ways in which marginalization contributes to crime. What of the obverse? What of the way in which crime contributes to marginalization? This is what hate crime accomplishes. It constructs the relative identities of both offender and victim by simultaneously asserting one and subordinating, if not annihilating the other.

Marxist-informed analyses of crime also fail as an explanatory schema in another crucial respect. Although seen as an outcome of broader socio-economic processes, crime itself is not regarded as a process. The criminal event itself is seen as a static, singular event. While placed in its broad historical context, crime is not also placed in its immediate subjective context. It is crucial to examine hate crime in terms of the meanings it has not just for the impersonal structural imperatives of capitalism, but also for the perpetrator, victim and their respective reference communities. This latter ability does not inhere in critical criminology.

Summing Up

As the foregoing critique has implied, criminology has yet to come to terms with the phenomenon we have come to know as hate crime. Existing theory tends to neglect either or both the structural underpinnings of hate crime, and the situated process that it entails. To fully understand hate crime, one must put it in its sociocultural context. In particular, hate crime must be understood as one among an array of mechanisms by which deeply ingrained sets of power relationships are maintained. It is, in short, constituted of and by difference. In fact, as the remainder of this chapter will argue, hate crime is a vitally important mechanism for "doing difference."

Structured Action Theory: Doing Difference

Structures of power and oppression permeate society. They inform and are reinforced by a myriad of institutional forms. Moreover, power and privilege are unequally allocated along hierarchies shaped by such dimensions as race, class and gender. Hegemonic visions of "how the world should be" find substance and support most strongly in dominant structures: labor, power, sexuality (Connell, 1987; Messerschmidt, 1993, 1997) and culture (Martin & Jurik, 1996). It is these contexts—labor, power, sexuality and culture—that specifically condition human action, identity and place in such a way that hierarchies of difference may be maintained or challenged. These structures of oppression and their supporting institutional patterns provide the context and constraints within which we "do difference" as human actors. Moreover, it is the "interactions between individuals and groups (that) is the medium for much institutional functioning" (Acker, 1992:568). These structural arrangements define the standards to which we hold ourselves and others accountable with respect to the appropriate enactment of categories of difference (West & Fenstermaker, 1997).

At all times, in all situations, actors are concerned with whether their behavior *will be seen to be* in accordance with approved standards for their assigned identity. Within the essentialist understanding that dominates Western notions of identities, there is very little space for ambiguity, or crossing the boundaries between categories of difference. Speaking of gender, specifically, West and Zimmerman (1987:136) contend that "a person engaged in virtually any activity may be held accountable for performance of that activity as a *woman* or a *man*, and their incumbency in one or the other sex category can be used to legitimate or discredit their other activities." In other words, accountability involves the assessment of behavior as either conforming or deviating from culturally normative standards. So it is that we are discouraged from the "attempt to cross the line, to transgress, desert or quit" (Bourdieu, cited in Fine, 1997:58). Consequently, when individuals or groups cross those boundaries, when they fail to perform their identity in normative ways, they are held to be doing difference inappropriately, and thereby leave themselves open to censure. It is in this context that hate crime emerges as a resource for doing difference, and punishing those who do difference inappropriately. In other words, hate motivated violence is used to police the boundaries between groups by reminding the Other of his/her "place." Perpetrators thus recreate their own masculinity, or whiteness, for example, while punishing the victims for their deviant identity performance.

Doing Difference, Doing Hate Crime

First and foremost, there are extensive cultural mythologies that facilitate inequities and corresponding hate motivated violence. It is within culture that we find "a range of rules: "is's" and "oughts," "do's" and "dont's," "cans" and "cannots," "thou shalts" and "thou shalt nots" (Goldberg, 1990:297). Cultural discourses normalize particular representations of groups independently and in relation to others—in ways that reinforce hierarchical structures. Thus, presumed characteristics of groups are institutionalized in ideologies and stereotypes of racial or gender inferiority, in laws that marginalize or exclude particular groups and individuals, in media depictions which demonize the Other.

Where the popular image of the Other is constructed in negative terms—as it frequently is—group members may be victimized on the basis of those perceptions. For example, cultural assumptions about men, women and the relationships between them condone and often encourage victimization of women as women, because they commonly objectify and minimize the value of women. In other words, "men physically and emotionally abuse women because they *can*, because they live in a world that gives them permission" (Pharr, 1988:14). Cultural constructs surrounding women's experiences of violence overwhelmingly lay blame on the victim. If only she had not been out alone; if only she had prepared a hot, appetizing meal; if only she had not dressed so provocatively, she would not have been assaulted, battered or raped. In other words, if she had "done femininity" appropriately rather than oppositionally, she would not have suffered. Violence is a predictable response to women who violate the gender order. In contrast, the male offender is exonerated, often rewarded. He is "doing masculinity" normally; he is performing masculinity is a socially sanctioned, legitimate manner, in accordance with his right and duty to chasten "uppity women" (Sheffield, 1989).

Moreover, the implied good/bad woman dichotomy is especially problematic for women of color, who, according to strictures of the racial hierarchy, can never achieve "goodness." More so even than white women, women of color are characterized as inviting violent assault. The latitude allowed them for enacting femininity is even more circumscribed than that allowed white women. African-American women, for example, are "safe" only when enacting the roles of *mule* or *Mammy*. So narrow are these notions of black womanhood that few women could possibly live up to them. Consequently, strong black women are assigned the labels—often by black and white cultures alike—of *Jezebels, Matriarchs* or *Uppity Black Women* who transcend both racial and gender boundaries. It is this intersection of race, gender and sexuality which shapes the victimization of black women and other women of color (Crenshaw, 1994; Collins, 1993). The Jezebel image of the black prostitute is perhaps most damning, since it constructs black women as sexually promiscuous and therefore enticing, seductive. It is "impossible" to rape a prostitute since she is always on the job.

In short, race conditions the gender imagery to which women are held accountable, especially in terms of their sexuality. While both white women and women of color are vulnerable to gendered violence, the cultural permission for such victimization varies dramatically. As argued above, white women are often victimized because they are perceived to have crossed some boundary of appropriate feminine behavior; women of color because they are perceived to be, "by nature," sexually available and provocative.

Because categorical differences between groups are assumed to be accompanied by differences in capacities, there are also dramatic discrepancies in the place and treatment of groups in the context of labor. The division of labor thus becomes a potential source of identification and of empowerment, or conversely, disempowerment (Messerschmidt, 1993). For example, the presumption of racial hierarchies has had, and continues to have, a profound impact on the place of minority groups within the labor process. In particular, people of color have traditionally been marginalized and exploited as free, cheap and malleable labor (Young, 1990). People of color who presume to advance on the economic ladder are perceived as unfair and undeserving competitors, and takers of "white" jobs. They are seen to have "overstepped" the economic boundaries which have long contributed to their marginalization. Consequently, white fear and resentment are frequently and viciously translated into racial violence. Ethnoviolence is an attempt to reclaim the advantages of whiteness. It is an assertion of racial superiority and, more important, proprietorship: to the white man belong the spoils, not some "third world invader." Violence motivated by the resentment of labor competition provides the perpetrator with the opportunity to publicly announce his indignation, and correspondingly, his "right to work."

Part of this agenda to regain white privilege involves a backlash against immigrants. While immigrants have historically been associated with moral and cultural threats, they have also been targets of racial animus on the basis of their perceived economic threat. Key to the hostility is the assumption that immigrants will not work hard, but will nonetheless steal valuable employment opportunities from white workers. Interestingly, even as immigrants attempt to create for themselves a productive racial identity, they are demonized. Rather than reward their initiative, the white hosts punish them through harassment and violence. In recent years, those of Hispanic and Asian descent have taken the brunt of the anti-immigrant violence, for slightly different reasons.

Hispanics—Mexicans in particular—are often held responsible for the dual threats of wage depression and competition for unskilled and semi-skilled jobs. There is an abundance of examples to illustrate the link between job competition and racially motivated violence. Hispanic day laborers and those living in migrant worker camps are frequent victims. In 1992, six white males armed with baseball bats beat a Hispanic man in an Alpine, CA migrant workers' camp. They later bragged about "kicking Mexican ass" (Southern Poverty Law Center, 1997:223). It was not only the particular victim that was being admonished. The beating also served notice that Mexicans as a class were not welcome. The victim was but one symbol of the unwillingness of his people to say in their place, i.e., across the border.

The economic activity of Asian immigrants and Asian Americans provokes similar resentment. However, in this case, it emerges out of hostility toward the perceived success of the "model minority." Regardless of their diversity and uneven performance in the United States, Asians are inscribed with the mantle of prosperity. They risk reprisal when they become viable, if not superior competitors. The months of violence, harassment and intimidation experienced by Vietnamese shrimpers in Texas illustrates the point. Supported by the KKK, local white shrimpers engaged in a campaign of violence from 1979 to 1980, which included sinking the boats belonging to the Vietnamese, cutting their fishing nets, assaults and harassment. Gilbert Pampa, then director of the federal Community Relations Service, observed that

> There was displeasure on the part of the other fishermen con-
> cerning the overindulgence of refugees. [The American fisher-
> men] did not feel that the refugees were competing in the Amer-
> ican way. The refugees worked on Sundays, stayed longer hours on
> the bay, and sometimes caught shrimp outside certain demarcat-
> ed areas of the bay. [The Americans] felt that this was unfair to
> them, and the competition turned to open conflict (cited in the
> U.S. Commission on Civil Rights, nd:51).

To white workers, Asian laborers have the appearance of overachievers who must be curbed if white workers are to retain their image as disciplined and worthy laborers.

The importance of power as a cornerstone of the politics of difference goes beyond purely economic concerns. "Power" is a much broader con-cept, encompassing "the ability to impose a definition of the situation, to set the terms in which events are understood and issues discussed, to formulate ideas and define morality, in short, to assert hegemony" (Connell, 1995:107). Power, then, consists in the ability to set the terms of discourse and action, and to impose a particular type of order. Consequently, relations of power are fre-quently contested arenas in the struggles over subordination and domination.

Racially motivated violence is directly implicated in efforts to maintain unequal relations of power. It is itself a mechanism of social power by which white males in particular assert a particular version of hegemonic whiteness. It is not difficult to trace the history of racially motivated violence during periods when the dominance of whites was perceived to be at risk—periods in which this identity was reconstructed through the exercise of vio-lence as a resource for "doing race." Nor is it difficult to identify contem-porary illustrations.

Violence in general has long been accepted as a means of flexing one's muscles, both literally and figuratively. Racially motivated violence, specifi-cally, continues to be a mechanism for doing so in such a way as to reinforce the privilege of whiteness and the subjugation of color. It represents a "will to power" by which the very threat of otherwise unprovoked acts of vio-lence "deprives the oppressed of freedom and dignity" (Young, 1995:83). Conversely, both the threat and use of violence by white perpetrators enhance their authority in the eyes of the communities of both the victim and the offender. Violence is empowering for its users: physical dominion implies a corresponding cultural mastery. Gunner Lindberg boasted in a let-ter of his killing of a Vietnamese man, Thien Minh Ly:

> Oh I killed a jap a while ago. I stabbed him to death at Tuslin High
> School . . . I walked right up to him and he was scared . . . he got
> happy that he wasn't gona get jumped. Then I hit him . . . I
> stabbed him about 7 or 8 times he rolled over a little so I stabbed
> his back out 18 or 19 times then he layed flat and I slit one side of
> his throat on his jugular vein . . . I stabbed him about 20 or 21
> times in the heart (cited in Phan, online:2).

The murderer's use of the derogatory label "jap" implies the racial distancing and animosity that underlie Lindberg's motive. He signifies his dominant whiteness by derogating Ly's Asian identity. That Ly was in fact Vietnamese and not Japanese further confirms Lindberg's presumption of superiority and hauteur. It is enough to know that Ly was Asian—no need to discern his true ethnicity or national origin. Any Asian could be at risk. Thus, the entire community is put on notice. Moreover, Lindberg's awareness that his racial identity was reinforced by his acts is clear in his pretentious statement within the letter: ". . . here's the clippings from the newspaper we were on all the channels." Lindberg assumes that his audience—upon learning of his exploits in the media—will judge his whiteness and not find him lacking. He is appropriately accountable to his race, given his eagerness to destroy the Other. No race traitor there; rather Lindberg announces through his actions that he is in solidarity with the white race, thereby preserving white privilege and position.

Such racial constructions, however, are dynamic and relational. Not only does this example illustrate how perpetrators empower whiteness through violence. It is also suggestive of the opposite: disempowering the victims' communities. Ly's death—like other hate motivated assaults—also represents an effort to render impotent the targeted group. Individual assaults are as a warning sign to others like the victim—you could be next. Richard Wright, in his now classic *Black Boy,* speaks to the vicarious experience of racial violence, when he says that "the things that influenced my conduct as a Negro did not have to happen to me directly; I needed but to hear of them to feel their full effects in the deepest layers of my consciousness." A black person or a Korean person or an Hispanic person need not have been a victim personally. Like Wright they are all too aware of their consistent vulnerability because of their race. The immutability of their racial identity invokes hopelessness—they are victimized for reasons they cannot change. In the midst of the "Dot Busters" campaign of terror against Asian Indians in Jersey City, an open letter made clear the generalized vulnerability of a group: "If I'm walking down the street and I see a Hindu and the setting is right, I will just hit him or her" (cited in "Racial Violence Against Asian Americans," 1993). Thus, hate crimes have the potential to throw an entire community into paralysis, forcing them to withdraw further into themselves. The victimized group may redefine itself as powerless in the face of the racist onslaught.

Paradoxically, efforts to render minority communities impotent can backfire. Rather than hobbling the victim group, they may in fact mobilize the community. This was the case in New York City, for example, where Haitians accompanied by other Caribbeans demonstrated angrily, vocally and visibly against the racist violence represented by Louima's brutal beating and sodomization at the hands of police officers. While innumerable victims had previously remained silent out of fear and intimidation, the publicity surrounding Louima's victimization galvanized the community into action.

Unfortunately, this posture of empowerment is often seen as an affront to white power. The victim community is perceived to be violating the anticipated rules of behavior. Instead of accepting their subordination, they resist it. In such a context, incidents of hate crime may escalate in retaliation. Consider the case of Farmington, New Mexico in the mid-1970s. In response to the vicious murders of three American Indian men, local Navajo activists established the Coalition for Navajo Liberation. As the coalition dug in its heels and intensified its demands for justice, the antagonism of the white community became clear. Rather than discourage anti-Navajo violence, the activism of the Coalition for Navajo Liberation seemed to inspire it, as became evident in the increase in the number of drive-by shootings at hogans, and at sheep tended by Navajo people (Barker, 1992). Seen in this light, hate crime is a reactionary tool, a resource for the reassertion of whiteness over color. It is a form of "resistance to any diminishment in the authorial claims of a particular white identity" (Hesse, Rai, Bennett & McGilchrist, 1992:172).

The final major axis upon which structural patterns of inequality rests is sexuality. To the extent that hegemonic forms of identity exist at any historical period, they serve to create a hierarchy around sexual values and practices. In short, each culture can be characterized by a series of definitions of "appropriate" and "inappropriate" sexual forms. Given these definitions—which might include prohibitions on racial or gendered couplings—certain behaviors and identities become marginalized at best, stigmatized and demonized at worst. "Doing gender," for example, is explicitly concerned with structuring differences between males and females, with creating "essential" natures specific to each gender. Consequently, contemporary sexuality (and marriage) is predicated upon the normalcy of opposite sex relationships. Homosexuals, for example, refuse to be forced into these "natural" binary categories of masculine or feminine. Thus, by definition, homosexuality transcends the boundaries our culture has so conscientiously erected between the genders, lapsing into the category of deviance. This violation ultimately make them vulnerable to stigmatization and finally to violent repression. Hate crime victim William Hassel's two teenage assailants were clearly hostile to his refusal to "be a man." Throughout the attack—at knifepoint—the pair continuously challenged his masculinity, berating him for crossing the gender line, for being a failed man. They threatened to complete his emasculation physically. According to Hassel's (1992:144-145) account,

> They made me address them as "Sir." They made me beg them to
> be made into a real woman. They threatened to castrate me. They
> threatened to emasculate me. They called me "Queer," "Faggot."
> One of them urinated on me. They threatened me with sodomy.

Homophobia and gay-bashing can thus be explained by "the degree to which the fact of homosexuality threatens the credibility of a naturalized ideology of gender and a dichotomized social world" (Connell, 1987:248). Violations of the normative rules of sexuality provide an important motive for violence against gays. In West's terms, homosexuals are "called to account for" their failure to do gender as prescribed (West & Zimmerman, 1987).

Moreover, gay-bashing provides an ideal context in which the perpetrators can conclusively establish what they *are*, i.e., manly, virile men. Recall the importance of accountability here: one must be seen (and interpreted) to be masculine in the prevailing sense of the term. And violence is a tried and true means to this end. Moreover, gay-bashers are most at pains to prove the very essence of their masculinity: heterosexuality. This may take the form of "cruising for chicks," or boasting of their (hetero)sexual exploits. But it often asserts itself in the form of violence against homosexuals. To quote a confirmed gay-basher interviewed by Collins, "I tell you, (the) Blue Boys are male. We're heteros. We have girlfriends and wives. We're out there fucking chicks every night and we have nothing to do with any fag shit" (Collins, 1992:193). Again, denial of the "unnatural" reinforces the "natural" heterosexuality of their emerging masculinity. Ironically, then, gay-bashers are not so much violating the norms of society (re: violence), as they are reaffirming a much more important set of norms revolving around sexuality. Their activities reflect the performance of the most salient features of a culturally approved hegemonic masculinity: aggression, domination and heterosexuality.

Conclusion

The sort of sociological and cultural analysis of hate crime suggested herein allows us to recognize that it is nested in a structural complex of relations of power grounded simultaneously in race, class, gender and sexuality. Structured action theory enables us to see hate crime as a forceful illustration of what it is to engage in situated conduct. The interactions between subordinate and dominant groups provides a context in which both compete for the privilege to define difference in ways which either perpetuate of reconfigure hierarchies of social power. Simultaneous and oppositional efforts to do difference set up tensions, in which the act of victimization co-constructs the victim and perpetrator. This confrontation is informed by the broader cultural and political arrangements which "allocate rights, privilege and prestige according to biological or social characteristics" (Sheffield, 1995:438). Perpetrators attempt to reaffirm their dominant identity, their access to resources and privilege, while at the same time limiting the opportunities of the victims to express their own needs.

However, the communities bearing the brunt of hate motivated crime have not been passive victims of the varied forms of violence they experienced. On the contrary, in recent years many have become very active in asserting the legitimacy of their identities, challenging heterosexism, patriarchy, racism and bigotry, and resisting the cultural and individual forms of violence to which they are subjected. It is not surprising that such challenges have emerged in response to hate crime, since hegemonic formations are subject to ongoing crisis tendencies which open up space for counter-hegemonic strategies. In other words, hegemony implies its own potential demise, since any hegemonic formation is subject to ongoing strain, resistance and transformation. It is a process of struggle. It is in this space that campaigns against the negative and violent politics of difference must be waged in order to transform current patterns into a positive politics of difference. The perceived threats to which hate crimes are a response are themselves indicative of the crisis tendencies that constantly throw the hegemonic order into question. Civil rights movements, wage and employment gains, political empowerment—all these and more represent the thin end of the wedge that holds the potential for further rending the fabric of a racist, sexist culture. I remain optimistic that the structures and images underlying hate crime can be mitigated through a positive politics of difference.

Connell (1992) refers to the "practical politics" of difference, which include educational and institutional initiatives, as well as deeper structural changes which are intended to begin breaking down the hierarchical and dichotomous structures of difference. Until we are able, as culture, to celebrate difference rather than denigrate it, until we blur those boundaries, we will continue to force people into rigid categories of male/female, straight/gay, white/not white, normal/deviant—often through violence. What we must seek to create through long and short term initiatives is a culture in which we are not forced to "choose" an identity on the basis of reified and privileged categories. However, "the goal should not be to transcend race," or difference in general, but "to transcend the biased meanings associated with" difference (Dyson, 1991). In other words, we must begin to think of and enact difference differently.

Discussion Questions

1. What do you think accounts for the failure of criminologists to try to explain hate crime theoretically?

2. Which of the theories evaluated in this chapter do you think holds the most promise for helping us to understand hate crime?

3. Select one theory discussed in the book and in this chapter. Discuss its contributions and limitations in theorizing hate crime.

4. Identify and explain the four "dominant structures" to which Perry refers. Provide illustrative examples.

5. Explain how each of the dominant structures noted above contributes to hate crime. Provide illustrative examples.

6. What does Perry mean when she refers to "structure" and "agency?" What are the distinctions and connections between the two concepts?

7. What is meant by "doing difference?" How does hate crime shape how we "do difference?"

8. Identify a recent case of hate crime and apply the perspective of doing difference as a mechanism for explaining the offense.

9. How does hate crime reproduce relations of inequality?

10. Given Perry's account of hate crime—especially the four dominant structures—how might we intervene to prevent hate crime?

References

Abbe, M. (1994). "Walker's Erotic Torture Heated Up National Debate." *Minneapolis Star Tribune*, December 28.

Acker, J. (1992). "Gendering Organizational Theory." In A.J. Mills & P. Tancred (eds.) *Gendering Organizational Analysis,* pp. 248-260. Newbury Park, CA: Sage.

ADCA (1996b). *Best Practice in the Diversion of Alcohol and other Drug Offenders.* Canberra, Australia: The Alcohol and Other Drugs Council of Australia.

ADCA (1996a). *Case Studies in the Diversion of Alcohol and Other Drug Offenders: A Preliminary Report.* Canberra, Australia: The Alcohol and Other Drugs Council of Australia.

Akers, R. (1997). *Criminological Theories.* Los Angeles, CA: Roxbury.

Alder, C. & K. Polk (2001). *Child Victims of Homicide.* Melbourne, Australia: Cambridge University Press.

Alder, C. & J. Wundersitz (eds.) (1994). *Family Conferencing and Juvenile Justice: The Way Forward or Misplaced Optimism?* Australian Studies in Law, Crime and Justice, Canberra, Australia: Australian Institute of Criminology.

ALRC (1997). *Review of the Adversarial System of Litigation: Rethinking Legal Education And Training.* Australian Law Reform Commission Issues Paper 21, August 1997.

ALRC (1986). *The Recognition of Aboriginal Customary Laws, Report No. 31.* Australian Law Reform Commission, Canberra: Australian Government Publishing Service, 3 volumes.

Alvi, S., W.S. DeKeseredy & D. Ellis (2000). *Contemporary Social Problems in North American Society.* Toronto, CN: Addison Wesley Longman.

Arrigo, B.A. (2000). "Social Justice and Critical Criminology: On Integrating Knowledge." *Contemporary Justice Review*, 3(1):7-37.

Arrigo, B.A. (1999). "In Search of Social Justice: Toward an Integrated (Critical) Criminological Theory." In B.A. Arrigo (ed.) *Social Justice/Criminal Justice: The Maturation of Critical Theory in Crime, Law, and Deviance*, pp. 253-272. Belmont, CA: West/Wadsworth.

Arrigo, B.A. (1997). "Dimensions of Social Justice in a Single Room Occupancy (SRO): Contributions Form Chaos Theory, Policy, and Practice." In D. Milovanovic (ed.) *Chaos, Criminology, and Social Justice*, pp. 179-194. New York, NY: Praeger.

Arrigo, B.A. (1996). *The Contours of Psychiatric Justice.* New York/London: Garland.

Arrigo, B.A. (1995). "The Peripheral Core of Law and Criminology: On Postmodern Social Theory and Conceptual Integration." *Justice Quarterly*, 12(3):447-472.

Arrigo, B.A. (1994). "Rooms for the Misbegotten: On Social Design and Social Deviance." *Journal of Sociology and Social Welfare*, 21(4):95-113.

Arrigo, B.A. & T.J. Bernard (1997). "Postmodern Criminology in Relation to Radical and Conflict Criminology." *Critical Criminology: An International Journal*, 8(2):39-60.

Arrigo, B.A. & D.O. Friedrichs (1997). "Can Students Benefit from an Intensive Engagement with Postmodern Criminology?" In J.R. Fuller & E. Hickey (eds.) *Current Issues in Criminology*, pp. 149-166. Needham Heights, MA: Allyn & Bacon.

Arrigo, B.A. & R.C. Schehr (1998). "Restoring Justice for Juveniles: A Critical Analysis of Victim Offender Mediation, *Justice Quarterly*, 15(4):629-666.

Arrigo, B.A. & C.R. Williams (1999). "Law, Ideology, and Critical Inquiry: The Case of Treatment Refusal for Incompetent Prisoners Awaiting Execution." *New England Journal on Criminal and Civil Confinement*, 25(2):367-412.

Arrigo, B.A., D. Milovanovic & R. Schehr (2000). "The French Connection: Implications for Law, Crime, and Social Justice." *Humanity & Society*, 24(2):163-203.

Aulette, J.R. & R.J. Michalowski (1993). "Fire in Hamlet: A Case Study of State-Corporate Crime." In Kenneth D. Tunnell, *Political Crime in Contemporary America*, pp. 171-206. New York, NY: Garland.

Banfield, E.C. (1974). *The Unheavenly City Revisited*. Boston, MA: Little Brown.

Barak, G. (1998). *Integrating Criminologies*. Boston, MA: Allyn and Bacon.

Barak, G. (ed.) (1994). *Media, Process, and the Social Construction of Crime: Studies in Newsmaking Criminology*. New York, NY: Garland.

Barak, G. (1991). *Crimes by the Capitalist State*. Albany, NY: State University of New York Press.

Bargen, J. (1995). "A Critical View of Conferencing." *Australian and New Zealand Journal of Criminology*. Special Supplementary Issue, 100-103.

Barker, R. (1992). *The Broken Circle*. New York, NY: Simon and Schuster.

Basran, G.S., G. Charan & B.D. MacLean (1995). *Farm Workers and Their Children*. Vancouver, CN: Collective Press.

Bazemore, G. & M. Umbreit (1994). *Balanced and Restorative Justice: Program Summary*. Washington, DC: U.S. Department of Justice Office of Juvenile Justice and Delinquency Prevention.

Beauchesne, E. (2000). "61% of Unemployed Don't Receive EI: Most Aren't Eligible Due to Tightened Requirements: Stats Can Report." *Ottawa Citizen*, July 11, A10.

Becker, H.S. (1963). *Outsiders: Studies in the Sociology of Deviance*. New York, NY: Free Press.

Beirne, P. & J. Messerschmidt (1995). *Criminology*, Second Edition. Fort Worth, TX: Harcourt Brace.

Bianchi, H. (1994). *Justice as Sanctuary: Toward a New System of Crime Control*. Bloomington, IN: Indiana University Press.

Bibbings, L. & P. Alldridge (1993). "Sexual Expression, Body Alteration, and the Defense of Consent." *Journal of Law and Society*, 20(3):356-370.

Blagg, H. (1998). "Restorative Visions and Restorative Justice Practices: Conferencing, Ceremony and Reconciliation in Australia." *Current Issues in Criminal Justice*, 10(1):5-14.

Bohm, R.M. (1997). "Review of Stuart Henry and Dragan Milovanovic's Constitutive Criminology." *The Criminologist*, 22:15-16.

Bonger, W. (1916). *Criminality and Economic Conditions*. Boston, MA: Little Brown.

Bottoms, A. (1994). "Avoiding Injustice, Promoting Legitimacy and Relationships." In J. Burnside & N. Baker (eds.) *Relational Justice: Repairing the Breach*, pp. 53-68. Winchester: Waterside Press.

Bourgois, P. (1995). *In Search of Respect: Selling Crack in El Barrio*. Cambridge, UK: Cambridge University Press.

Braithwaite, J. (1999). "Restorative Justice: Assessing Optimistic and Pessimistic Accounts." In M. Tonry (ed.) *Crime and Justice: A Review of Research*, 25. Chicago, IL: University of Chicago Press.

Braithwaite, J. (1994). "Thinking Harder About Democratising Social Control." In C. Alder & J. Wundersitz (eds.) *Family Conferencing and Juvenile Justice: The Way Forward or Misplaced Optimism?*, pp. 199-216. Australian Studies in Law, Crime and Justice, Canberra, Australia: Australian Institute of Criminology.

Braithwaite, J. & S. Mugford (1994). "Conditions of Successful Reintegration Ceremonies: Dealing with Young Offenders." *British Journal of Criminology*, 342:139-171.

Breslauer, J. (1994). "The Body Politics." *Los Angeles Times*, July 2.

Brogden, M. & C. Shearing (1993). *Policing for a New South Africa*. London, England: Routledge.

Burnside, J. & N. Baker (eds.) (1994). *Relational Justice: Repairing the Break*. Winchester, England: Waterside Press.

Butler, J. (1992). "Contingent Foundations: Feminism and the Question of 'Postmodernism'." In J. Butler and J.W. Scott (eds.) *Feminists Theorize the Political*. London, England: Routledge.

Cain, M. & A. Hunt (1979). *Marx and Engels on Law*. New York, NY: Academic Press.

Califia, P. (1994). *Public Sex: The Culture of Radical Sex*. San Francisco, CA: Cleis Press.

Campbell, A. (1993). *Men, Women, and Aggression*. New York, NY: Basic Books.

Carlen, P. (1992). "Women, Crime, Feminism, and Realism." In J. Lowman & B.D. MacLean (eds.) *Realist Criminology: Crime Control and Policing in the 1990s*, pp. 203-220. Toronto, CN: University of Toronto Press.

Carlson, S.M. & R.J. Michalowski (1997). "Crime, Unemployment, and Social Structures of Accumulation: An Inquiry into Historical Contingency." *Justice Quarterly*, 14:101-133.

Chambliss, W. (1994). "Policing the Ghetto Underclass: The Politics of Law and Order Enforcement." *Social Problems*, 41:177-194.

Chambliss, W.J. (1975). "Toward a Political Economy of Crime." *Theory and Society*, 2:149-170.

Chambliss, W.J. & M.S. Zatz (1993). *Making Law: The State, the Law and Structural Contradictions*. Bloomington, IN: University of Indiana Press.

Chesney-Lind, M. (1997). *The Female Offender: Girls, Women, and Crime*. Thousand Oaks, CA: Sage Publications.

Christie, N. (1977). "Conflicts as Property." *British Journal of Criminology*, 171:1-15.

Cohen, S. (1993). "Human Rights and the Crimes of the State: The Culture of Denial." *Australian and New Zealand Journal of Criminology*, 26:97-115.

Cohen, S. (1988). *Against Criminology*. New Brunswick, NJ: Transaction Books.

Cohen, S. (1972/1980). *Folk Devils and Moral Panics*. London, England: Macgibbon and Kee.

Cohen, S. (ed.). (1971). *Images of Deviance*. Harmondsworth, UK: Penguin Books.

Collier, R. (1998). *Masculinities, Crime and Criminology*. London, England: Sage.

Collins, M. (1992). "The Gay-Bashers." In G. Herek & K. Berrill (eds.) *Hate Crimes: Confronting Violence Against Lesbians and Gay Men*, pp. 191-200. Newbury Park, CA: Sage.

Collins, P.H. (1993). "The Sexual Politics of Black Womanhood." In P. Bart & Eileen Moran (eds.) *Violence Against Women*, pp. 85-104. Newbury Park, CA: Sage.

Collins, P.H. (1990). *Black Feminist Thought: Knowledge, Consciousness and the Politics of Empowerment*. New York, NY: Routledge.

Colvin, M. (1997). "Review of Stuart Henry and Dragan Milovanovic's Constitutive Criminology." *American Journal of Sociology*, 102:1448-1450.

Comstock, G. (1991). *Violence Against Lesbians and Gay Men*. New York, NY: Columbia University Press.

Connell, R. (1995). *Masculinities*. Berkeley, CA: University of California Press.

Connell, R. (1992). "Drumming Up the Wrong Tree." *Tikkun*, 7(1):31-36.

Connell, R. (1990). "The State, Gender and Sexual Politics: Theory and Appraisal." *Theory and Society*, 19(4):507-544.

Connell, R. (1987). *Gender and Power*. Stanford, CA: Stanford University Press.

Cook, P.J. & M.H. Moore (1999). "Guns, Gun Control, and Homicide." In M.D. Smith & M.A. Zahn (eds.) *Studying and Preventing Homicide: Issues and Challenges*, pp. 246-273. Thousand Oaks, CA: Sage.

Cornell, D. (1991). *Beyond Accommodation*. New York, NY: Routledge.

Crenshaw, K.W. (1994). "Mapping the Margins: Intersectionality, Identity and Violence Against Women of Color." In M.A. Fineman & R. Mykitiuk (eds.) *The Public Nature of Private Violence*, pp. 93-118. New York, NY: Routledge.

Croall, H. (1997). "Crime: Understanding More and Condemning Less?" *Reviewing Sociology*, 10(3).

Cunneen, C. (1998, November). *Restorative Justice and the Recognition of Indigenous Rights*. Paper presented to the Second Annual International Conference on Restorative Justice for Juveniles, Fort Lauderdale, FL.

Cunneen, C. & D. McDonald (1997). "Keeping Aboriginal and Torres Strait People Out of Custody." Canberra, Australia: Aboriginal and Torres Strait Islander Commission.

Currie, E. (1998). *Crime and Punishment in America: Why the Solutions to America's Most Stubborn Social Crisis Have Not Worked—and What Will*. New York, NY: Metropolitan Books.

Currie, E. (1997). "Market Society and Social Disorder." In B. MacLean & D. Milovanovic (eds.) *Thinking Critically About Crime*, pp. 37-42. Vancouver, BC: The Collective Press.

Currie, E. (1992). "Retreatism, Minimalism, Realism: Three Styles of Reasoning on Crime and Drugs in the United States." In J. Lowman & B.D. MacLean (eds.) *Realist Criminology: Crime Control and Policing in the 1990s*, pp. 88-97. Toronto, CN: University of Toronto Press.

Currie, E. (1985). *Confronting Crime*. New York, NY: Pantheon.

Daly, K. (2000). "Feminist Theoretical Work in Criminology." *DivisioNews*. Newsletter of the Division of Women and Crime, American Society of Criminology, August. ⟨http://www.ou.edu/soc/dwc/newsletter.htm⟩.

Daly, K. (1998). "From Gender Ratios to Gendered Lives: Women and Gender in Crime and Criminological Theory." In Tonry, Michael (ed.) *The Handbook of Crime and Justice*, pp. 85-108. Oxford, England: Oxford University Press.

Daly, K. & M. Chesney-Lind (1988). "Feminism and Criminology." *Justice Quarterly*, 5:497-538.

Daly, K. & L. Maher (eds.) (1998). *Criminology at the Crossroads: Feminist Readings in Crime and Justice*. Oxford, England: Oxford University Press.

Daly, M. & M. Wilson (1988). *Homicide*. New York, NY: Aldine de Gruyter.

DeKeseredy, W.S. (2000b). *Women, Crime and the Canadian Criminal Justice System*. Cincinnati, OH: Anderson Publishing Co.

DeKeseredy, W.S. (2000a). "Current Controversies On Defining Non-Lethal Violence Against Women in Intimate Heterosexual Relationships: Empirical Implications." *Violence Against Women*, 6:728-746.

DeKeseredy, W.S. (1996). "The Left Realist Perspective on Race, Class, and Gender." In M.D. Schwartz & D. Milovanovic (eds.) *Race, Gender, and Class in Criminology: The Intersection*, pp. 49-72. New York, NY: Garland.

DeKeseredy, W.S. & M.D. Schwartz (1996). *Contemporary Criminology*. Belmont, CA: Wadsworth.

DeKeseredy, W.S. & M.D. Schwartz (1991). "British Left Realism on the Abuse of Women: A Critical Appraisal." In H. Pepinsky & R. Quinney (eds.) *Criminology as Peace-Making*, pp. 154-174. Bloomington, IN: Indiana University Press.

DeKeseredy, W.S., S. Alvi, M.D. Schwartz & B. Perry (1999). "Violence Against and the Harrassment of Women in Canadian Public Housing: An Exploratory Study." *Canadian Review of Sociology & Anthropology*, 36:499-516.

DeKeseredy, W.S., B.D. MacLean & M.D. Schwartz (1997). "Thinking Critically About Left Realism." In B.D. MacLean & D. Milovanovic (eds.) *Thinking Critically About Crime*, pp. 19-27. Vancouver, BC: Collective Press.

DeKeseredy, W.S., M.D. Schwartz & S. Alvi (2000). "The Role Of Pro-Feminist Men in Dealing With Woman Abuse on the Canadian College Campus." *Violence Against Women*, 6:918-935.

DeLeon-Granados, W. (1999). *Travels Through Crime and Place: Community Building as Crime Control*. Boston, MA: Northeastern University Press.

Dennis, N. (ed.) (1997). *Zero-Tolerance: Policing in a Free Society*. London, England: Institute of Economic Affairs.

Deutschmann, L.B. (1998). *Deviance and Social Control*, Second Edition. Toronto, CN: IPC.

Devine, J.A. & J.D. Wright (1993). *The Greatest of Evils: Urban Poverty and the American Underclass*. Hawthorne, NY: Aldine de Gruyter.

Dobash, R.P. & R.E.Dobash (1992). *Women, Violence and Social Change*. New York, NY: Routledge.

Dyson, M.E. (1991). *Reflecting Back: African-American Cultural Criticism*. Minneapolis, MN: University of Minnesota Press.

Editorial (1996). "An Escape from Criminal Justice Rituals?" *Criminal Law Review*, 1-3.

Eglash, A. (1977). "Beyond Restitution: Creative Restitution." In J. Hudson & B. Galaway (eds.) *Restitution in Criminal Justice*. Lexington, MA: Lexington Books.

Einstadter, W. & S. Henry (1995). *Criminological Theory: An Analysis of Its Underlying Assumptions*. Fort Worth, TX: Harcourt Brace.

Ellis, D. (2000). "Credit the Economy for a Big Drop in Attacks." *The Globe and Mail*, July 27, A13.

Eubanks, V. (1996). "Zones of Dither: Writing the Postmodern Body." *Body and Society*, 2(3):73-88.

Favazza, A. (1996). *The Body Under Siege: Self-Mutilation and Body Modification in Culture and Psychiatry*. Baltimore, MD: John Hopkins University Press.

Fenstermaker, S., C. West & D. Zimmerman (1991). "Gender Inequality: New Conceptual Terrain." In Rae Lesser Blumberg (ed.) *Gender, Family and Economy: The Triple Overlap*, pp. 289-307. Newbury Park, CA: Sage.

Ferrell, J. (1999b). "Cultural Criminology." *Annual Review of Sociology*, 25:395-418.

Ferrell, J. (1999a). "Anarchist Criminology and Social Justice." In Bruce A. Arrigo (ed.) *Social Justice/Criminal Justice*, pp. 91-108. Belmont, CA: West/Wadsworth.

Ferrell, J. (1998). "Criminalizing Popular Culture." In F. Bailey and D. Hale (eds.) *Popular Culture, Crime, and Justice*, pp. 71-83. Belmont, CA: West/Wadsworth.

Ferrell, J. (1997). "Youth, Crime, and Cultural Space." *Social Justice*, 24:21-38.

Ferrell, J. (1996). *Crimes of Style*. Boston, MA: Northeastern.

Ferrell, J. & C.R.Sanders (eds.) (1995). *Cultural Criminology*. Boston, MA: Northeastern.

Fine, M. (1997). "Witnessing Whiteness." In M. Fine, L. Weis, L. Powell & L.M. Wong (eds.) *Off White: Readings on Race, Power and Society*, pp. 57-65. New York, NY: Routledge.

Fine, M., L. Weis & J. Addelston (1997). "(In)Secure Times: Constructing White Working Class Masculinities in the Late Twentieth Century." *Gender and Society*, 11(1):52-68.

Fisher, T. (1993). "Victim/Offender Mediation: Survey of Overseas Practices and Research 1993." *Australian Dispute Resolution Journal*, 125.

Fisher, T., P. O'Malley & A. Leigh (1992). *Alternative Dispute Resolution Strategies for Dealing With Young Offenders*. Bundoora Vic: National Centre for Socio-Legal Studies, La Trobe University.

Fishman, M. & G. Cavender (eds.) (1998). *Entertaining Crime*. New York, NY: Aldine de Gruyter.

Foucault, M. (1978). *The History of Sexuality, Volume 1: An Introduction*, (Translated by Robert Hurley). New York, NY: Pantheon.

Fox, J.A. & M.W. Zavitz (2000). *Homicide Trends in the United States: 1998 Update*. Bureau of Justice Statistics Crime Data Brief. Washington, DC: U.S. Department of Justice.

Freeman, J.C. (1988). "Criminal Justice and the Community." *Australian Crime Prevention Council Journal*, August, 13-16.

Freire, P. (1972). *Pedagogy of the Oppressed*. New York, NY: Herder and Herder.

Friedrichs, D.O. (1996b). "Governmental Crime, Hitler, and White-Collar Crime: A Problematic Relationship." *Caribbean Journal of Criminology and Social Psychology*, 1(2):44-63.

Friedrichs, D.O. (1996a). *Trusted Criminals: White Collar Crime in Contemporary Society*. New York, NY: Wadsworth.

Friedrichs, D.0. (1996). "Critical Criminology and Progressive Pluralism: Strength in Diversity for These Times." *Critical Criminology*, 7:121-128.

Friedrichs, D.O. (1992). "State Crime or Governmental Crime: Making Sense of the Conceptual Confusion." In J.I. Ross (ed.) *Controlling State Crime*, pp. 53-80. New York, NY: Garland.

Friedrichs, D.O. (1998b). *State Crime: Volumes I and II*. Aldershot, UK: Ashgate/Dartmouth.

Friedrichs, D.O. (1998a). "New Directions in Critical Criminology and White Collar Crime." In J.I. Ross (ed.) *Cutting the Edge: Current Perspectives in Radical/Critical Criminology and Criminal Justice*, pp. 77-94. Westport, CT: Praeger.

Friedrichs, D.O. (1983). "Victimology: A Consideration of the Radical Critique." *Crime & Delinquency*, April, pp. 283-294.

Funk, R.E. (1993). *Stopping Rape: A Challenge for Men*. Philadelphia, PA: New Society Publishers.

Gelles, R.J. (2000). "Estimating the Incidence and Prevalence of Violence Against Women: National Data Systems and Sources." *Violence Against Women*, 6:784-804.

Gibbons, D.C. (1994) *Talking About Crime and Criminals: Problems and Issues in Theory Development in Criminology*. Englewood Cliffs, NJ: Prentice Hall.

Giroux, H. (1992). *Border Crossings: Cultural Workers and the Politics of Education*. New York, NY: Routledge.

Gleick, J. (1987). *Chaos: Making a New Science*. New York, NY: Penguin.

Goffman, E. (1963). *Stigma: Notes on the Management of Spoiled Identity*. New York, NY: Touchstone Books.

Gold, D.A., C.Y.H. Lo & E.O. Wright (1975, October/November). "Recent Developments in Marxist Theories of the Capitalist State." *Monthly Review*, 27:23-43/36-51.

Goldberg, D.T. (1995). "Afterword: Hate or Power?" In R.K. Whillock & D. Slayden (eds.) *Hate Speech*, pp. 267-276. Thousand Oaks, CA: Sage.

Goldberg, D.T. (1990). "The Social Formation of Racist Discourse." In D.T. Goldberg (ed.) *Anatomy of Racism*, pp. 295-318. Minneapolis, MN: University of Minnesota Press.

Gottfredson, M.R. & T. Hirschi (1990). *A General Theory of Crime*. Stanford, CA: Stanford University Press.

Gottlieb, R. (1992). *Marxism: Origins, Betrayal, Rebirth*. New York, NY: Routledge.

Greenberg, D. (1981). *Crime and Capitalism*. Palo Alto, CA: Mayfield Publishing Company.

Grosz, E. (1999). "Bodies-Vities." In Price, Janet and Shildrick, Margrit, (eds.) *Feminist Theory and the Body*, pp. 381-387. New York, NY: Routledge.

Grosz, E. (1984). *Volatile Bodies: Towards a Corporeal Feminism*. London, England: Routledge.

Hagan, J., A.R. Gillis & J. Simpson (1985). "The Class Structure of Gender and Delinquency: Toward a Power-Control Theory of Common Delinquent Behavior." *American Journal of Sociology*, 90:1151-1178.

Hall, S. (1996). "Introduction: Who Needs Identity?" In Hall, Staurt, and Gay, Paul du, (eds.) *Questions of Cultural Identity*, pp. 1-17. London, England: Sage.

Hamm, M.S. (1994b). *Hate Crime: International Perspectives on Causes and Control*. Cincinnati, OH: Anderson Publishing Co.

Hamm, M.S. (1994a). *American Skinheads: The Criminology and Control of Hate Crime*. Westport, CT: Praeger.

Handler, J. (1992). "The Presidential Address, 1992, Law and Society: Postmodernism, Protest and the New Social Movement." *Law and Society Review*, 26:697-731.

Harding, S. (ed.) (1987). *Feminism and Methodology*. Bloomington, IN: Indiana University Press.

Hartmann, U. (1996). "Victim Offender Reconciliation With Adult Offenders in Germany." In C. Sumner, M. Israel, M. O'Connell & R. Sarre (eds.) *International Victimology: Selected Papers from the Eighth International Symposium on Victimology*, pp. 321-327. Adelaide 1994, Conference Proceedings No. 27, Canberra, Australia: Australian Institute of Criminology.

Hassel, W. (1992). "Survivors Story." In G. Herek & K. Berrill (eds.) *Hate Crimes: Confronting Violence Against Lesbians and Gay Men*, pp. 144-148. Newbury Park, CA: Sage.

Hatfield, M. (1999). *Canadian Urban Poverty Tables*. Ottawa, CN: Human Resources and Development Canada.

Hatty, S.E. (2000). *Masculinities, Violence, and Culture*. Thousand Oaks, CA: Sage.

Heilbroner, R. (1980). *Marxism, For and Against*. New York, NY: Norton.

Heimer, K. & S. De Coster. (1999). "The Gendering of Violent Delinquency." *Criminology*, 37:277-317.

Henderson, J. (2000). "Personal Communication with Dragan Milovanovic." August 29.

Henry, S. (1999). "Is Left Realism a Useful Theory for Addressing the Problems of Crime?: No." In J.R. Fuller & E.W. Hickey (eds.) *Controversial Issues in Criminology*, pp. 137-144. Boston, MA: Allyn & Bacon.

Henry, S. & D. Milovanovic (1999). *Constitutive Criminology at Work: Applications to Crime and Justice*. Albany, NY: SUNY Press.

Henry, S. & D. Milovanovic (1996). *Constitutive Criminology*. London, England: Sage.

Henry, S. & D. Milovanovic (1994). "The Constitution of Constitutive Criminology." In D. Nelken (ed.) *The Futures of Criminology*. London, England: Sage.

Henry, S. & D. Milovanovic (1991). "Constitutive Criminology." *Criminology*, 29:293-316.

Herek, G. (1992). "The Social Context of Hate Crimes: Notes on Cultural Heterosexism." In G. Herek and K. Berrill (eds.) *Hate Crimes: Confronting Violence Against Lesbians and Gay Men*, pp. 89-104. Newbury Park, CA: Sage.

Hesse, B., D. Rai, C. Bennett & P McGilchrist (1992). *Beneath the Surface: Racial Harassment*. Aldershot, UK: Avebury Press.

Hewitt, Kim. (1997). *Mutilating the Body: Identity in Blood and Ink*. Bowling Green, OH: Popular Press.

Hill, G.D. & E.M. Crawford (1990). "Women, Race and Crime." *Criminology*, 28:601-623.

Hirschi, T. (1969). *Causes of Delinquency*. Berkeley, CA: University of California Press.

Hirst, P. (1975). "Marx and Engels on Law, Crime and Morality. In I. Taylor, P. Walton & J. Young (eds.) *Critical Criminology*. London, England: Routledge and Kegan Paul.

Hobsbawm, E. (1994). *The Age of Extremes*. London, England: Michael Joseph.

Howe, A. (1997). "Criminology Meets Postmodern Feminism (and Has a Nice Day)." In B.D. MacLean & D. Milovanovic (eds.) *Thinking Critically About Crime*. Vancouver, BC: Collective Press.

Hunt, A. (1991). "Postmodernism and Critical Criminology." In B.D. MacLean & D. Milovanovic (eds.) *New Directions in Critical Criminology*, pp. 79-85. Vancouver, BC: The Collective Press.

Hunt, A. (1990). "The Big Fear: Law Confronts Postmodernism." *McGill Law Journal*, 35:507-540.

Hurtado, A. (1989). "Relating to Privilege: Seduction and Rejection in the Subordination of White Women and Women of Color." *Signs*, 14:833-855.

Hurtig, M. (1999). *Pay the Rent or Feed the Kids: The Tragedy and Disgrace of Poverty in Canada*. Toronto, CN: McClelland & Stewart.

International Court of Justice (1996). *The Legality of the Threat or Use of Nuclear Weapons* (Request for advisory opinion submitted by the General Assembly of the United Nations). General List, No. 95, Advisory Opinion of 8 July 1996.

Irigaray, L. (1993). *Je, Tous, Nous*. Ithaca, NY: Cornell University Press.

Irwin, J. & J. Austin (1997). *It's About Time: America's Imprisonment Binge*, Second Edition. Belmont, CA: Wadsworth.

Isaacson, W. (1999). "Who Mattered and Why." In *Time Magazine's Person of the Century*, 154(27):48-60. New York, NY: Time Inc.

Jargowsky, P.A. (1997). *Poverty and Place*. New York, NY: Russell Sage Foundation.

Jeffries, S. (1994). Sadomasochism, Art and the Lesbian Sexual Revolution. *Artlink*, 14(1).

Jenkins, P. (1999). "Fighting Terrorism as if Women Mattered: Anti-Abortion Violence as Unconstructed Terrorism." In J. Ferrell and N. Websdale (eds.) *Making Trouble*, pp. 319-346. New York, NY: Aldine de Gruyter.

Jones, A. (1998). *Body Art: Performing the Subject*. Minneapolis, MN: University of Minnesota Press.

Jones, T., B.D. MacLean & J. Young (1986). *The Islington Crime Survey*. London, England: Gower.

Jurik, N.C. (1999). "Socialist Feminism, Criminology, and Social Justice." In B.A. Arrigo (ed.) *Social Justice/Criminal Justice*, pp. 31-50. Belmont, CA: West/Wadsworth.

Justice Fellowship (1989). *Restorative Justice: Theory, Principles, Practice*. Washington DC: Fellowship Communications.

Kane, S. (1998). *AIDS Alibis: Sex, Drugs and Crime in the Americas*. Philadelphia, PA: Temple University Press.

Kappeler, V.E. & P.B. Kraska (1999). "Policing Modernity: Scientific and Community Based Violence on Symbolic Playing Fields." In S. Henry & D. Milovanovic (eds.) *Constitutive Criminology at Work*. Albany, NY: SUNY Press.

Kauzlarich, D. (1995). "A Criminology of the Nuclear State." *Humanity and Society*, 19 (August):37-57.

Kauzlarich, D. & R.C. Kramer (1998). *Crimes of the American Nuclear State: At Home and Abroad.* Boston, MA: Northeastern University Press.

Kauzlarich, D., R.A. Matthews & W.J. Miller (2001). "Toward a Victimology of State Crime." *Critical Criminology*, 10(3):173-194.

Kelling, G. & C. Coles (1997). *Fixing Broken Windows.* New York, NY: Free Press.

Kelly, R. (ed.) (1993). *Bias Crime: American Legal Responses*, Second Edition. Chicago, IL: Office of International Criminal Justice.

Kinsey, R., J. Lea & J. Young (1986). *Losing the Fight Against Crime.* Oxford, UK: Blackwell.

Kleese, C. (1999). " 'Modern Primitivism': Non-Mainstream Body Modification and Racialized Representation." *Body and Society*, 5(2-3):15-38.

Kramer, R.C. & D. Kauzlarich (1999). "The World Court's Decision on Nuclear Weapons: Implications for Criminology." *Contemporary Justice Review*, 4(2):395-413.

Kraska, P.B. (1996). "Enjoying Militarism." *Justice Quarterly*, 13:405-429.

Kraska, P.B. & V.E. Kappeler (1995). "To Serve and Pursue." *Justice Quarterly*, 12:85-111.

Krivo, L.J., R.D. Peterson, H. Rizzo & J.R. Reynolds (1998). "Race, Segregation, and the Concentration of Disadvantage." *Social Problems*, 45:61-80.

Kruttschnitt, C. (1996). "Contributions of Quantitative Methods to the Study of Gender and Crime, or Bootstrapping Our Way Into the Theoretical Thicket." *Journal of Quantitative Criminology*, 12:135-161.

La Prairie, C. (1996). "Sentencing Circles and Family Group Conferences." *Australian and New Zealand Journal of Criminology*, March, 74-75.

La Prairie, C. (1995). "Altering Course: New Directions in Criminal Justice." *Australian and New Zealand Journal of Criminology,* Special Supplementary Issue: 78-99.

Laclau, E. (2000). "Constructing Universality." In Judith Butler, Ernesto Laclau and Slavoj Zizek (eds.) *Contingency, Hegemony, Universality.* New York, NY: Verso.

Lanier, M.M. & S. Henry (1998). *Essential Criminology.* Boulder, CO: Westview Press.

Laster, K. & E. Erez (2000). "The Oprah Dilemma: The Use and Abuse of Victims." In D. Chappell & P. Wilson (eds.) *Crime and the Criminal Justice System in Australia: 2000 and Beyond*, pp. 240-258. Sydney, Australia: Butterworths.

Lea, J. & J. Young (1984). *What Is to Be Done About Law and Order?* Harmondsworth, UK: Penguin.

Lederach, J.P. (1999). *The Journey Toward Reconciliation.* Scottdale, PA: Herald Press.

Lederach, J.P. & R. Kraybill (1995). "The Paradox of Popular Justice: A Practitioner's View." In S. Merry & N. Milner (eds.) *The Possibility of Popular Justice: A Case Study of Community Mediation in the United States*, pp. 357-378. Ann Arbor, MI: University of Michigan Press.

Levin, J. & McDevitt (1993). *Hate Crimes: The Rising Tide of Bigotry and Bloodshed.* New York, NY: Plenum.

Lewis, O. (1966). "The Culture of Poverty." *Scientific American*, October, 19-25.

Lippens, R. (2000). *Who Owns Criminology? A Short Note on Gaps, Divides and Bridges.* http://www.tryoung.com/journal-pomocrim/lippens.html

Lippens, R. (1999). "Into Hybrid Marshlands." *International Journal for the Semiotics of Law*, 34:59-89.

Lippens, R. (1998). *Grenze/n/Loze Kriminologie (Borderless Criminology)*. Ghent, Belgium: Academia Press.

Lynch, M. & B. Groves (1989). *A Primer in Radical Criminology*. Albany, NY: Harrow and Heston.

Lynch, M.J. & P. Stretesky (1999). "Marxist and Social Justice: Thinking About Social Justice, Eclipsing Criminal Justice." In B.A. Arrigo (ed.) *Social Justice/Criminal Justice*, pp. 13-29. Belmont, CA: West/Wadsworth.

Lynch, M.J., R.A. Lynch & D. Milovanovic (1995). "Deconstruction and Radical Criminology: An Analysis of Postmodernism and Its Possible Uses in Criminology." In W.R. Janikowski and D. Milovanovic (eds.) *Legality and Illegality: Semiotics, Postmodernism, and Law*, pp. 199-232. New York, NY: Peter Lang.

Lyng, S. (1998). "Dangerous Methods: Risk Taking and the Research Process." In J. Ferrell and M.S. Hamm (eds.) *Ethnography at the Edge*, pp. 221-251. Boston, MA: Northeastern.

Lyng, S. & M.L. Bracey (1995). "Squaring the One Percent." In J. Ferrell and C.R. Sanders (eds.) *Cultural Criminology*, pp. 235-276. Boston, MA: Northeastern.

MacKendrick, K. (1998). "Technoflesh, or Didn't That Hurt?" *Fashion Theory*, 2(1):3-24.

MacRae, L. (1994). "Victim-Offender Mediation: Is it an Option for Your Client?" *Proctor*, 144:12.

Maher, L. (1997). *Sexed Work: Gender, Race and Resistance in a Brooklyn Drug Market*. Oxford: Clarendon Press.

Mann, C.R. (1993). *Unequal Justice: A Question of Color*. Bloomington, IN: Indiana University Press.

Manning, P.K. (1998). "Media Loops." In F. Bailey and D.Hale (eds.) *Popular Culture, Crime, and Justice*, pp. 25-39. Belmont, CA: West/Wadsworth.

Manning, P.K. (1995). "Postmodernism and Law." In W.R. Janikowski and D. Milovanovic (eds.) *Legality and Illegality: Semiotics, Postmodernism, and Law*, pp. 5-21. New York, NY: Peter Lang.

Manning, P.K. (1988). "Symbolic Communication: Signifying Calls and the Police Response." Cambridge, MA: MIT Press.

Marshall, T.F. & S. Merry (1990). *Crime and Accountability: Victim/Offender Mediation in Practice*, London, England: HMSO.

Martin, S. & N. Jurik (1996). *Doing Justice, Doing Gender*. Thousand Oaks, CA: Sage.

Martinson, R. (1974). "What Works? Questions and Answers About Prison Reform." *The Public Interest*, 35:22-54.

Matthews, R.A. & D. Kauzlarich (2000). "The Crash of ValuJet Flight 592: A Case Study in State-Corporate Crime." *Sociological Focus*, 33:281-298.

Matthews, R. & J. Young (eds.) (1992). *Issues in Realist Criminology*. London, England: Sage.

Matthews, R. & J. Young (1992). "Reflections on Realism." In Jock Young & Roger Matthews (eds.) *Rethinking Criminology: The Realist Debate*. London, England: Sage.

Mattley, C. (1998). "(Dis)Courtesy Stigma." In J. Ferrell & M.S. Hamm (eds.) *Ethnography at the Edge*, pp. 146-158. Boston, MA: Northeastern.

McRobbie, A. & S.L. Thornton (1995). "Rethinking 'Moral Panic' for Multi-Mediated Social Worlds." *British Journal of Sociology*, 46:559-574.

Mead, G.H. (1917). *Selected Writings*. Edited by A.J. Reck. Chicago, IL: University of Chicago Press, 1964.

Medhurst, A. & S. Munt (1998). *The Lesbian and Gay Studies Reader*. London, England: Cassell.

Melichar, K. (1990). "Deconstruction: Critical Theory or an Ideology of Despair?" *Humanity & Society*, 12(4):366-385.

Mendoza-Denton, N. (1996). "'Muy Macha': Gender and Ideology in Gang-Girls' Discourse About Makeup." *Ethnos*, 61:47-63.

Messerschmidt, J. (1993). *Masculinities and Crime: Critique and Reconceptualization of Theory*. Lanham, MD: Rowman & Littlefield.

Messner, S.F. & R. Rosenfeld (1997). *Crime and the American Dream*, Second Edition. Belmont, CA: Wadsworth.

Michalowski, R.J. (1998). "Foreword." In D. Kauzlarich & R.C. Kramer, *Crimes of the Nuclear State: At Home and Abroad*, pp. ix-xv. Boston, MA: Northeastern University Press.

Michalowski, R. (1991). "'Niggers, Welfare Scum and Homeless Assholes:' The Problems of Idealism, Consciousness and Context in Left Realism." In B.D. MacLean & D. Milovanovic (eds.) *New Directions in Critical Criminology*, pp. 31-38. Vancouver, BC: Collective Press.

Michalowski, R. (1985). *Order, Law and Crime*. New York, NY: McGraw-Hill.

Mike, B. (1976). "Wilhelm Adrian Bonger's Criminality and Economic Conditions: A Critical Appraisal" *International Journal of Criminology and Penology*, 4:211-238.

Miller, J. (1995). "Struggles Over the Symbolic." In J. Ferrell and C.R. Sanders (eds.) *Cultural Criminology*, pp. 213-234. Boston, MA: Northeastern.

Miller, J. (2001). *One of the Guys: Girls, Gangs and Gender*. New York, NY: Oxford University Press.

Milovanovic, D. (ed.) (1997). *Chaos, Criminology, and Social Justice*. New York, NY: Praeger.

Milovanovic, D. (1996b). "Rebellious Lawyering." *Legal Studies Forum*, 20(3):295-321.

Milovanovic, D. (ed.) (1996a). *Chaos, Criminology and Social Justice*. Westport, CT: Praeger.

Milovanovic, D. (1988). "Jailhouse Lawyers and Jailhouse Lawyering." *International Journal of the Sociology of Law*, 16:455-475.

Ministry of Justice New Zealand (1995). "Restorative Justice: Discussion Paper." Wellington, NZ: Ministry of Justice, October 1995.

Molina, L.F. (1995). "Can States Commit Crimes? The Limits of Formal International Law." In J.I. Ross (ed.) *Controlling State Crime*, pp. 349-388. New York, NY: Garland.

Moore, D. (1996). "Criminal Action – Official Reaction: Affect Theory, Criminology and Criminal Justice." In D.L. Nathanson (ed.) *Knowing Feeling*, NY: WW Norton.

Moore, D. (1993). "Shame, Forgiveness and Juvenile Justice." *Criminal Justice Ethics*, 12:3-25.

Murphy, T. (1994). *Ethics in an Epidemic: AIDS, Morality, and Culture*. Berkeley, CA: University of California Press.

Murray, C. (1984). *Losing Ground*. New York, NY: Basic Books.

Murray, G. (1991). "Mediation and Reparation Within the Criminal Justice System." A discussion paper prepared for the Department of the Attorney-General, Queensland, Australia.

Myers, J. (1992). "Non-Mainstream Body Modification." *Journal of Contemporary Ethnography,* 21:267-307.

Naffine, N. (1996). *Feminism and Criminology.* Philadelphia, PA: Temple University Press.

National Council of Welfare (2000). *Justice and the Poor.* Ottawa, CN: National Council of Welfare.

Norris, C. (2000). *Quantum Theory and the Flight from Realism.* New York, NY: Routledge.

Note (1995). "Racial Violence Against Asian Americans." *Harvard Law Review,* 106:1926-1943.

O'Carroll, P.W. & J.A. Mercy (1986). "Patterns and Recent Trends in Black Homicide." In D.F. Hawkins (ed.) *Homicide Among Black Americans.* Lanham, MD: University Press of America.

Pearce, F. & S. Tombs (1992). "Realism and Corporate Crime." In R. Matthews & J. Young (eds.) *Issues in Realist Criminology,* pp. 70-101. London, England: Sage.

Pepinsky, H. (1999). "Peacemaking Primer." In B.A. Arrigo (ed.) *Social Justice/Criminal Justice,* pp. 51-70. Belmont, CA: West/Wadsworth.

Pham, M. Another Senseless Hate Crime (online). www.avl.umd.edu/staff/nowk/hate_crime.html

Pharr, S. (1995). "Homophobia as a Weapon of Sexism." In Paula Rothenberg (ed.) *Race, Class and Gender in the United States,* Third Edition, pp. 481-490. New York, NY: St. Martin's.

Pharr, S. (1988). *Homophobia: A Weapon of Sexism.* Inverness, CA: Chardon Press.

Pitts, V.L. (1999). "Body Modification, Self-Mutilation and Agency in Media Accounts of a Subculture." *Body and Society,* 5(2-3):291-303.

Pitts, V.L. (1998). "Reclaiming the Female Body: Embodied Identity Work, Resistance and the Grotesque." *Body and Society,* 4(3):67-84.

Pitts, V., S. Hatty & M.D. Schwartz (2000). "Power, Gender and Place." A paper presented to the American Sociological Association, Washington, DC.

Platt, A. & P. Takagi (1981). "Intellectuals for Law and Order: A Critique of the New Realists." In A. Platt & P. Takagi (eds.) *Crime and Social Justice.* London, England: Macmillan.

Polk, K. (1994). "Family Conferencing: Theoretical and Evaluative Questions." In Alder, C. and J. Wundersitz (eds.) *Family Conferencing and Juvenile Justice: The Way Forward Or Misplaced Optimism?,* pp. 123-140. Australian Studies in Law, Crime and Justice, Canberra: Australian Institute of Criminology.

Polk, K. (1994). *When Men Kill: Scenarios of Masculine Violence.* Melbourne, Australia: Cambridge University Press.

Price, J. & M. Shildrick (eds.) (1999). *Feminist Theory and the Body: A Reader.* New York, NY: Routledge.

Ptacek, J. (1999). *Battered Women in the Courtroom: The Power of Judicial Responses.* Boston, MA: Northeastern University Press.

Quinney, R. (1999). "The Prophetic Meaning of Social Justice." In B.A. Arrigo (ed.) *Social Justice/Criminal Justice*, pp. 73-90. Belmont, CA: West/Wadsworth.

Quinney, R. (1977). *Class, State, and Crime*. New York, NY: Longman.

Radosh, P. (1990). "Woman and Crime in the United States: A Marxian Explanation." *Sociological Spectrum*, 10:105-131.

Reiman, J. (1998). *The Rich Get Richer and the Poor Get Prison: Ideology, Class, and Criminal Justice*, Fifth Edition. Boston, MA: Allyn & Bacon.

Renzetti, C.M. & S.L. Maier (2002). "Private Crime in Public Housing." *Women's Heath & Urban Life*, 1(2):46-65.

Richie, B.E. (1996). *Compelled to Crime: The Gender Entrapment of Battered Black Women*. New York, NY: Routledge.

Rose, D. (1996). *In the Name of the Law: The Collapse of Criminal Justice*, Revised Edition. London, England: Vintage.

Rosen, S. (1992). "Police Harassment of Homosexual Women and Men in New York City 1960-1980." In W.D. Dynes & S. Donaldson (eds.) *Homosexuality: Discrimination, Criminology and the Law*, pp. 505-536. New York, NY: Garland.

Rosenau, P.A. (1992). *Postmodernism and the Social Sciences: Insights, Inroads, and Intrusions*. Princeton, NJ: Princeton University Press.

Rosenblatt, D. (1997). "The Antisocial Skin: Structure, Resistance, and Modern Primitive Adornment in the United States." *Cultural Anthropology*, 12(3):287-334.

Ross, J.I. (1995). *Controlling State Crime*. New York, NY: Garland.

Ross, J.I., G. Barak, J. Ferrell, D. Kauzlarich, M.S. Hamm, D.O. Friedrichs, R.A. Matthews, S. Pickering, M. Presdee, P. Kraska & V. Kappeler (1999). "The State of State Crime Research: A Commentary." *Humanity and Society*, 23(3):273-281.

Royal Commission (1991). "Royal Commission into Aboriginal Deaths in Custody." *National Report*. Canberra, Australia: Australian Government Publishing Service, 5 volumes.

Ruggiero, V. (1992). "Realist Criminology: A Critique." In J. Young & R. Matthews (eds.) *Rethinking Criminology: The Realist Debate*, pp. 123-140. London, England: Sage.

Ruller, S. (1997). "Review of Stuart Henry and Dragan Milovanovic's Constitutive Criminology." *Contemporary Criminology*, 26:496-97.

Rushton, J.P. (1999). *Race, Evolution & Behavior*. New Brunswick, NJ: Transaction Books.

Russell, K.K. (1999). "Critical Race Theory and Social Justice." In Bruce A. Arrigo (ed.) *Social Justice/Criminal Justice*, pp. 178-188. Belmont, CA: West/Wadsworth.

Russell, S. (1997). "The Failure of Postmodern Criminology." *Critical Criminology* 8(2):61-90.

Sampson, R.J., S.W. Raudenbush & F. Earls (1998). *Neighborhood Collective Efficacy—Does it Help Reduce Violence?* Washington, DC: U.S. Department of Justice.

Sampson, R.J., S.W. Raudenbush & F. Earls (1997). "Neighborhoods and Violent Crime: A Multilevel Study of Collective Efficacy." *Science*, 277:918-924.

Sampson, R. & J. Laub (1993). *Crime in the Making*. Cambridge, MA: Harvard University Press.

Sanchez, L. (1999) "Sex, Law and the Paradox of Agency and Resistance in the Everyday Practices of Women in the 'Evergreen' Sex Trade." In S. Henry and D. Milovanovic (eds.) *Constitutive Criminology at Work*. Albany, NY: SUNY Press.

Sarre, R. (2000b). "Beyond What Works?: A 25-Year Jubilee Retrospective of Robert Martinson's
Famous Article." *The Australian and New Zealand Journal of Criminology*, 34(1):38-
46.

Sarre, R. (2000a). "Diversionary Programs in the Criminal Justice System and Their Effects on
Victims." In O'Connell, M.J. (ed.) *Victims of Crime: Working Together to Improve Services*. Conference proceedings. South Australian Institute of Justice Studies, Victim Support Service, Inc. & the Australasian Society of Victimology, Adelaide, 68-80.

Sarre, R. (1999c). "Family Conferencing as a Juvenile Justice Strategy." *The Justice Professional*,
11:259-271.

Sarre, R. (1999b). "Restorative Justice: Translating the Theory into Practice." *University of
Notre Dame Australia Law Review*, 11:11-25.

Sarre, R. (1999a, February). "Restorative Justice: Exploring Its Theological Roots." Unpublished
paper presented at the Shaping Australian Institutions Conference, Research School of
Social Sciences, ANU, Canberra, Australia.

Sarre, R. (1997b). "Is There a Role for the Application of Customary Law in Addressing Aboriginal Criminality in Australia?" *Critical Criminology: An International Journal*,
8(2):91-102.

Sarre, R. (1997a). "Justice as Restoration: Exploring New Themes for the Criminal Justice System." *Peace Review*, 94:541-548.

Sarre, R. (1996). "The State of Community Based Policing in Australia: Some Emerging
Themes." In D. Chappell & P. Wilson, (eds.) *Australian Policing: Contemporary
Issues*, 2nd ed., pp. 26-41. Sydney, Australia: Butterworths.

Sarre, R. (1994). *Uncertainties and Possibilities: A Discussion of Selected Criminal Justice
Issues in Contemporary Australia*. School of Law, University of South Australia, Adelaide.

Schmalleger, F. (1999). *Criminology Today*, 2nd ed. Upper Saddle River, NJ: Prentice Hall.

Schwartz, D.F., J.A. Grisso & C.G. Miles (1994). "A Longitudinal Study of Injury Morbidity in
an African-American Population." *Journal of the American Medical Association*, 271:755-
760.

Schwartz, M.D. (1991). "The Future of Criminology." In B.D. MacLean & D. Milovanovic
(eds.) *New Directions in Critical Criminology*. Vancouver, BC: Collective Press.

Schwartz, M.D. & W.S. DeKeseredy (1991). "Left Realist Criminology: Strengths, Weaknesses,
and the Feminist Critique." *Crime, Law and Social Change*, 15:51-72.

Schwartz, M. & D.O. Friedrichs (1994). "Postmodern Thought and Critical Discontent: New
Metaphors for Understanding Violence." *Criminology*, 32:221-246.

Schwartz, M.D. & D. Milovanovic (eds.) (1996). *Race, Gender, and Class in Criminology: The
Intersection*, New York, NY: Garland Publishing.

Schwendinger, H. & J. Schwendinger (1970). "Defenders of Order or Guardians of Human
Rights?" *Issues in Criminology*, 7(1):71-81.

Schwendinger, J. & H. Schwendinger (1983). *Rape and Inequality*. Beverly Hills, CA: Sage.

Shapiro, B. (1999). "The Crime Wave." In M.L. Fisch (ed.) *Annual Editions: Criminology, 99/00*, pp. 24-25. Guilford, CT: Duskin/McGraw-Hill.

Sharkansky, I. (1995). "A State Action May Be Nasty But Is Not Likely to Be a Crime." In J.I. Ross (ed.) *Controlling State Crime*, pp. 35-52. New York, NY: Garland.

Sheffield, C. (1995). "Hate Violence." In P. Rothenberg (ed.) *Race, Class and Gender in the United States*, Third Edition, pp. 432-441. New York, NY: St. Martin's.

Sheffield, C. (1989). "Sexual Terrorism." In J. Freeman (ed.) *Women: A Feminist Perspective*, pp. 3-19. Mountain View, CA: Mayfield Publishing.

Shelton, A. (1996). "Fetishism's Culture." In N. Sinclair (ed.) *The Chameleon Body*, pp. 82-112. London, England: Lund Humphries.

Shilling, C. (1993). *The Body and Social Theory*. London, England: Sage.

Shon, P.C. (2000). "Hey You C'me Here!" Subjectivization, Resistance, and the Interpellative Violence of Self-Generated Police-Citizen Interaction. *International Journal for the Semiotics of Law*, 13(2).

Sim, J., P. Scraton & P. Gordon (1987). "Introduction: Crime, the State and Critical Analysis." In P. Scraton (ed.) *Law, Order and the Authoritarian State*, pp. 1-70. Philadelphia, PA: Open University Press.

Simpson, S. (2000). "Gendered Theory and Single Sex Research." *DivisioNews*. Newsletter of the Division of Women and Crime, American Society of Criminology, August. (http://www.ou.edu/soc/dwc/newsletter.htm).

Simpson, S. (1991). "Caste, Class and Violent Crime: Explaining Differences in Female Offending." *Criminology*, 29:115-135.

Simpson, S. (1989). "Feminist Theory, Crime and Justice." *Criminology*, 27:605-631.

Simpson, S. & L. Elis (1995). "Doing Gender: Sorting Out the Caste and Crime Conundrum." *Criminology*, 33:47-81.

Smith, D.A. & R. Paternoster (1987). "The Gender Gap in Theories of Deviance: Issues and Evidence." *Journal of Research in Crime and Delinquency*, 24:140-172.

Social Justice Commissioner (1995). *Darwin Report 19-21 April 1995 on the National Aboriginal and Islander Legal Field Officer Training Program*. Office of the Aboriginal and Torres Strait Islander Social Justice Commissioner, unpublished.

South Australia (1999a). *Statistical Report on Aboriginal Over-Representation in the Criminal Justice System in South Australia 1997/98*. Adelaide, Australia: Division of State Aboriginal Affairs.

South Australia (1999b). *Aboriginal Community Justice*. Scoping Document, Adelaide, Australia: Division of State Aboriginal Affairs.

Southern Poverty Law Center (1997f). "Anti-Immigrant Violence." In V. Cyrus (ed.) *Experiencing Race, Class and Gender in the United States*, pp. 223-228. Mountain View, CA: Mayfield.

Southern Poverty Law Center (1997e). *SPLC Report*. Montgomery, AL: SPLC.

Southern Poverty Law Center (1997d). *Intelligence Report*, 88. Montgomery, AL: SPLC.

Southern Poverty Law Center (1997c). *Intelligence Report*, 87. Montgomery, AL: SPLC.

Southern Poverty Law Center (1997b). *Intelligence Report*, 86. Montgomery, AL: SPLC.

Southern Poverty Law Center (1997a). *Intelligence Report*, 85. Montgomery, AL: SPLC.

Sparks, R. (1995). "Entertaining the Crisis: Television and Moral Enterprise." In D. Kidd-Hewitt & R. Osborne (eds.) *Crime and the Media*, pp. 49-66. London, England: Pluto.

Spitzer, S. (1975). "Toward a Marxian Theory of Deviance." *Social Problems*, 22:638-651.

Steele, V. (1996). *Fetish: Fashion, Sex and Power*. New York, NY: Oxford University.

Stockdill, B. (1999). "AIDS, Queers, and Criminal (In)Justice: Repressing Radical Aids Activism." In B.A. Arrigo (ed.) *Social Justice/Criminal Justice*, pp. 224-250. Belmont, CA: West/Wadsworth.

Stohl, M. & G.A. Lopez (eds.) (1984). *The State as Terrorist: The Dynamics of Governmental Violence and Repression*. Westport, CT: Greenwood Press.

Strang, H. (2000). "The Future of Restorative Justice." In D. Chappell & P. Wilson (eds.) *Crime and the Criminal Justice System in Australia: 2000 and Beyond*, pp. 22-23. Sydney, Australia: Butterworths.

Straus, M.A. & R.J. Gelles (1990). *Physical Violence in American Families: Risk Factors and Adaptations to Violence in 8,145 Families*. New Brunswick, NJ: Transaction Publishers.

Sweetman, P. (1999). "Only Skin Deep? Tattooing, Piercing, and the Transgressive Body." In M.A. Edinburgh, (ed.) *The Body's Perilous Pleasures: Dangerous Desires and Contemporary Culture*, pp. 15-30. Edinburgh University Press.

Taylor, I. (1999). *Crime in Context*. Cambridge, UK: Polity Press.

Taylor, I. (1992). "Left Realist Criminology and the Free Market Experiment in Britain." In J. Young & R. Matthews (eds.) *Rethinking Criminology*, pp. 95-122. London, England: Sage.

Taylor, W., I. Walton & J. Young (1973). *The New Criminology: For a Social Theory of Deviance*. Boston, MA: Routledge and Keagan Paul.

Thomson, A. (1997, June). "Post-Modernism and Social Justice." Paper presented at the annual meeting of the Society of Socialist Studies, St. John's, Newfoundland. A shorter version published in *Canadian Journal of Sociology*, 23(1998):109-113.

Thorne, B. (1993). *Gender Play: Girls and Boys in School*. New Brunswick, NJ: Rutgers University Press.

Thorne-Finch, R. (1992). *Ending the Silence: The Origins and Treatment of Male Violence Against Women*. Toronto, CN: University of Toronto Press.

Tifft, L. & D. Sullivan, (1980). *The Struggle to Be Human: Crime, Criminology, and Anarchism*. Sanday, Orkney, UK: Cienfuegos Press.

Tomaszewski, E.A. (1999). "Review of When Work Disappears." *Justice Quarterly*, 16:239-243.

Tong, R. (1998). *Feminist Thought*, Second Edition. Boulder, CO: Westview Press.

Townsend, C. (1994). "Believing in Justice." In J. Burnside & N. Baker (eds.) *Relational Justice: Repairing the Breach*, pp. 133-146. Winchester, England: Waterside Press.

Tunnell, K.D. (1993). *Political Crime in Contemporary America*. New York, NY: Garland.

Turk, A. (1995). "Foreword." In J.I. Ross (ed.) *Controlling State Crime*, pp. ix-x. New York, NY: Garland.

Turner, B.S. (1999). "The Possibility of Primitiveness: The Sociology of Body Marks in Cool Societies." *Body and Society*, 5(2-3):39-50.

U.S. Commission on Civil Rights (n.d.). *Recent Actions Against Citizens and Residents of Asian Descent.*

Umbreit, M.S. (1994). *Victim Meets Offender—The Impact of Restorative Justice And Mediation.* Monsey, NY: Criminal Justice/Willow Tree Press.

United Nations Alliance (1995, May). "Working Party on Restorative Justice." Paper presented by R. Claassen at the United Nations Alliance of Non-governmental Organizations on Crime Prevention and Criminal Justice.

United Nations (2000). *Human Development Report, 1999.* New York, NY: United Nations.

Vale, V. & A. Juno (1990). "Art Controversy Is About Freedom of Expression." *The San Francisco Chronicle,* March 23.

Van Ness, D.W. (1990). "Restorative Justice." In B. Galaway & J. Hudson (eds.) *Criminal Justice, Restitution and Reconciliation,* pp. 7-14. Monsey, NY: Criminal Justice/Willow Tree Press.

Van Ness, D.W. & K.H. Strong (1997). *Restoring Justice.* Cincinnati, OH: Anderson Publishing Co.

Victoria (1993). *Restitution for Victims of Crime.* Law Reform Committee, Melbourne, Australia: Government Printer.

Vold, G.B., J.T. Bernard & J.B. Snipes (1998). *Theoretical Criminology,* Fourth Edition. New York, NY: Oxford University.

Walker, S. (1998). *Sense and Nonsense about Crime and Drugs: A Policy Guide,* Fourth Edition. Belmont, CA: West/Wadsworth.

Wallace, A. (1986). *Homicide: The Social Reality.* Sydney, Australia: New South Wales Bureau of Crime Statistics and Research.

Warner, K. (1994). "Family Group Conferences and the Rights of the Offender." In C. Alder & J. Wundersitz, J. (eds.) *Family Conferencing and Juvenile Justice: The Way Forward or Misplaced Optimism?,* pp. 141-152. Australian Studies in Law, Crime and Justice, Canberra, Australia: Australian Institute of Criminology.

Websdale, N. (1999). "Police Homicide Files as Situated Media Substrates." In J. Ferrell & N. Websdale (eds.) *Making Trouble,* pp. 277-300. New York, NY: Aldine de Gruyter.

West, C. & D. Zimmerman (1987). "Doing Gender." *Gender and Society,* 1(2):125-151.

West, C. & S. Fenstermaker (1995). "Doing Difference." *Gender and Society,* 9(1):8-37.

West, C. & S. Fenstermaker (1993). "Power, Inequality and the Accomplishment of Gender: An Ethnomethodological View." In P. England (ed.) *Theory on Gender/Feminism on Theory,* pp. 151-174. Hawthorne, NY: Aldine de Gruyter.

Western Australia. (1992). *The Role of Community-Based Corrections in Restorative Justice.* Perth: Department of Corrective Services.

Wilkerson, A. (1998). *Diagnosis Difference: The Moral Authority of Medicine.* Ithaca, NY: Cornell University Press.

Williams, C.R. & B.A. Arrigo (2001). *Law, Psychology, and Justice: Chaos Theory and the New (dis)Order.* Albany, NY: SUNY Press.

Wilson, J.Q. (1985). *Thinking About Crime.* New York, NY: Vintage.

Wilson, W.J. (1996). *When Work Disappears.* New York, NY: Knopf.

Wilson, W.J. (1987). *The Truly Disadvantaged: The Inner City, the Underclass, and Public Policy*. Chicago, IL: University of Chicago Press.

Wonders, N.A. (1999). "Postmodern Feminist Criminology and Social Justice." In B.A. Arrigo (ed.) *Social Justice/Criminal Justice*, pp. 111-128. Belmont, CA: West/Wadsworth.

Wundersitz, J. (1996). *The SA Juvenile Justice System: A Review of Its Operation*. Office of Crime Statistics, Attorney-Generals Department.

Young, I.M. (1995). "Social Movements and the Politics of Difference." In J. Arthur & A. Shapiro (eds.) *Campus Wars: Multiculturalism and the Politics of Difference*, pp. 199-225. Boulder, CO: Westview.

Young, I.M. (1990). *Justice and the Politics of Difference*. Princeton, NJ: Princeton University Press.

Young, J. (1999). *The Exclusive Society*. London, England: Sage.

Young, J. (1998). "Left Realist Criminology: Radical in its Analysis, Realist In its Policy." Paper presented at the annual meetings of the American Society of Criminology, San Diego.

Young, J. (1997). "Left Realism: The Basics." In B.D. MacLean & D. Milovanovic (eds.) *Thinking Critically about Crime*, pp. 28-36. Vancouver, BC: The Collective Press.

Young, J. (1986). "The Failure of Criminology: The Need for a Radical Realism." In R. Matthews & J. Young (eds.) *Confronting Crime*, pp. 4-30. London, England: Sage.

Zehr, H. (1990). *Changing Lenses: A New Focus for Crime and Justice*. Scottdale, PA: Herald Press.

Zehr, H. (1985). "Retributive Justice, Restorative Justice." In *New Perspectives on Crime and Justice: Occasional Papers of the MCC Canada Victim Offender Ministries Program and the MCC Office of Criminal Justice,* (Issue No. 4). Akron, PA: Mennonite Central Committee.

Zorza, J. (1991). "Woman Battering: A Major Cause of Homelessness." *Clearinghouse Review*, 25. Available: http:/wwwpovertylaw.org/articles/tableofcontents/1991/2504.htm.

Contributors' Biographical Information

Bruce A. Arrigo is Professor and Chair of the Department of Criminal Justice at the University of North Carolina—Charlotte, with additional faculty appointments in the Psychology Department, the Public Policy Program, and the Center for Applied and Professional Ethics. Formerly the Director of the Institute of Psychology, Law, and Public Policy at the California School of Professional Psychology-Fresno, Dr. Arrigo began his professional career as a community organizer and social activist for the homeless, the mentally ill, the working poor, the frail elderly, the decarcerated, and the chemically addicted. Dr. Arrigo received his Ph.D. from Pennsylvania State University, and he holds a master's degree in psychology and in sociology. He is an internationally recognized scholar who has authored more than 100 journal articles, academic book chapters, and scholarly essays. These works explore theoretical, applied, and policy topics in social psychology, criminal justice and mental health, and socio-legal studies. He is the author, co-author, or editor of 11 books; including, *Madness, Language, and the Law* (1993), *The Contours of Psychiatric Justice* (1996), *Social Justice/Criminal Justice* (1998), *The Dictionary of Critical Social Sciences* (with T.R. Young, 1999), *Introduction to Forensic Psychology* (2000), *Law, Psychology, and Justice* (with Christopher R. Williams, 2001), *The Power Serial Rapist* (with Dawn J. Graney, 2001), *Punishing the Mentally Ill: A Critical Analysis of Law and Psychiatry* (2002), *Criminal Competency on Trial* (with Mark C. Bardwell, 2002), *Psychological Jurisprudence: Critical Exploration in Law, Crime, and Society* (in press), and *Criminal Behavior: A Systems Perspective* (in press). Dr. Arrigo is the past Editor of *Humanity & Society* and founding and acting Editor of the peer-reviewed quarterly, *Journal of Forensic Psychology Practice*. He was recently named the Critical Criminologist of the Year (2000), sponsored by the Critical Criminology Division of the American Society of Criminology. Dr. Arrigo is also a Fellow of the American Psychological Association through the Law-Psychology Division (Div. 41) of the APA.

Walter S. DeKeseredy is Professor of Sociology at Ohio University and is the Chair of the American Society of Criminology's Division on Critical Criminology. DeKeseredy and Katharine Kelly conducted the first Canadian national representative sample survey of woman abuse, including sexual assault, in university/college dating. For this work he was given the Division's Critical Criminologist of the Year Award in 1995. DeKeseredy, who received his Ph.D. in Sociology from York University in Toronto, has also published dozens of scientific articles and book chapters on woman abuse, criminological theory, and crime in public housing. He is the author of *Woman Abuse in Dating Relationships: The Role of Male Peer Support* and is the co-author of *Woman Abuse: Sociological Perspectives*, the second edition of *The Wrong Stuff: An Introduction to the Sociological Study of* Deviance, *Woman Abuse: A Sociological Story*, *Sexual Assault on the College Campus: The Role of Male Peer Support*, *Woman Abuse on Campus: Results from the Canadian National Survey*, *Contemporary Criminology*, and *Contemporary Social Problems in North American Society*. In 1993, he received Carleton University's Research Achievement Award. Currently he serves on the Editorial Boards of *Criminal Justice, Women & Criminal Justice, Violence Against Women: An International and Interdisciplinary Journal*, and *Crime & Delinquency*.

Jeff Ferrell received his Ph.D. in Sociology from the University of Texas at Austin, and is currently a visiting professor of sociology at Southern Methodist University. He is the author of *Crimes of Style: Urban Graffiti and the Politics of Criminality* (Garland, 1993; Northeastern University Press, 1996) and *Tearing Down the Streets* (St. Martin's/Palgrave, 2001); editor, with Clinton R. Sanders, of *Cultural Criminology* (Northeastern University Press, 1995), a finalist for the American Society of Criminology's 1996 Michael J. Hindelang Award for Most Outstanding Contribution to Criminology; editor, with Mark S. Hamm, of *Ethnography at the Edge: Crime, Deviance, and Field Research* (Northeastern University Press, 1998); and editor, with Neil Websdale, of *Making Trouble: Cultural Constructions of Crime, Deviance, and Control* (Aldine de Gruyter, 1999). His scholarship has also appeared in a range of edited collections, and in journals including *Theoretical Criminology, Contemporary Justice Review, Social Justice, Justice Quarterly, Annual Review of Sociology, Youth and Society, Public Art Review, Social Anarchism, Radical America, Alternatives Journal, Humanity and Society, Labor History*, the *Journal of Folklore Research*, the *Journal of Popular Culture*, and the *Journal of Criminal Justice and Popular Culture*. He is the recipient of the 1998 Critical Criminologist of the Year Award, presented by the Division on Critical Criminology of the American Society of Criminology, and is founding editor of the New York University Press book series, Alternative Criminology.

David O. Friedrichs is Professor of Sociology/Criminal Justice at the University of Scranton (Pennsylvania). He is the author of *Trusted Criminals: White Collar Crime in Contemporary Society* (1996) and *Law in Our Lives: An Introduction* (2001), and Editor of *State Crime: Volumes I & II* (1998). He is also the author of some 85 articles, book chapters, and essays on such topics as legitimation of legal order, radical/critical criminology, victimology, violence, postmodern theory, narrative jurisprudence, white-collar crime, and state crime. He has served as Editor of *Legal Studies Forum*, as Vice President of the Association for Humanist Sociology, and as Vice Chair of the Division on Critical Criminology, American Society of Criminology. He is President (2002-2004) of the White-Collar Crime Research Consortium.

John Randolph Fuller has been Professor of Criminology and Sociology at the State University of West Georgia for the past 22 years. He has had experience in the criminal justice system as a probation and parole officer as well as a criminal justice planner. His writings include *Criminal Justice: A Peacemaking Perspective, Controversial Issues in Criminology* (co-editor), and the forthcoming *Corrections, Peacemaking and Restorative Justice: Transforming Individuals and Institutions* (co-author). Dr. Fuller is a certified mediator in the Georgia courts.

Suzanne Hatty is Professor of Culture, Epistemology and Medicine in the Department of Social Medicine, the College of Medicine at Ohio University. Prior to taking up this position in 1998, she held the position of Associate Professor in Social Sciences and Chair, Center for Humanities and Human Sciences, Southern Cross University, Australia. Dr. Hatty received a Ph.D. in Psychology in 1982 from the University of Sydney and has a strong record of research and publishing. Her research achievements to date are decidedly eclectic and span the broad spectrum of topics and issues including masculinity and health; women's health and public policy; community strategies to reduce intentional and unintentional injury; access, prevention and treatment of incarcerated and institutionalized populations; behavioral risk and health outcomes in underserved and neglected populations; cultural competency and health care services; the cultures of medicine, the body and society, bioethics and biotechnologies, posthumanism and future studies, and crime and popular culture. Dr. Hatty has received numerous research grants. Her two most recent books are *The Disordered Body: Epidemic Disease and Cultural Transformation* (SUNY 1999; coauthored with James Hatty), and *Masculinities, Violence and Culture* (Sage, 2000).

Stuart Henry is Professor and Chair of the Department of Interdisciplinary Studies in the College of Urban, Labor and Metropolitan Affairs at Wayne State University in Detroit. He has researched varieties of marginalized knowledge and informal institutions including: mutual aid groups, informal economies, non-state systems of discipline and social control, and cooperatives. Most recently, he examined the relationship between social norms, private discipline and public law. Dr. Henry has 20 books published and more than 70 of his articles have appeared in professional journals or as book chapters. His books include the classic works *The Hidden Economy* (1978), and *Informal Institutions* (1981) and the *Informal Economy*

(1987). His most recent works include: *Criminological Theory: An Analysis of its Underlying Assumptions* (with Werner Einstadter, 1995) and *Constitutive Criminology: Beyond Postmodernism* (1996) and *Constitutive Criminology at Work* (1999) (both with Dragan Milovanovic), *Essential Criminology* (1998), *School Violence* (2000) and *Careers in Criminal Justice* (2001, both with Bill Hinkle) and *Degrees of Deviance* (2001, with Roger Eaton). Dr. Henry serves on the editorial board of *Theoretical Criminology* and *The Critical Criminologist*.

David Kauzlarich is Associate Professor of Sociology and Criminal Justice Studies at Southern Illinois University, Edwardsville. He was formerly Assistant Professor of Sociology and Director of the graduate and undergraduate Criminal Justice programs at Saint Joseph's University. He received the Ph.D. in Sociology from Western Michigan University in 1994. He has authored or co-authored 15 journal articles and two books, *Crimes of the American Nuclear State: At Home and Abroad* (with Ronald C. Kramer) and *Introduction to Criminology, 8th Edition* (with Hugh D. Barlow). His major areas of interest are state crime, human rights, and criminal justice policy. He is currently working on a primer in criminological theory.

Rick A. Matthews is an associate professor of sociology and criminal justice at Carthage College. He has published in the areas of governmental and corporate crime, the political economy of street crime, and juvenile delinquency. Currently, he is researching corporate involvement in the Holocaust.

Jody Miller is Associate Professor of Criminology and Criminal Justice at the University of Missouri-St. Louis. She specializes in feminist theory and qualitative research methods. Her research focuses on gender, crime and victimization, particularly in the contexts of youth gangs, urban communities, and the commercial sex industry. Recent publications include *One of the Guys: Girls, Gangs and Gender* (Oxford University Press, 2001) and articles in *Criminology, Theoretical Criminology*, and *Violence Against Women*.

Dragan Milovanovic is Professor of Criminal Justice at Northeastern Illinois University. He is the author of 17 books and contributes regularly to scholarly journals. In 1993 he received the Distinguished Service Award from the Division on Critical Criminology of the American Society of Criminology for his research and contributions to critical criminology. He is Editor of the *International Journal for the Semiotics of Law*. His recent works include: *Critical Criminology at the Edge: Postmodern Perspectives, Integrations and Applications* (2002); *Introduction to the Sociology of Law, 3ed.* (2003); and a forthcoming, co-edited book with Ellie Ragland, Lacan: *Topologically Speaking* (2003).

Victoria Pitts received her Ph.D. in Sociology from Brandeis University. She is Assistant Professor of Sociology at Queens College, CUNY, where she teaches courses in social theory and seminars in gender and the sociology of the body. Her current research examines the cultural and identity politics of bodies and body image. She has published numerous articles and book chapters. Her most recent articles appear in the *Sociological Quarterly* and *Body and Society*, and her book, *In the Flesh: The Cultural Politics of Body Modification* is published by St. Martin's/Palgrave.

Barbara Perry is Associate Professor of Criminal Justice at Northern Arizona University. Her work emphasizes issues of inequality and (in)justice. Specifically, she has published in the area of hate crime and ethnoviolence. Her book, *In the Name of Hate: Accounting for Hate Crime* (Routledge) is a theoretical exploration of hate crime as a mechanism for constructing difference. *Hate Crime: A Reader* (Routledge, forthcoming) is a comprehensive collection of current theoretical and empirical literature. With Dr. Marianne Nielsen, Dr. Perry is the co-editor of *Investigating Difference: Human and Cultural Relations in Criminal Justice*.

Kenneth Polk is Professor of Criminology at the University of Melbourne in Australia. Before that he was, for many years, Professor of Sociology at the University of Oregon. His undergraduate degree was from San Diego State University, and his Ph.D. from UCLA. Much of his research over the past decade has focused on violence and homicide, including the books *When Men Kill* (1994) and *Child Victims of Homicide* (2001, with Christine Alder). In addition, his most recent work has examined art crime, including the problem of the international traffic in plundered archeological material.

Rick Sarre is Associate Professor of Law at the School of International Business, University of South Australia. He holds an L.L.B. from the University of Adelaide, an M.A. (Criminology) from the University of Toronto, Canada and the SJD from the University of Canberra, Australia. He lectures in media law, criminal justice and criminology, commercial and marketing law for the University of South Australia and, from time to time, Graceland University, Iowa and Hong Kong Baptist University. He is a former legal adviser to the Jesuit Refugee Service, and legal practitioner. His latest book is *Considering Crime and Justice* (edited with J. Tomaino), Crawford House Publishing: Adelaide, 2000.

Martin D. Schwartz is Professor of Sociology and holds the title of Presidential Research Scholar at Ohio University, where he has twice won the College of Arts and Sciences Outstanding Teacher Award, and been named the university's Outstanding Graduate Faculty Member. He has received the career research achievement award of the American Society of Criminology's Division on Critical Criminology, and the Thomas R. Ford Outstanding Alumni Award in Sociology from the University of Kentucky. Schwartz has published more than 100 articles, chapters, edited books and books on a variety of topics in such journals as *Criminology, Deviant Behavior, Violence Against Women, Justice Quarterly, Journal of Family Violence,* and *Journal of Interpersonal Violence.* Among his 11 books he is the co-author (all with Walter DeKeseredy) of *Contemporary Criminology; Sexual Assault on the College Campus: The Role of Male Peer Support;* and *Woman Abuse on Campus;* and (with Lawrence Travis) *Corrections: An Issues Approach,* now in its 4th edition; the editor of *Researching Sexual Violence Against Women: Methodological and Personal Perspectives,* and the co-editor (with Dragan Milovanovic) of *Race, Class and Gender in Criminology: The Intersections.* He is a former president of the Association for Humanist Sociology and Critical Criminology Division Chair for the American Society of Criminology and he has been associated with 12 journals, serving as co-editor of *Criminal Justice: The International Journal of Policy and Practice,* deputy editor of *Justice Quarterly* and the *Legal Studies Forum,* and on the editorial boards of *Criminology, Men and Masculinities, Critical Criminology, the Online Journal of Justice, Humanity & Society, Violence Against Women; Race, Class & Gender; Teaching Sociology,* and the *Journal of Criminal Justice Education.*

Index